DESSERT FOURPLAY

1

2

3

4

DESSERT FOURPLAY

SWEET QUARTETS FROM A FOUR-STAR PASTRY CHEF

JOHNNY IUZZINI
AND ROY FINAMORE

PHOTOGRAPHS BY GREGOR HALENDA

CLARKSON POTTER/PUBLISHERS

NEW YORK

Published in the United States by Clarkson Potter/Publishers,
an imprint of the Crown Publishing Group,
a division of Random House, Inc., New York.
www.crownpublishing.com
www.clarksonpotter.com

CLARKSON POTTER is a trademark and Potter with colophon
is a registered trademark of Random House, Inc.

Library of Congress Cataloging-in-Publication Data
Iuzzini, Johnny.
    Dessert fourplay : sweet quartets from a four-star pastry
chef / by Johnny Iuzzini and Roy Finamore
        p.   cm.
Includes index.
    1. Desserts.   2. Jean Georges (Restaurant).   I. Finamore, Roy.
II. Title.
TX773.I98   2008
641.8'6—dc22   2008002912

ISBN 978-0-307-35137-1

Printed in China

Design by Marysarah Quinn

10   9   8   7   6   5   4   3   2   1

FIRST EDITION

I DEDICATE THIS BOOK TO THE

LOVING MEMORY OF MY MOTHER,

DALE MARCIA IUZZINI,

THE KINDEST, STRONGEST,

MOST BENEVOLENT WOMAN

I HAVE EVER MET.

SHE IS MISSED DEARLY.

contents

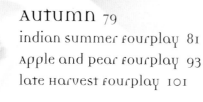

introduction

I was pretty young when I got into this food business. At fifteen, I got my working papers because I needed a job and the paycheck that came with it. I was soon riding my bike back and forth to the Osiris Country Club, near where I lived in the Catskills in New York. I didn't think for a moment that my job as a dishwasher would lead to finding my life's passion. That I'd be the pastry chef of a four-star restaurant by the time I was twenty-six. That I'd spend my days and nights dreaming up intricate new dessert tastings to elevate the ultimate course of a meal.

The chef at the country club, Brad Goulden, liked me, so he let me do some prep work, too. Things like peeling carrots and cutting vegetables. When Chef Goulden moved to a place called the Cavu Restaurant, I got on my bike and followed. I did more dishes, but I also got my introduction to actual cooking. Chef gave me some minor responsibilities: working the salamander (broiler) and the sauté station. I wasted a lot of food as I was learning what to do, and I got yelled at a lot. But Chef Goulden took me with him when he left Cavu for another country club, so clearly I was doing something right.

While I was in high school, I enrolled in the vo-tech program, which introduced students to a trade while they were still young. So for my junior and senior years, I studied culinary food trades, and I entered my first culinary competition. I took second place in the regionals when I was a senior, and I went to the New York State finals.

One day, Chef took me to lunch at the Culinary Institute of America—also known as CIA—the school he had graduated from, in Hyde Park, New York. After looking around, I was sure this was the place for me. I applied and was accepted.

I had six months to kill between graduation from high school and starting at CIA. The florist at Cavu also did the flowers for the River Café in Brooklyn, and she brought me there one day to meet John Loughran, the chef. By the end of the day, Chef Loughran had hired

me for the position of garde-manger. I was seventeen years old and "keeper of the food" (which mostly means making salads, but still) at one of New York's most talked-about restaurants!

Part of my job every morning was doing some minor butchering and killing lobsters, and I wasn't very comfortable with this. My mother was a wildlife rehabilitator, and I grew up nursing baby and wounded animals back to health. I found it extremely difficult to have to pull claws off live lobsters.

The pastry chef at the time was Eric Gouteyron. He worked in a barnlike building out back. I kept watching him making chocolate butterflies and chocolate mini Brooklyn Bridges—all I knew about chocolate then was Hershey's Kisses and Snickers bars—and I asked if I could help. He laughed and said, "What do you know? You're a cook." But I convinced him I wanted to learn. I started working with him for free every day after my shift. He taught me what "tempering chocolate" meant, how to make a cornet—the small parchment paper cones pastry chefs fill with chocolate and use for decorating. When he had an opening on his pastry team, I made the switch. I also called the CIA and made the change from the culinary program to the pastry program.

The CIA was a lot of fun. When it came time for my externship, I worked at a restaurant called Luxe, under Chef Lincoln Carson, a disciple of the "famed and feared" pastry chef François Payard. I loved every minute of my eighteen weeks working with Chef Carson, learning something new every day.

Once I got back to school, I was restless. I couldn't wait to get back to work. About two months before graduation, I asked Lincoln if he could get me an interview with François Payard—a third-generation pastry chef and arguably the best in the business at that time—who was then at Daniel Boulud's restaurant, Daniel. At that interview, I stood like a soldier, saying "Yes, Chef!" this and "Yes, Chef!" that. I spent the next day in the kitchen at Daniel, standing for sixteen hours until Chef Payard told me I was hired and that I should come back on Monday.

"Chef," I said, "I'm still in school."

"Why do you come here to waste my time, then," he asked, "and steal my recipes?"

"Chef, I want to work with you, but I don't graduate for two months."

Payard made me come to work for him every Saturday until graduation, after which I started full-time.

I stayed at Daniel with François for three and a half years, learning more techniques, developing my palate, and getting my butt handed to me every day. At one point, I was practically the only American in the kitchen. So I learned French. While I was at Daniel, the restaurant earned its fourth star from the *New York Times,* and François received the coveted James Beard Foundation Award for outstanding pastry chef. François left to open his own place, Payard Pâtisserie and Bistro, and he asked me to come with him as sous-chef. I did, and now I was working two jobs.

During those years, I wasn't making a lot of money and was having a hard time making ends meet. But I was determined to work for the best and learn everything I could instead of short-circuiting my career and taking a higher-paying job somewhere else. At the same time, I was working until at least 1 A.M. most nights—like everyone else in the kitchen—and needed to unwind after the dinner service. The whole team would go to a bar, but since I didn't smoke or drink, that didn't hold much attraction for me. What interested me were New York's megaclubs: Limelight, Club USA, Tunnel, Palladium. I fell in love with underground house music. So after putting in a twelve- to sixteen-hour day, I would go out and dance for another four to six hours a few nights a week. I met more and more people and soon was given the opportunity to make a little extra money by running a guest list. I needed the cash to supplement my paychecks and loved the excitement. Then I got the chance to work the door, which meant I was choosing who would and wouldn't be allowed in! This was craziness. I burned the candle at both ends for a while, working for François all morning and at Daniel all night and then doing the club thing. Pretty soon, I wasn't sure what I was—a pastry chef or a club kid—or what I wanted to be.

Daniel Boulud got word that I was planning to leave and find myself, and he made me the offer of a lifetime. "I'll make you a deal," he said. "I'll lend you $10,000 for a trip around the world, because I'm confident you will return eager to get back to the kitchen. I am closing Daniel to change locations and will reopen the old space as Café Boulud. You will help me open Café Boulud as sous-chef and then open the new Daniel as sous-chef as well." He offered me a substantial raise—as well as a huge responsibility for a kid who was only twenty-three—but the best part was that I would be repaying his loan interest-free out of my salary.

I took the money and ran. Hong Kong. Australia. Thailand. Russia. The Czech Republic. Italy. France. Spain. Switzerland. Austria. Germany. Holland. Belgium. England. For seven months I traveled, and all the time I found myself gravitating back to the kitchen, working a few days here, a few days there, for free—wherever anyone would take me. That led me to the kitchens at the Hôtel de Paris and Le Louis XV Restaurant in Monte Carlo, among other places, and to Paris's notable pastry shop Ladurée, under the famed Pierre Hermé.

Daniel had been right. Once I was home, I was itching to jump back into the fire of a four-star kitchen. First was Café Boulud, with Chef Rémy Funfrock, and then the new Daniel, under the tutelage of Chef Thomas Haas, a wiry and highly energetic fourth-generation pastry chef. I often reflect on just how much I learned under him as sous-chef; there are recipes I learned from him that remain part of my repertoire today, both as he taught them to me and as springboards for my own desserts. After just over a year and a half, Thomas Haas left to open his own chocolate business in Vancouver, British Columbia. Daniel brought in a new chef from Roger Vergé's celebrated Moulin de Mougins, but the restaurant and the new pastry chef weren't happy with each other, and the chef soon returned to France. I kept the team on track and we finished the year strong.

Daniel named an "employee of the month" for the front and the back of the house at each of our monthly meetings. But at our first meet-

ing of the new year, Daniel said he had an announcement to make. "Well," he said to the management team, "this month we have a new category, and it is Man of the Year." Then he turned to me. He said that I had done a great job over the past year, and that he was naming *me* "Man of the Year" and the new executive pastry chef! I was twenty-six years old.

After a year and a half in this new position, I realized that in order to grow as a pastry chef, I needed the challenges of a new kitchen. It was one of the most difficult things I've ever had to do, telling the man who had been like a second father to me that it was time for me to leave the nest. He was upset, but supportive, with his own ideas of where I should go. I hadn't had someplace lined up when I gave notice, but some amazing offers came my way. Until Jean-Georges Vongerichten called me, though, I wasn't very interested in any of them for one reason or another. After a few long, intense conversations, Jean-Georges offered me an opportunity I couldn't refuse.

When I began as the pastry chef at Restaurant Jean Georges, I was introduced to the notion of "tasting" desserts—three different desserts on one plate. At the time, they were simply classified as Tasting 1, Tasting 2, and Tasting 3. I added another tasting—or "fourplay"— which made it possible for sixteen different desserts to be served to one table. I also decided to make the menu more focused by highlighting a specific ingredient, for example, or combining the classic flavors of a particular season to make a harmonious dessert that was greater than the sum of its parts. I wanted to grab the diner with every bite of each element on the plate.

Strawberries, for example, are one of my favorite late-spring ingredients, and so I've created a tasting that explores the different ways flavors and textures can be coaxed out of the berry. The flavor is distilled and carbonated for a soda and intensified by slow-roasting the berries for a deconstructed strawberry shortcake. I play with texture by pairing creamy strawberry ice cream with chewy strawberry-lavender leather, and again with a combination of strawberry gelée, fresh strawberries, and strawberry sauce in a fourth dessert that also includes coconut cream and crisp chocolate pastry.

The result is a sophisticated explosion of a familiar flavor. You begin with the full flavor of strawberry rich on your tongue and end with an effervescent tingle of flavor in your nose.

For an autumnal theme, take the Indian Summer FourPlay. I've found that there are a lot of vegetables that fit comfortably on a dessert plate. Sweet corn is practically a fruit to my mind, and it makes an elegant panna cotta. Beets and chocolate have a complementary kind of earthiness; I pair them with bright, acidic raspberries in a beet parfait. Quince is a classic autumn fruit; I poach it gently and serve it with creamy farmer's cheese and refreshing sherry granité. Rounding out this tasting is a sweet potato cake. Inspired by, but not as heavy or sweet as, the old-time pie, this dessert has the added pop of acidity from cranberry foam.

My inspiration can come from seasonal fruits or produce from local growers (take a look at the Honey-Roasted Tomatoes on page 56), conversations during a late-night dinner (the Chocolate-Olive Panini on page 149, for example), or my desire to showcase the versatility of a family of flavors like citrus, as in the fourplay on page 113. Equally important is my drive to learn and share the new techniques that are possible in the pastry kitchen, transforming ingredients we know and love into something unexpected: espresso into an edible cloud, or rich, creamy praline paste into a powder. You'll find these cutting-edge techniques in a few recipes and I hope you'll be inspired to try them.

In the restaurant, there is no option for the diner. If you were to order the Exotic Tasting, you would get the four mini desserts, with no substitutions. With *Dessert FourPlay,* however, you can pick and choose. Each recipe in a tasting works on its own, and you can serve it alone. "Make It Simpler" boxes throughout the book give you ideas on how to streamline preparation of some of the more complicated desserts. Additionally, the "building block" recipes can also be served alone, or they can become the start of a dessert of your own creation. The shiny, smooth chocolate glaze that I use to finish cakes makes a killer hot fudge sauce. Instead of making traditional madeleines, I like to use the batter to make a lemony base for a layer cake.

I hope I help you shake things up a bit when it comes to the end of the meal—from what you make to how you eat it. Contrary to conventional wisdom, I suggest starting with the richest dessert, which is often the one that features chocolate, and tasting your way through to the lightest, which could be a soup or a soda or a fruit salad. That way, you finish your meal feeling refreshed. (As you look at the recipes, though, keep in mind that each fourplay begins with the lightest dessert and moves on to the richest.)

So make one dessert or make four, as you wish. For the adventurous, the multidessert presentation, with its careful construction and innovative techniques, will be a revelatory dessert experience.

ABOUT SERVING

I've tried to give you a lot of options in this book. You can make just one dessert, and that will be an ample ending to a meal. You might even make just one of the ice creams and serve that as a perfect ending to a meal for six diners.

Should you go the fourplay route, making all four desserts in a tasting, remember that the portions are small, so you won't be overwhelmed with sweets at the end of your dinner. They should be just enough to satisfy. Of course, tasting portions will serve

many more guests, so you may have leftovers. Keep anything you don't eat that night in the refrigerator (unless it's a frozen dessert) wrapped in plastic or in an airtight container. Most will keep for a day or two. I've indicated when leftovers will freeze well.

fourplays

spring

When the season is just beginning, the full arsenal of spring fruits is not yet at my disposal. Here I combine muscats—one of the earliest sweet spring flavors—with some stragglers from winter, like citrus, for a tasting that is seasonal and bright.

serves 10

early

spring

FOURPLAY

muscat grape soup ~ cape gooseberries

strawberry-rhubarb mochi ~ basil fluid gel

key lime parfait ~ graham cracker sablé

chocolate-beet cake ~ candied beets ~ raspberry-beet sauce

muscat grape soup ~ cape gooseberries

Muscat grapes mark the beginning of spring, and they're a prompt for me to start thinking of new menus, new ideas, and the other spring fruits to come. This soup is designed to keep the distinct musky flavor of these grapes in its purest form.

"Cape" refers to the papery husk the gooseberries are wrapped in, which makes them look like tiny Chinese lanterns.

For the Soup

MAKES ABOUT 2 CUPS

1 TEASPOON (5 G) VITAMIN C
POWDER (SEE NOTE)
17½ OUNCES (500 G) MUSCAT
GRAPES
1 TEASPOON POWDERED GELATIN
(OR 4.25 G SHEET GELATIN; SEE
PAGE 276)
⅓ CUP PLUS 1 TABLESPOON (95 G)
SIMPLE SYRUP (PAGE 184)

Put the vitamin C powder in the container you'll be juicing the grapes into.

Juice the grapes in a juicer and immediately mix the juice with the vitamin C powder.

Sprinkle the gelatin over the surface of the simple syrup and leave for about 1 minute to soften. Microwave for 45 seconds or heat gently in a saucepan until melted. Add the gelatin and syrup to the grape juice and stir well. Cover with plastic wrap immediately, pressing the wrap to the surface, and chill completely.

Note: Vitamin C powder will prevent the grape juice from discoloration. You can buy it at a drugstore.

To Serve

6 OUNCES (170 G) CAPE
GOOSEBERRIES, HUSKED,
RINSED, AND CHILLED

Put a few Cape gooseberries in small dessert bowls or glasses. Spoon in enough grape soup to cover halfway.

strawberry-rhubarb mochi ~ basil fluid gel

*Mochi are sweet, filled Japanese dumplings that are served
chilled. I've been fascinated by them from the first time I had one,
but I'd always been told that they could be made only in factories.
And since the commercial ones are artificially flavored and
colored and filled with ice-hard ice cream, that didn't surprise me.
One day, I promised my friend David Chang of Momofuku that I'd
make fresh mochi for him. It became a mission. Once I learned
how to do it, I found that it really wasn't difficult at all to make
the tender, sweet rice dough and flavor it naturally. And since I fill
mochi with a compote, they're fork-tender. The basil fluid gel is an
ideal herbal foil to the compote.*

*I use 2-inch demisphere molds when I make mochi, but I've
found that an egg carton works fine. The secret to the dough is
working quickly. This recipe makes twice as much as you need for
the fourplay, but I hardly consider leftover mochi a problem. The
mochi will keep for 1 day in the refrigerator.*

Bring a saucepan of water to a boil. Add the basil and blanch for
30 seconds. Drain and refresh immediately under cold running
water. Squeeze out all the water.

Set up an ice bath in a large bowl.

Put the basil in a blender with the simple syrup and the ⅓ cup
water. Blend until bright green, smooth, and thin in consistency.
Pour into a medium bowl, set it into the ice bath, and infuse for
20 minutes. Strain through a fine strainer, discarding the solids.

Blend the sugar and agar together well, then pour the syrup
into the blender. Turn the blender to low and sift the sugar and
agar into the vortex. Blend for 1 minute.

Pour into a small saucepan and bring to a boil over high heat.
Reduce the heat to medium-low and simmer for 5 minutes. Pour
into a baking dish, cover with plastic wrap, and refrigerate until
set, about 10 minutes.

Put the gel back into the blender and blend until very smooth.
Strain through a fine strainer. Store in an airtight container in
the refrigerator for up to 3 days.

CONTINUES . . .

SERVES 10 ON ITS OWN OR
20 AS PART OF A FOURPLAY

MAKE IT SIMPLER
In place of the compote, doctor
all-natural strawberry-
rhubarb preserves with some
grated lemon zest and diced
fresh strawberries. Instead
of making the basil fluid gel,
you could just puree the basil
with the simple syrup, strain
it, and use the puree as a sauce.

For the Basil Fluid Gel
PACKED ¾ CUP (37 G) FRESH
    BASIL LEAVES
⅓ CUP (80 G) SIMPLE SYRUP
    (PAGE 184)
⅓ CUP (80 G) WATER
1 TEASPOON (4 G) SUGAR
½ TEASPOON (2 G) AGAR

For the Mochi

POTATO STARCH

SCANT ½ CUP (10 G) FREEZE-DRIED
 STRAWBERRIES (SEE NOTE)

SCANT ⅓ CUP (60 G) SUGAR

1 CUP (140 G) MOCHIKO RICE
 FLOUR (SEE NOTE)

COARSE SALT

¾ TO 1 CUP (180 TO 240 G)
 COLD WATER

STRAWBERRY-RHUBARB
 COMPOTE (PAGE 250)

NOTE: Freeze-dried strawberries (sold as Just Strawberries) are available in many good grocery stores. Mochiko rice flour is milled from glutinous, short-grained, sweet mochi rice. I use Mochiko Blue Star Brand, which is available at many Asian markets and online from Quickspice.com.

Dust twenty 2-inch demisphere molds with potato starch or line two empty egg cartons with plastic wrap and dust lightly with potato starch.

Put the strawberries in a spice grinder and process to a fine powder.

Whisk the strawberry powder with the sugar, mochiko flour, and a pinch of salt in a microwave-safe bowl. Add ¾ cup cold water and mix into a smooth paste. Cover with plastic wrap and microwave for 90 seconds. Stir. If the dough is very tight, stir in a little more water. Cover with plastic wrap and microwave for 1 minute. The dough will darken and become opaque.

Dust a work surface heavily with potato starch. Working quickly, roll the warm dough ¹⁄₁₆ inch thick. Cut 3½-inch rounds of dough. Hold a round of dough in your palm and fill with 1 tablespoon strawberry-rhubarb compote. Pinch the dough closed, stretching it if necessary, and place, seam side down, in the mold. Repeat with the rest of the dough. Cover with plastic wrap and refrigerate until serving.

If desired, process a few strawberries in a spice grinder to a fine powder.

Make a smear of the basil fluid gel on a dessert plate and set a mochi on top. Garnish, if you want, with a few pinches of the strawberry powder and some basil leaves. Repeat for each serving.

To Serve

FREEZE-DRIED STRAWBERRIES
(OPTIONAL)
MICRO BASIL (OR THINLY SLICED
FRESH BASIL LEAVES;
OPTIONAL)

WHAT'S A FLUID GEL?

Set with agar and then run through a blender, fluid gels land right in the middle between being a liquid and a solid. Because they can hold a shape, fluid gels take us beyond the pool of sauce on a plate and make all kinds of interesting presentations possible. And they pack super-intense flavors.

key lime parfait ~ graham cracker sablé

SERVES 10

MAKE IT SIMPLER
If you're in a rush, replace the Graham Cracker Sablé Cookies with Carr's whole wheat biscuits.

I had never seen a key lime when I was growing up; I thought the juice was something that just came in bottles. Once I discovered the real fruit, though, I wanted to do something with it. So here's a fresh, brightly flavored version of key lime pie, with a crisp graham cracker sablé standing in for the usual soggy crust.

The sauce would also be great over sliced fresh apricots or nectarines.

A scale is a must for making this dessert. And you'll need ten 2 x 2-inch ring molds.

For the Italian Meringue
2 LARGE EGG WHITES
CREAM OF TARTAR
SCANT ¼ CUP (45 G) SUGAR
1 TABLESPOON (15 G) WATER

Combine the egg whites with a tiny pinch of cream of tartar and 1 teaspoon of the sugar in the bowl of a standing mixer fitted with the whisk. Beat the whites at low speed while you make the sugar syrup.

Place the remaining sugar and the water in a very small saucepan (like a butter warmer). Mix with your fingers until the sugar is like wet sand. Cook over medium-high heat until the syrup reaches 250°F.

When the syrup comes to a boil, increase the mixer speed to medium. When the syrup is ready and the whites are just shy of soft peaks, pour the syrup in a steady stream into the whites, avoiding the whisk and the sides of the bowl. Turn the speed to high and beat the whites until the sides of the bowl feel cool. Set aside while you make the base for the parfait.

For the Parfait
1 CUP (240 G) MILK
⅔ CUP (150 G) STRAINED FRESH KEY LIME JUICE
1 VANILLA BEAN, SPLIT AND SCRAPED
½ CUP PLUS 3 TABLESPOONS (135 G) GRANULATED SUGAR
9 LARGE EGG YOLKS
1 TABLESPOON (30 G) INVERT SUGAR (PAGE 185)
1½ CUPS (360 G) HEAVY CREAM

Line a baking sheet with a Silpat or parchment. Put ten 2 x 2-inch ring molds on the baking sheet and freeze while you prepare the parfait.

Set up an ice bath in a large bowl. Bring a saucepan half full of water to a simmer.

Put the milk, key lime juice, vanilla seeds, granulated sugar, yolks, and invert sugar in a heatproof large bowl and whisk together. Set the bowl over a pan of simmering water and cook, stirring occasionally with a heatproof rubber scraper, until the mixture reaches 181°F. Set the bowl into the ice bath, stirring often to chill down quickly.

Whip the cream to soft peaks.

Scale out 50 g of the Italian meringue and fold it into the key lime mixture. Fold in the whipped cream.

Fill a pastry bag (you don't need a tip) with the parfait mix and pipe into the prepared molds. Cover the molds with plastic wrap and freeze for at least 4 hours before serving or for up to 3 days.

Combine the verjus, simple syrup, lemongrass, ginger, and lime leaves in a saucepan. Bring to a simmer over medium heat. Simmer until thickened and reduced by half, about 25 minutes. Strain and chill for at least 1 hour before serving or for up to 3 days.

For the Sauce

MAKES ABOUT 1 CUP

½ CUP (120 G) VERJUS (SEE NOTE)

1¼ CUPS (350 G) SIMPLE SYRUP (PAGE 184)

1 STALK FRESH LEMONGRASS, TRIMMED, CRUSHED, AND CHOPPED

½ OUNCE (12 G) FRESH GINGER, PEELED AND SLICED

½ OUNCE (12 G) FRESH KAFFIR LIME LEAVES, CHOPPED (SEE NOTE)

Note: Verjus is available at gourmet markets and online from Amazon. Kaffir lime leaves are sold at many good grocery stores and gourmet markets.

CONTINUES . . .

To Serve

3 OR 4 RIPE PLUMS
10 GRAHAM CRACKER SABLÉ
COOKIES (PAGE 204)

Unmold the parfaits. Rubbing them briskly between your palms should heat the rings enough so you can push the parfaits out easily.

Cut the plums in half and remove the pits. Cut the plums into very thin slices and arrange on top of each parfait in concentric circles, beginning at the outside and working in, to form a rose. Set each parfait on a cookie, place on a dessert plate, and drizzle a little of the sauce around.

chocolate-beet cake ~ candied beets ~ raspberry-beet sauce

Chef Alex Lee of Daniel taught me his way of starting to create recipes: taking an ingredient and then making a list of all the other flavors or ingredients that go well with it. He also prompted me to start thinking about the possibilities of pairing vegetables with sweets.

In this dessert, I match the earthiness of chocolate with the earthiness of beets.

When you make the candied beets, use a mixture of red, golden, and chiogga (the candy-striped ones) for the prettiest presentation. You'll need separate batches of Simple Syrup for each type of beet to keep the colors intact.

You'll be roasting more beets than you need for the cake. Use the extra puree to make Raspberry-Beet Sauce.

Peel the beets and slice them about ⅛ inch thick. A vegetable slicer or mandoline works well for this.

Bring the simple syrup to a boil in a saucepan over medium heat. Add the beets and bring to a simmer. Reduce the heat and simmer the beets gently until they're translucent, about 1 hour. Keep the heat low, so the beets don't curl as you cook them. Let cool completely in the syrup.

Line a baking sheet with a Silpat or parchment.

Drain the beets gently, so they don't break, and dredge them in sugar. Arrange on the baking sheet and place in a cold oven overnight to dry.

Store in an airtight container for up to a week.

SERVES 8 TO 10

MAKE IT SIMPLER
You could skip the candied beets if need be. As an act of desperation, you could substitute a store-bought chocolate cake for the cake here.

For the Candied Beets
2 BUNCHES BABY BEETS
2 CUPS (560 G) SIMPLE SYRUP
 (PAGE 184)
SUGAR

CONTINUES . . .

Heat the oven to 425°F or 400°F on convection.

3 LARGE BEETS

COARSE SALT

1 OUNCE (28 G) UNSWEETENED
  CHOCOLATE (PREFERABLY
  VALRHONA COCOA PASTE),
  CHOPPED

½ CUP PLUS 2 TABLESPOONS (80 G)
  ALL-PURPOSE FLOUR

½ TEASPOON (2 G) BAKING SODA

¾ CUP PLUS 1 TABLESPOON
  (160 G) SUGAR

1 LARGE EGG

6 TABLESPOONS (80 G) GRAPESEED
  OIL

1 TEASPOON (2 G) VANILLA
  EXTRACT

Trim the tops from the beets, leaving about 1 inch of the stems. Tear off a large piece of aluminum foil and make a bed of coarse salt in the center. Set the beets on the salt, wrap the foil to make a tight package, and roast the beets until very tender, about 1 hour.

Let the beets cool. Peel them and cut them into chunks. Put them in a food processor and process to a very fine puree. Strain and measure out ½ cup. Reserve the rest for the sauce.

Heat the oven to 350°F or 325°F on convection. Butter and sugar a 9-inch square baking pan.

Melt the chocolate in the microwave, in 30-second bursts, stirring after each burst.

Whisk the flour, baking soda, and ⅛ teaspoon salt together in a bowl.

Put the sugar, egg, and oil in the bowl of a standing mixer fitted with the whisk. Whisk for 2 minutes at medium-high speed, until pale and light. Beat in the vanilla extract, then the dry ingredients, then the chocolate, then the beet puree, mixing well after each addition.

Scrape the batter into the pan and rap it on the counter to remove air bubbles. Bake until a knife comes out clean, 18 to 20 minutes, rotating the pan after 10 minutes. Let cool completely before removing the cake from the pan

To Serve

Cut the cake into cubes.

RASPBERRY-BEET SAUCE
  (PAGE 273)

Dip one cube in the raspberry-beet sauce, coating it completely. Pair it with a plain piece of cake on a dessert plate and garnish with a few candied beets, crumbling some of the beets if you want, and a spoonful of sauce.

This tasting combines textures and temperatures, moving from the warm tart to the icy and refreshing vacherin *to the creamy and crisp pairing of panna cotta and rhubarb and finishing up with a light consommé.*

serves 8

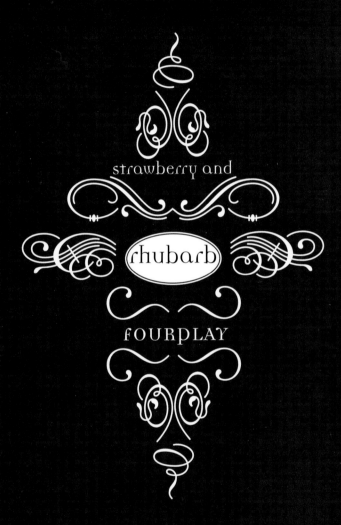

strawberry and **rhubarb** FOURPLAY

strawberry-rhubarb consommé ~ basil tapioca
~ rhubarb foam

fromage blanc panna cotta ~ rhubarb two ways
~ crispy almond phyllo

pink peppercorn meringues ~ white chocolate ice cream
~ rhubarb sorbet

rhubarb-flan tarts ~ graham streusel
~ mustard-rhubarb jam

strawberry-rhubarb consommé ~ basil tapioca ~ rhubarb foam

SERVES 4 ON ITS OWN OR
8 AS PART OF A FOURPLAY

MAKE IT SIMPLER
You could serve the consommé without the basil tapioca and foam, just with the Thai basil.

Maybe I like rhubarb so much because I started eating it when I was a child; my mother's strawberry-rhubarb pie is one of my earliest memories. And I love summer fruit soups; that's something I learned from François Payard. So this combination is a natural for me.

You need just the pod from the vanilla bean for this dessert, so if you have saved some used pods, now is the time to recycle. And you will need a whipped cream charger (see page 279) for the foam.

You will have leftover consommé (which you can freeze) and foam; you simply can't successfully foam less liquid than is in the recipe.

For the Rhubarb Foam

2 POUNDS (900 G) VERY RIPE
    RHUBARB
GRENADINE
2 TEASPOONS POWDERED GELATIN
    (OR 9 G SHEET GELATIN; SEE
    PAGE 276)

Cut the rhubarb into small pieces and put it through a juicer. Rhubarb fibers can clog the juicer, so you may need to clean it about halfway through this process. Strain the juice and measure out 2 cups. Adjust the color with grenadine to make it a light pink.

Pour about ½ cup of the juice into a small glass bowl and sprinkle the gelatin over the surface. Let it sit for about 1 minute, then microwave for 45 seconds or heat gently in a saucepan until melted. Pour into the rest of the rhubarb juice and stir for about 1 minute.

Pour into a whipped cream maker and screw on a fresh N_2O charger. Shake vigorously for about 2 minutes. Refrigerate for at least 2 hours, shaking vigorously every 30 minutes or so, as the gelatin sets, or for up to 1 week.

Remove the zest from the orange and lemon with a vegetable peeler. Tie the zest in cheesecloth along with the vanilla pod and lemongrass. Juice the orange and lemon. Strain the juices and reserve.

Put the strawberries, rhubarb, elderflower cordial, Moscato d'Asti, water, and grenadine in a saucepan and bring to a boil over medium-high heat. Add the cheesecloth sachet, reduce the heat, and simmer the soup for 10 minutes. Remove from the heat and let cool to room temperature.

Remove the sachet and liquefy the soup with an immersion blender. Strain through a fine strainer set over a bowl or pitcher (discard the solids). Whisk in the orange and lemon juices and chill thoroughly before serving or for up to 3 days.

For the Consommé

MAKES 2½ CUPS

½ ORANGE

½ LEMON

DRIED POD FROM ½ SCRAPED VANILLA BEAN

½ STALK FRESH LEMONGRASS, TRIMMED, CRUSHED, AND CHOPPED

6 OUNCES (170 G) FRESH STRAWBERRIES, HULLED AND HALVED

1½ POUNDS (680 G) RIPE RHUBARB, CHOPPED

⅓ CUP (85 G) ELDERFLOWER CORDIAL (SEE NOTE)

½ CUP (120 G) MOSCATO D'ASTI

½ CUP (120 G) WATER

1 TABLESPOON (15 G) GRENADINE

NOTE: Elderflower cordial is available at gourmet markets and online from English Delights.

CONTINUES . . .

For the Basil Tapioca

MAKES ABOUT 1 CUP

4 CUPS (960 G) WATER

1/3 CUP (30 G) SMALL (OR LARGE) PEARL TAPIOCA

1 1/4 CUPS (350 G) SIMPLE SYRUP (PAGE 184)

PACKED 1/2 CUP (25 G) FRESH BASIL LEAVES

Bring 2 cups of the water to a boil in a small saucepan. Add the tapioca and simmer, stirring occasionally, for about 10 minutes. The tapioca will have lost about half its opacity. Drain and rinse the tapioca. Bring the remaining 2 cups water to a boil and add the tapioca. Cook until the tapioca has lost all its opacity, another 2 to 3 minutes. Large pearls will take longer to cook. Drain, and rinse well in cold water to remove the excess starch. Put the tapioca in a container with 1 cup of the simple syrup and refrigerate until you're ready to serve.

Blanch the basil in boiling water for 15 seconds. Drain, refresh in ice water, and drain again. Squeeze out all of the water and put the basil in a blender. Add the remaining 1/4 cup simple syrup and blend on high for at least 1 minute, to make a smooth puree. Line a strainer with a few layers of cheesecloth. Strain the basil syrup (discard the solids) and refrigerate until you're ready to serve or for up to 1 week.

To Serve

FRESH THAI BASIL LEAVES, THINLY SLICED (OPTIONAL)

Drain the tapioca. Stir the basil syrup into the tapioca and add a spoonful to a small glass. Pour in the consommé over the back of a spoon to help keep the layers distinct. Shake the whipped cream maker and top the glass with a shot of rhubarb foam. Sprinkle with sliced basil, if desired. Repeat for each serving.

Fromage Blanc Panna Cotta ~
Rhubarb Two Ways ~ Crispy Almond Phyllo

This dessert showcases the versatility of rhubarb, its acidity balanced by a silky, creamy cheese panna cotta. The recipe scales up quite easily if you want to make more for a crowd.

Line an 8 x 4-inch loaf pan with plastic wrap.

Pour a couple of tablespoons of the cream into a small bowl and sprinkle the gelatin over the surface. Let it sit for about 1 minute, then microwave for 45 seconds or heat gently in a saucepan until melted.

Put the remaining cream, the sugar, and the vanilla pod and seeds in a small saucepan and bring to a boil over medium-high heat. Add the cream and gelatin and stir.

Put the cheese in a heatproof bowl and pour in the hot cream. Emulsify with an immersion blender. Strain through a fine strainer.

Pour the panna cotta mixture into the prepared pan and chill overnight.

Unmold the panna cotta. Slice into rectangles and use a spatula to transfer it to dessert plates. Garnish each with a few batons of rhubarb, a few blackberries (it looks nice when you cut the blackberries in half), and a shard or two of the crispy phyllo. Drizzle a few drops of the port poaching liquid on the plate.

SERVES 4 ON ITS OWN OR
8 AS PART OF A FOURPLAY

For the Panna Cotta
SCANT ½ CUP (112 G) HEAVY
   CREAM
½ TEASPOON POWDERED GELATIN
   (OR 2.25 G SHEET GELATIN; SEE
   PAGE 276)
¼ CUP (50 G) SUGAR
½ VANILLA BEAN, SPLIT AND
   SCRAPED
8 OUNCES (225 G) FROMAGE BLANC

To Serve
PORT-POACHED RHUBARB
   (PAGE 248)
RHUBARB PICKLES (PAGE 249)
BLACKBERRIES
CRISPY ALMOND PHYLLO
   (PAGE 211)

MAKE IT SIMPLER
You could serve the panna cotta with the almond phyllo and just fresh berries, or pair it with the Strawberry-Rhubarb Compote (page 250). If you want, you could replace the almond phyllo with a thin, crisp store-bought cookie, but the phyllo is so easy to make.

pink peppercorn meringues ~
white chocolate ice cream ~ rhubarb sorbet

SERVES 8

MAKE IT SIMPLER
You could buy meringues from a good pastry shop (you won't find them perfumed with pink peppercorns, though). You could also crumble the meringues and layer the components in a parfait glass, like a trifle. Just make sure to keep the amount of each component the same.

For the Meringues

MAKES ABOUT 24 MERINGUES
¼ CUP (62 G) EGG WHITES
CREAM OF TARTAR
5 TABLESPOONS (62 G)
   GRANULATED SUGAR
½ CUP (60 G) CONFECTIONERS'
   SUGAR
¾ TEASPOON PINK PEPPERCORNS,
   COARSELY GROUND IN A SPICE
   GRINDER

I started making vacherins *when I was in the south of France, at Pâtisserie Chéreau in Nice, and fell in love with this combination of meringue, creamy ice cream, fruit, sorbet, and whipped cream. We made big ones in France, but I like individual* vacherins *best.*

I use a stencil when I make these meringues in the restaurant, but I've adapted the recipe for a pastry bag here. The recipe makes more than you will need for the dessert, but it's nearly impossible to whip any less egg white successfully.

The meringues will keep for several days if you store them airtight, and they're a great snack. Make as many of the composed desserts as you like. You will have enough sorbet and ice cream for up to 24.

Heat the oven to 150°F.

Line a baking sheet with parchment and trace twenty-four 2-inch circles onto the paper. Turn the parchment over, so the ink won't bleed into the meringues.

Put the egg whites and a tiny bit of cream of tartar in the bowl of a standing mixer fitted with the whisk. Turn it on to low, and beat the whites gently for 2 minutes, to start establishing a structure. The whites will look frothy but still a bit wet. Turn the speed up to medium and add 2 tablespoons of the granulated sugar. Continue to beat at medium speed until the whites have body and are just shy of having soft peaks. Add 2 more tablespoons of the sugar and continue beating until the whites have formed firm peaks. Add the remaining 1 tablespoon sugar and beat until the whites are glossy and smooth and almost stiff. Keep your eye on the whites, so you don't overbeat them. If the whites get grainy, they're useless.

Sift the confectioners' sugar over the whites and sprinkle on the ground peppercorns. Fold in gently but thoroughly.

Transfer the meringue to a pastry bag fitted with a small plain round tip (#803 is perfect) and pipe out neat concentric circles from the outside in, using the circles you drew as a guide. Keep inside the tracings so the finished meringues will fit into 2-inch ring molds. Bake the meringues for about 1 hour, until crisp. Cool completely and store in an airtight container.

Set a meringue in the bottom of a 2 x 2-inch ring mold. Fill the mold about half full with sorbet, using the back of a spoon to press the sorbet up against the sides all the way to the top, leaving a well in the center. Clean the edges and freeze for at least 2 hours until firm. Repeat for each serving.

Put a spoonful of strawberries in the sorbet well of each mold and cover with white chocolate ice cream, filling the mold to the top and evening it off. Return to the freezer for at least 2 hours or up to 2 days.

Rub each mold briskly between your hands to release the *vacherin.* Set it on a small plate and top with some vanilla whipped cream. Crumble a few leaves of crystallized verbena over the top as a garnish, if you want, and serve.

For the Vacherins
RHUBARB SORBET (PAGE 235)
DICED FRESH STRAWBERRIES
WHITE CHOCOLATE ICE CREAM
    (PAGE 221)

To Serve
VANILLA WHIPPED CREAM
    (PAGE 184)
CRYSTALLIZED VERBENA (PAGE
    186; OPTIONAL)

Rhubarb-Flan Tarts ~ Graham Streusel ~ Mustard-Rhubarb Jam

SERVES 8

This is a riff on Jean-Georges's grandmother's rhubarb tart. It's not her recipe for the pastry or the streusel, but the notion of macerating the rhubarb before baking and adding the flan came from her. Mustard may not be a traditional ingredient for desserts, but it adds a definite edge to the jam and it's my nod to Alsace, from where Jean-Georges hails.

You'll have leftover jam. Try pairing it with cheese or with a sizzling steak.

MAKE IT SIMPLER
Try making this as a single large tart in a 9-inch tart pan. You could doctor some good all-fruit jam from the grocery store with crushed mustard seeds instead of making the jam.

For the Mustard-Rhubarb Jam
MAKES ABOUT 1½ CUPS

1 CINNAMON STICK
1 WHOLE CLOVE
½ TEASPOON (1 G) GROUND MACE
1 TABLESPOON (9 G) YELLOW MUSTARD SEEDS, CRUSHED
1½ CUPS (357 G) SWEET MUSCAT WINE
½ CUP (120 G) RED WINE VINEGAR
1½ POUNDS (680 G) RIPE RHUBARB, PEELED AND CHOPPED
2 TABLESPOONS (25 G) SUGAR
½ TEASPOON (0.85 G) XANTHAN GUM

Tie the cinnamon, clove, mace, and mustard seeds in a few layers of cheesecloth. Put the spice sachet in a saucepan with the wine and vinegar and bring to a boil over medium heat. Add the rhubarb, bring to a simmer, and simmer for 5 minutes. Remove from the heat and let cool to room temperature.

Drain to get rid of the excess liquid. Remove the spice sachet and puree the rhubarb in a food processor.

Set up an ice bath in a large bowl.

Bring the rhubarb back to a simmer. Mix the sugar and xanthan gum and whisk in, a few grains at a time (you don't want the xanthan gum to clump). Scrape out into a medium bowl and set into the ice bath, stirring often to chill down quickly. Once cool, refrigerate until ready to serve or for up to 1 week.

For the Rhubarb Filling
8 OUNCES (227 G) RIPE RHUBARB
⅓ CUP (65 G) SUGAR

Peel the rhubarb and cut into tiny dice. Toss it with the sugar and macerate for at least 2 hours.

Set up an ice bath in a large bowl.

Put the cream and vanilla seeds (rinse, dry, and save the pod for another use) in a small saucepan and heat to just below a simmer.

Whisk the sugar and cornstarch together.

In a separate bowl, whisk the egg until smooth; gradually whisk in the dry ingredients, beating until smooth.

Slowly add half the warm cream to the egg mixture and whisk for about 1 minute to temper it. Off of the heat, scrape the egg mixture into the pan and mix well with an immersion blender. Strain into a small bowl and set into the ice bath to chill down quickly, stirring often. Refrigerate until ready to use or for up to 1 day.

Roll half the dough $\frac{1}{16}$ inch thick on a lightly floured work surface. Transfer to a Silpat- or parchment-lined baking sheet and chill for 30 minutes. Cut out eight $2\frac{1}{4}$ x 4-inch rectangles and line eight $\frac{3}{4}$ x $3\frac{1}{4}$-inch tart molds with the dough (or cut $3\frac{1}{2}$-inch circles and line $2\frac{1}{4}$-inch tart rings). Place them on the baking sheet and chill for 30 minutes.

Heat the oven to 375°F or 350°F on convection.

Strain the rhubarb filling and fill the tart shells to overflowing. Bake until the rhubarb is starting to brown, about 20 minutes.

Reduce the oven temperature to 325°F (300°F if you're using convection).

Pour some of the flan into each tart and top each with a generous amount of the graham streusel. Bake until the streusel is browned and the filling is bubbling, about 20 minutes.

Let cool for at least a few minutes before unmolding. You can serve the tarts warm or at room temperature.

Spoon some mustard-rhubarb jam onto dessert plates and spread it with the back of a spoon. Dust the tarts with confectioners' sugar, set them on the jam, and serve.

For the Flan

¼ CUP (60 G) HEAVY CREAM
½ VANILLA BEAN, SPLIT AND
  SCRAPED
3 TABLESPOONS (37 G) SUGAR
1 TABLESPOON (10 G) CORNSTARCH
1 LARGE EGG

For the Tarts

PÂTE BRISÉE (PAGE 180)
GRAHAM STREUSEL (PAGE 214)
CONFECTIONERS' SUGAR

I love seeing how much can be done with a single ingredient. This tasting is a playful experiment in textures, with each dessert capturing the essence of strawberry flavor in a different form.

serves 12

strawberry

FOURPLAY

strawberry soda ~ birch beer cream

strawberry ice cream ~ strawberry-lavender leather

strawberry shortcakes ~ slow-roasted strawberries
~ vanilla whipped cream

strawberry gelée ~ coconut cream ~ crispy chocolate

strawberry soda ~ birch beer cream

SERVES 6 ON ITS OWN OR
12 AS PART OF A FOURPLAY

Recently, I've become infatuated with bubbles and carbonation, and I've been on a mission to find ways to introduce bubbles as a texture in desserts. So adding a soda to the menu was a natural. With the help of David Arnold, Director of Culinary Technology at the French Culinary Institute, I've built a carbonation rig for the pastry kitchen at Jean Georges.

Don't let that scare you from trying this recipe, though. All you need at home is a soda siphon. Using a half-size hotel pan and perforated hotel pan (which you can buy online from BigTray) ensures that the strawberry water freezes and defrosts evenly during the clarification process.

For the Soda

MAKES ABOUT 3 CUPS

17 OUNCES (500 G) FRESH
STRAWBERRIES, HULLED
2 CUPS PLUS 1 TABLESPOON
(500 G) WATER
1/2 CUP (100 G) SUGAR
1 1/4 TEASPOONS POWDERED
GELATIN (OR 5.5 G SHEET
GELATIN; SEE PAGE 276)

Put the strawberries, water, and sugar in a saucepan and bring to a boil. Remove from the heat and puree with an immersion blender.

Ladle out about 3/4 cup of the strawberry puree into a small heatproof bowl. Sprinkle the gelatin over the surface and let sit for about 1 minute. Microwave for 45 seconds or heat gently in a saucepan until melted. Stir the gelatin into the rest of the strawberries and pour into a half-size hotel pan. Let cool to room temperature. Cover with plastic wrap and freeze overnight.

Line a perforated hotel pan with several layers of cheesecloth and turn the frozen puree out into it. Wash the hotel pan, set the perforated pan into it, and refrigerate to drain for 2 days.

Discard the solids. Load the strawberry water into a soda siphon and charge with a CO_2 charger. Shake vigorously for 1 minute. Refrigerate until you're ready to serve or for up to 3 days.

Put the cream in a chilled bowl with the sugar and birch beer extract and whip to soft peaks.

For the Birch Beer Cream
½ CUP (120 G) HEAVY CREAM
2 TEASPOONS (6 G)
   CONFECTIONERS' SUGAR
½ TEASPOON (2.5 G) BIRCH BEER
   EXTRACT (SEE NOTE) OR
   VANILLA EXTRACT

NOTE: Birch beer extract is available online from Terra Spice Company.

Put a few diced strawberries in the bottom of each glass and fill with the soda. Top with a dollop of the birch beer cream.

To Serve
DICED FRESH STRAWBERRIES

strawberry ice cream ~ strawberry-lavender leather

SERVES 6 ON ITS OWN OR
12 AS PART OF A FOURPLAY

In this dessert, you get the same flavor twice but with different textures: creamy ice cream and slightly chewy strawberry leather. Fruit leathers are an ideal way to incorporate secondary flavors, like herbs, and making leathers is really easy.

For the Strawberry-Lavender Leather

MAKES 12 PIECES

13 OUNCES (370 G) FRESH
  STRAWBERRIES
6 TABLESPOONS (75 G) SUGAR
5 SPRIGS FRESH LAVENDER,
  BUDS ONLY (SEE NOTE)

NOTE: Make sure your lavender hasn't been sprayed.

Heat the oven to 150°F. Line a 9 x 12-inch rimmed baking sheet with a Silpat.

Hull the strawberries and process them in a food processor to a fine puree.

Put the puree and sugar in a small saucepan and bring to a boil over medium-high heat. Reduce the heat to low and simmer until reduced by a bit more than half, stirring and scraping often with a heatproof rubber scraper. Work the puree through a fine strainer (discard the solids) and stir in the lavender. Spread into a thin layer on the Silpat.

Dry in the oven until leathery, about 4 hours. It will still be slightly tacky and flexible. Let cool.

Alternatively, set a dehydrator to 130°F. Line trays with acetate and spray lightly with cooking spray. Spread the puree into thin layers and dry for 3 hours.

To make curls, cut 2 x 4-inch-wide strips as soon as you take the leather out of the oven, roll them loosely, and place them in something to hold the shape as it sets. I use baguette forms in the restaurant. You could use something similar at home, or wrap the leather around a rolling pin. It will take about 1 hour to set.

If you are not serving right away, peel the strawberry film off the Silpat and lay it on a piece of parchment. Roll it up and wrap in plastic. It will keep for a few days.

To Serve

STRAWBERRY ICE CREAM
  (PAGE 228)
2 SPRIGS FRESH LAVENDER,
  BUDS ONLY

Scoop the ice cream into dessert bowls. Garnish with a curl or piece of the leather and some lavender.

strawberry shortcakes
~ slow-roasted strawberries ~ vanilla whipped cream

I'm not a fan of angel food cake or sponge cake for shortcakes; I prefer the texture and bite of biscuits, which I like to shape into small squares instead of large rounds. And I love gently roasted fruit. The long, slow roasting eliminates a lot of the water content of the fruit, concentrating the flavor and opening it up. The tangy crème fraîche in the whipped cream rounds out the flavors on the plate.

SERVES 6 ON ITS OWN OR
12 AS PART OF A FOURPLAY

MAKE IT SIMPLER
You could replace the biscuits with refrigerator biscuits. Brush them with an egg wash (an egg and an egg yolk beaten together) and sprinkle them with sugar and salt before baking. Fresh berries or stone fruit is another option in place of the roasted berries.

Put the flour, baking powder, baking soda, and salt in a food processor. Pulse a few times to combine. Add the shortening and pulse until the texture resembles fine crumbs. Whisk the milk and beaten egg together and pour through the feed tube, hitting the pulse button until the dough comes together evenly.

Turn the dough out onto a lightly floured work surface and form into a square. Wrap in plastic and refrigerate for at least 1 hour or up to 8 hours.

CONTINUES . . .

For the Shortcakes
MAKES TWENTY-FOUR
1½-INCH SQUARES

2⅓ CUPS (290 G) ALL-PURPOSE
FLOUR
4 TEASPOONS (16 G) BAKING
POWDER
½ TEASPOON (3 G) BAKING SODA
½ TEASPOON (2 G) COARSE SALT
6 TABLESPOONS (70 G) VEGETABLE
SHORTENING, CUT INTO PIECES
AND CHILLED
⅔ CUP (156 G) MILK
1 LARGE EGG AND 1 LARGE EGG
YOLK, BEATEN

To Serve

2 TABLESPOONS (28 G) UNSALTED
   BUTTER, MELTED
COARSE PINK SALT
SLOW-ROASTED STRAWBERRIES
   (PAGE 245)
VANILLA WHIPPED CREAM
   (PAGE 184)

Set the oven rack in the top position. Heat the oven to 450°F or 425°F on convection. Line a baking sheet with a Silpat or parchment.

Flour the work surface lightly and roll the dough into a square about ½ inch thick. Cut into twenty-four 1½-inch squares and place on the baking sheet. Brush the tops with melted butter and sprinkle with pink salt. Bake until risen and lightly browned, 4 to 5 minutes, rotating the pan halfway through baking.

Serve the shortcakes warm, with the strawberries and vanilla whipped cream, and drizzle some of the berry maceration liquid on the plate.

strawberry gelée ~ coconut cream ~ crispy chocolate

The flavor combinations here—particularly the strawberry and coconut—remind me of some Caribbean cocktail, the kind with an umbrella in it.

Roll the dough between two sheets of parchment until ¹⁄₁₆ inch thick. Slide onto a baking sheet and refrigerate for 30 minutes.

Cut the dough into twelve 2½-inch squares or 1 x 3-inch rectangles and separate them on the parchment, giving them room to spread. Refrigerate on the pan while you heat the oven.

Heat the oven to 375°F or 350°F on convection.

Lay a Silpat (top side down) on the squares to weight them down. Bake until just crisp, 12 to 15 minutes. Let cool on the baking sheet.

Cut the gelée into squares or rectangles to match the pastry and set onto the pastry.

Fill a pastry bag with the coconut cream and pipe two dollops on top of the gelée. Fill the remaining spaces with strawberries. Top with the chocolate décor.

Spoon some strawberry sauce onto dessert plates, set the desserts on top, and garnish with strawberries and, if you want, a few pinches of coconut milk powder.

SERVES 12

For the Dough
½ RECIPE CHOCOLATE SALT
    BUTTER SHORTBREAD dough
    (PAGE 203)

To Serve
STRAWBERRY GELÉE (PAGE 253)
COCONUT CREAM (PAGE 256)
FRESH STRAWBERRIES, HULLED
    AND CUT IN HALVES OR
    QUARTERS
CHOCOLATE DÉCOR (PAGE 265)
STRAWBERRY SAUCE (PAGE 272)
COCONUT MILK POWDER
    (OPTIONAL, SEE NOTE)

MAKE IT SIMPLER
Though it will change the dessert a lot, you could replace the pastry with a thin, crumbly shortbread from the store. Or substitute all-natural strawberry preserves for the gelée. Or top the dessert with shaved chocolate instead of the décor.

Note: Coconut milk powder is available online from Terra Spice Company.

summer

I turn a few things on their heads in this tasting. Figs are treated as if they were a vegetable and are grilled. Sangria, usually a drink, becomes a frozen counterpoint to the figs. And the tomatoes here are combined with blackberries in a fruit salad.

serves 12

cherry, fig, and tomato FOURPLAY

Tart cherry soup ~ frozen yogurt ~ sesame tuiles

Grilled figs ~ Raspberry-fig sangria granité

Honey-Roasted tomatoes ~ two sorbets ~ Almond streusel

White chocolate and cacao nib soufflés
~ Black peppermint crème Anglaise

tart cherry soup ~ frozen yogurt ~ sesame tuiles

SERVES 4 ON ITS OWN OR
12 AS PART OF A FOURPLAY

MAKE IT SIMPLER
You can certainly buy frozen
yogurt. And instead of making
the tuiles, garnish with
toasted sesame seeds or
crumble some great halvah
over the top.

I've adapted this dessert from one of Jean-Georges Vongerichten's recipes. It starts with his base soup, and I've added the tanginess of yogurt and the toasted nuttiness of sesame for depth of flavor and contrasting textures.

For the Soup

MAKES ABOUT 2 CUPS

1¼ POUNDS (567 G) SOUR
  CHERRIES
¾ CUP (180 G) WATER
⅓ CUP PLUS 2 TABLESPOONS (90 G)
  SUGAR

Pit the cherries. Put them in a saucepan with the water and sugar and stir. Bring to a boil to dissolve the sugar.

Transfer to a bowl, cover with plastic wrap, and chill overnight.

To Serve

FROZEN YOGURT (PAGE 230)
SESAME TUILES (PAGE 208)

Spoon some of the soup into a small glass or bowl. Top with a scoop of frozen yogurt and garnish with a tuile. Repeat for each serving.

grilled figs ~ raspberry-fig sangria granité

Ripe figs are delicious right off the tree, but in this recipe, I'm applying a touch of heat just to make them that much more tender.

Heat a griddle, preferably cast iron, over medium-high heat.

Cut the figs in half lengthwise and brush the cut sides with olive oil.

Cook the figs on the griddle, cut side down, until tender and lightly browned, about 3 minutes.

Divide the figs among dessert plates and sprinkle lightly with fleur de sel. If you want, garnish with some freeze-dried raspberries and cilantro. Serve with a small bowl (or Chinese soupspoon) of granité. If you want a sauce, melt a little of the granité to drizzle onto the plate.

SERVES 4 TO 6 ON ITS OWN
OR 12 AS PART OF A FOURPLAY

For the Figs
24 FRESH MISSION FIGS
OLIVE OIL

To Serve
FLEUR DE SEL
FREEZE-DRIED RASPBERRIES
  (SEE NOTE; OPTIONAL)
MICRO CILANTRO (OR CHOPPED
  FRESH CILANTRO LEAVES;
  OPTIONAL)
RASPBERRY-FIG SANGRIA
  GRANITÉ (PAGE 240)

NOTE: Freeze-dried raspberries (sold as Just Raspberries) are available at many grocery stores.

Honey-Roasted Tomatoes ~ Two Sorbets ~ Almond Streusel

SERVES 4 TO 6 ON ITS OWN OR 12 AS PART OF A FOURPLAY

MAKE IT SIMPLER
You could substitute your favorite salty-buttery cookie for the almond streusel, and crumble it on top.

This dessert was inspired by "Tomato Tim" Stark of Eckerton Hill Farm at the Union Square farmers' market in New York City. We were talking one morning and he gave me some tomatoes that were so sweet they tasted like berries. So I roasted them and paired them with super-ripe blackberries for an after-dinner fruit salad. Use a mix of tiny tomatoes for the best-looking and -tasting dessert.

For the Streusel

3 TABLESPOONS (42 G) UNSALTED BUTTER, SOFTENED
3 TABLESPOONS (37 G) SUGAR
SCANT ½ CUP (55 G) ALL-PURPOSE FLOUR
2 TABLESPOONS (15 G) ALMOND FLOUR
2 TABLESPOONS (17 G) SLICED ALMONDS, CHOPPED
½ TEASPOON (2 G) COARSE SALT

Heat the oven to 350°F or 325°F on convection. Line a small rimmed baking sheet with a Silpat or parchment.

Put the butter and sugar in the bowl of a standing mixer fitted with the paddle. Beat at medium speed until creamy. Add the all-purpose flour, almond flour, chopped almonds, and salt and mix at low speed until crumbly.

Gather the streusel by the handful and compact it in your hands. Break it into small clumps onto the baking sheet.

Bake until golden brown, about 20 minutes, stirring the streusel about halfway through baking. Let cool on a rack.

For the Tomatoes

1 PINT (453 G) RIPE RED GRAPE OR CURRANT TOMATOES
2 TABLESPOONS (40 G) HONEY, PREFERABLY LAVENDER
2 TEASPOONS (17 G) EXTRA-VIRGIN OLIVE OIL
COARSE SALT

Heat the oven to 200°F or 175°F on convection.

Put the tomatoes in a small baking dish. Toss with the honey, the olive oil, and salt to taste.

Roast until the tomatoes start to collapse but still look intact, 1½ to 2 hours (currant tomatoes will roast more quickly). Let cool on a rack.

Combine equal amounts of the sorbets in a bowl, stirring just enough to make swirls.

Cut some of the tomatoes and blackberries in half. Toss the blackberries with the tomatoes. Spoon into small bowls. Top each with a scoop of the mixed sorbets and sprinkle streusel over everything.

To Serve
TOMATO SORBET (PAGE 237)
LEMON-BASIL SORBET (PAGE 233)
6 OUNCES (170 G) BLACKBERRIES

white chocolate and cacao nib soufflés ~
black peppermint crème anglaise

SERVES 4 ON ITS OWN OR
12 AS PART OF A FOURPLAY

Cacao nibs give the flavor of chocolate without added sweetness, and they're a great side texture to this airy soufflé.

MAKE IT SIMPLER
Buy the Brandied Cherries.

For the Soufflés

BRANDIED CHERRIES (PAGE 246)
4 OUNCES (112 G) WHITE
  CHOCOLATE (PREFERABLY
  VALRHONA), FINELY CHOPPED
¼ CUP (60 G) HEAVY CREAM
2 LARGE EGG WHITES
1 TABLESPOON (6 G) EGG WHITE
  POWDER
CREAM OF TARTAR
¼ CUP PLUS 2 GENEROUS
  TABLESPOONS (75 G) SUGAR
2 TABLESPOONS (12 G) CACAO NIBS

Heat the oven to 400°F or 375°F on convection. Butter and sugar four 6-ounce ramekins or twelve 2-ounce ramekins. Place 2 drained Brandied Cherries in each ramekin.

Put the chocolate in a glass bowl and microwave for 30 seconds. Stir, then microwave another 30 seconds. The chocolate may not be completely melted. Bring the cream to a boil in a small saucepan.

Pour one-third of the hot cream into the center of the chocolate. Use a heatproof rubber spatula to stir, starting in the center and gradually working out. Pour in another third of the cream and continue to stir from the center out. Add the remaining cream and stir, from the center out, until the mixture is completely smooth.

In the bowl of a standing mixer fitted with the whisk, combine the egg whites with the egg white powder, a tiny pinch of cream of tartar, and 1 tablespoon of the sugar. Beat the whites at medium speed while you make the sugar syrup.

Place the remaining sugar in a small saucepan (a butter warmer is good here). Drizzle in a tablespoon or so of water. Mix with your fingers until the sugar is like wet sand. Cook over medium-high heat until the syrup reaches 250°F.

With the mixer still at medium speed (the egg whites should be holding whip marks, like whipped cream, at this point), pour the syrup in a steady stream into the whites, avoiding the whisk and the sides of the bowl. Turn the speed to high and beat the whites until the sides of the bowl feel only slightly warm.

Transfer the chocolate mixture to a large, wide bowl and fold in the cacao nibs. Fold in about one-quarter of the egg whites to lighten the mixture, then fold in the remaining egg whites carefully, so you maintain their volume and lightness.

Fill a pastry bag with the soufflé batter and pipe into the ramekins. Wet your finger and pat down any peaks. Set the ramekins on a baking sheet and bake until risen and just starting to brown on top. Small soufflés will take 5 to 6 minutes. Larger ones will take 12 to 18 minutes.

Serve the soufflés immediately, with some cherries and a pitcher of the crème anglaise. Garnish with some nibs, if desired.

To Serve
BRANDIED CHERRIES (PAGE 246)
BLACK PEPPERMINT CRÈME
  ANGLAISE (PAGE 269)
CACAO NIBS (OPTIONAL)

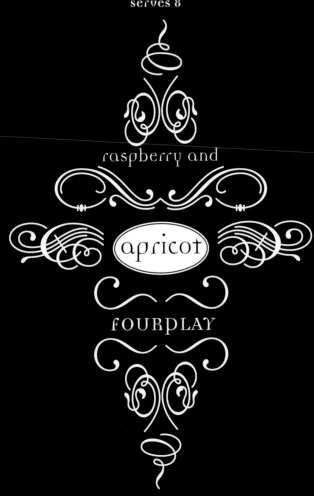

Raspberries and apricots are both bright flavors with a pleasant acidity, so this tasting explores their qualities on their own and in combination. And since each is a classic foil for chocolate, I've added a spicy, creamy "cake" to round out the fourplay.

serves 8

raspberry and

apricot

FOURPLAY

Raspberry—Rose water soup ~ champagne sorbet
~ Diced Apricots

Apricot panna cotta ~ Black peppermint gelée ~ Apricot sauce

Salt Butter shortbread ~ Almond cream
~ slow-Roasted Apricots

chocolate-chile cake

Raspberry–Rose Water Soup ~
champagne sorbet ~ Diced Apricots

SERVES 4 ON ITS OWN OR
8 AS PART OF A FOURPLAY

These ingredients all strike floral notes and to my mind are a natural combination. Raspberries contribute sweetness; champagne, acidity; rose water, depth of flavor; and the apricots, texture.

MAKE IT SIMPLER
You could float icy cold champagne on the soup instead of making the sorbet.

For the Apricots

¾ CUP (210 G) SIMPLE SYRUP (PAGE 184)
6 TABLESPOONS (90 G) WATER
4 OUNCES (113 G) DRIED TURKISH APRICOTS

Bring the simple syrup and water to a boil over medium heat. Add the apricots and bring to a simmer. Reduce the heat to low and simmer very gently for 5 minutes.

Pour the apricots and poaching liquid into a bowl, cover with plastic wrap, and refrigerate overnight to plump.

For the Soup

MAKES ABOUT 2 CUPS

24 OUNCES (680 G) FRESH RASPBERRIES
5 TABLESPOONS (87 G) SIMPLE SYRUP (PAGE 184), OR MORE TO TASTE
¾ TEASPOON POWDERED GELATIN (OR 3.3 G SHEET GELATIN; SEE PAGE 276)
1 TEASPOON (2 G) ROSE WATER

Put the raspberries in a food processor and process to a very smooth puree. Strain (discard the solids) and measure out 2 cups. Pour into a small saucepan and bring to a boil over medium-high heat, skimming off any impurities that rise to the surface. Strain through a fine strainer, then through a strainer lined with several layers of cheesecloth.

Put the simple syrup in a small glass bowl and sprinkle the gelatin over the surface. Let sit for at least 1 minute. Microwave for 30 seconds or heat gently in a saucepan to melt.

Add the syrup and gelatin to the raspberry puree and whisk for about 45 seconds. Stir in the rose water and taste. Add more syrup if necessary.

Chill completely before serving.

Spoon the soup into small dessert bowls or glasses. Cut the apricots into tiny dice and add to the soup with some fresh raspberries. Top with a scoop of the sorbet.

To Serve

FRESH RASPBERRIES

CHAMPAGNE SORBET (PAGE 238)

Apricot panna cotta ~
Black peppermint gelée ~ Apricot sauce

SERVES 4 TO 6 ON ITS OWN OR
8 AS PART OF A FOURPLAY

When I go to the farmers' markets in summer and see all the bounty, I start asking myself, "What can work with what?" and "What would balance that fruit?" Apricots and peppermint are both refreshing flavors. In this dessert, the mint livens the apricot, providing an herbal contrast to the natural sweetness of the fruit.

For the Gelée

PACKED 1½ CUPS (60 G) FRESH
BLACK PEPPERMINT LEAVES
6 TABLESPOONS (105 G) SIMPLE
SYRUP (PAGE 184)
6 TABLESPOONS (90 G) WATER
1¼ TEASPOONS POWDERED
GELATIN (OR 5.6 G SHEET
GELATIN; SEE PAGE 276)

Set up a bowl of ice water.

Bring a saucepan of water to a boil. Blanch the peppermint for 15 seconds, drain, and shock it in the ice water. Drain again and squeeze all the water out of the mint.

Put the mint in a blender with the simple syrup and the 6 tablespoons water. Blend at high speed for at least 1 minute to make a smooth puree. Strain through a fine strainer, pressing hard on the solids to get out all the mint syrup.

Put about 2 tablespoons of the mint syrup in a small glass bowl and sprinkle the gelatin over the top. Let sit for at least 1 minute to soften. Microwave for 30 seconds or heat gently in a saucepan until melted. Add the gelatin to the rest of the syrup and mix well. Divide the gelée among four 6-ounce ramekins, six 4-ounce custard cups, or 8 small glasses and refrigerate until set, at least 2 hours. (For the photograph, I poured the gelée into tall shot glasses and leaned them on their sides in an egg carton while the gelée set.)

Mix the sugar and gelatin together in a small bowl.

    Put the apricot puree, milk, and cream in a small saucepan and bring to a boil over medium heat. Turn off the heat and whisk in the sugar and gelatin, stirring for at least 1 minute.

    Let the panna cotta mixture cool to room temperature.

    Pour the panna cotta over the peppermint gelée, dividing it evenly and leaving a little room at the top of each. Refrigerate overnight to set.

Spoon a layer of apricot sauce over the panna cotta and garnish with some mint, if you want.

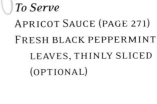

For the Panna Cotta

3 TABLESPOONS PLUS 1 TEASPOON (40 G) SUGAR

1 TEASPOON POWDERED GELATIN (OR 4.5 G SHEET GELATIN; SEE PAGE 276)

1 CUP (250 G) APRICOT PUREE (SEE PAGE 276)

½ CUP (120 G) WHOLE MILK

½ CUP (120 G) HEAVY CREAM

To Serve

APRICOT SAUCE (PAGE 271)

FRESH BLACK PEPPERMINT LEAVES, THINLY SLICED (OPTIONAL)

salt butter shortbread ~
almond cream ~ slow-roasted apricots

SERVES 8

The shortbread in this dessert provides the texture as well as the base for the tender apricots and delicate almond cream.

For the Almond Cream

⅓ CUP (65 G) SUGAR

4 TABLESPOONS PLUS 1 TEASPOON (62 G) UNSALTED BUTTER, SOFTENED

½ CUP PLUS 2 TABLESPOONS (64 G) ALMOND FLOUR

1 EXTRA-LARGE EGG

2 TABLESPOONS (16 G) ALL-PURPOSE FLOUR

Put the sugar and butter in the bowl of a standing mixer fitted with the paddle. Beat at medium speed until light. Add the almond flour and beat just to combine. Add the eggs and beat to combine. Add the all-purpose flour and beat well, scraping down the sides of the bowl.

Refrigerate until you're ready to finish the dessert.

For the Lemon Thyme Honey

½ CUP (120 G) WATER

3 TABLESPOONS (60 G) HONEY

4 OR 5 SPRIGS FRESH LEMON THYME

Stir the water and honey together in a small saucepan. Add the thyme. Bring to a boil over medium-high heat. Reduce the heat to low and cook until you have a thick syrup, about 10 minutes.

To Serve

SLOW-ROASTED APRICOTS (PAGE 244)

SALT BUTTER SHORTBREAD (PAGE 202)

CRYSTALLIZED LEMON THYME SPRIGS (SEE PAGE 186)

FLEUR DE SEL

Set the oven rack in the highest position. Heat the oven to 400°F or 375°F on convection.

Fill a pastry bag with the almond cream and pipe it into the cavities of 8 roasted apricots. Set the apricots on a baking sheet and bake on the top rack until the cream has just a touch of color, about 5 minutes.

Set a shortbread on a dessert plate and spoon on a little of the lemon thyme honey. Top with a filled apricot. Garnish with the crystallized thyme, salt, and a drizzle of the honey.

MAKE IT SIMPLER
You could replace the Salt Butter Shortbread with a store-bought cookie. Look for something that's not too crisp and not too soft.

chocolate-chile cake

SERVES 8

Inspiration here comes from my many Mexican friends who add chocolate to savory dishes. I thought I'd return the favor and add chiles to dessert. This frozen chocolate cake has a gentle heat, tamed by the chocolate and its hidden apricot center.

MAKE IT SIMPLER
Though you won't get the same results, you could replace the apricots with all-fruit apricot preserves. Doctor them up with some salt, a hit of lemon zest and juice, and a pinch of cayenne.

For the Chile Syrup

1 CUP (240 G) WATER
1¼ CUPS (250 G) SUGAR
½ HABANERO CHILE, CHOPPED
½ THAI BIRD CHILE, CHOPPED
¼ VANILLA BEAN, SPLIT AND
   SCRAPED
½ SMALL SPRIG FRESH ROSEMARY

Combine the water, sugar, chiles, vanilla seeds and pod, and rosemary in a small saucepan. Bring to a boil. Turn off the heat and infuse overnight. Strain before using.

For the Apricots

½ POUND (227 G) RIPE APRICOTS
CHILE SYRUP
1 TABLESPOON (14 G) UNSALTED
   BUTTER
COARSE SALT

Pit the apricots and cut into 1-inch chunks.

Warm a sauté pan over medium heat. When the pan is hot, add a slick of chile syrup and the apricots. Cook, tossing, until the apricots are barely tender. Add the butter and shake the pan until the butter melts and coats the fruit. Add a pinch of salt. Transfer to a strainer set over a bowl and let cool.

For the Cake

3 EXTRA-LARGE EGG YOLKS
⅓ CUP CHILE SYRUP
1¼ CUPS (300 G) HEAVY CREAM
4½ OUNCES (125 G) MILK
   CHOCOLATE (PREFERABLY
   VALRHONA JIVARA 40% CACAO),
   CHOPPED
3 OUNCES (87 G) BITTERSWEET
   CHOCOLATE (PREFERABLY
   VALRHONA MANJARI 64%
   CACAO), CHOPPED

Put eight 2 x 2-inch ring molds on a small baking pan and freeze them while you make the chocolate mousse.

Put the egg yolks in the bowl of a standing mixer fitted with the whisk and beat at medium speed.

Heat the chile syrup in a saucepan to 250°F. Pour the syrup into the beating yolks, avoiding the whisk and the sides of the bowl. Crank the mixer up to high and beat until the bowl is cool to the touch.

Whip the cream to medium peaks in a large bowl.

Melt the chocolates in a glass bowl in 30-second spurts in the microwave, or melt in a double boiler. After each spurt, let the chocolate sit for a minute or so, then stir it with a heatproof rubber scraper. Let the chocolate cool to 113°F.

Fold the yolk mixture into the cream, then fold in the chocolate.

Fill a pastry bag with the chocolate mousse and pipe into the molds, filling them about two-thirds full. Use the back of a small spoon to make a well in the center of each ring and bring the mousse up the sides to the top. Fill the centers with the apricots and top with more mousse to fill the molds. Level off the tops. Cover with plastic wrap and freeze overnight.

Put the butter, sugar, lemon zest, and a pinch of salt in the bowl of a standing mixer fitted with the paddle. Beat at medium-high speed until creamy.

Whisk the flour and baking powder together and add to the butter mixture. Mix at low speed until crumbly. Form into a brick, wrap in plastic, and freeze overnight.

Heat the oven to 375°F or 350°F on convection. Line a baking sheet with a Silpat or parchment and set eight 2½-inch tart rings on it.

Grate the streusel on the big holes of a box grater. Put a thin layer, about ¼ inch, in the bottom of each ring and press it down so it will stick together. Bake until crisp, about 8 minutes, rotating the pan halfway through baking. Let cool completely.

Glaze the tops of the cakes with a thin layer of the ganache. When the ganache sets, rub the rings briskly between your hands and unmold the cakes, pushing them out carefully.

Cut 2-inch rounds of the devil's food cake to match the size of the chocolate-chile cakes.

Place a round of streusel on each dessert plate. Top with the devil's food and then with the chocolate-chile cake.

Garnish with a drizzle of chile syrup and some chile seeds, if you want.

For the Streusel

7 TABLESPOONS (103 G) UNSALTED BUTTER, SOFTENED
SCANT ½ CUP (94 G) SUGAR
GRATED ZEST OF 1 LEMON
COARSE SALT
1½ CUPS (187 G) ALL-PURPOSE FLOUR
1 TEASPOON (4 G) BAKING POWDER

To Serve

CHOCOLATE GLAZING GANACHE (PAGE 183)
DEVIL'S FOOD CAKE (PAGE 192)
CHILE SEEDS (OPTIONAL)

There comes a time in the summer when the fruit at the farmers' market is so good that I really don't want to do anything more than provide a counterpoint to it, something to heighten the natural flavors and textures of the fruits. The only fruit cooked in this tasting is the cherries—and those only barely. Creamy farmer's cheese, pungent blue cheese, and nutty and mellow sticky rice all provide contrast.

serves 8 to 9

market fruit and

cheese

FOURPLAY

watermelon mosaics ~ blue cheese
~ strawberry-moscato granité

peach-basil compote ~ black sticky rice ~ coconut glaze

summer peaches ~ farmer's cheese ~ candied pistachios

cherry-chocolate linzer tarts ~ Thai basil ice cream

watermelon mosaics ~
blue cheese ~strawberry-moscato granité

Chef Alex Lee used to serve a tomato mosaic at Daniel, and when I got two super-ripe watermelons, one yellow and one red, I mimicked the appearance of his savory dish on my dessert menu. The cheese and granité add depth of flavor.

I'm not giving you a yield here, since this is more of a combination of flavors than anything, and you can make as many as you like.

To Serve

YELLOW SEEDLESS WATERMELON
RED SEEDLESS WATERMELON
FLEUR DE SEL OR MALDON SALT
BELVEDERE BLUE CHEESE OR
    OTHER CRUMBLY BLUE
STRAWBERRY-MOSCATO GRANITÉ
    (PAGE 239)

Cut the melons into 1½-inch slices to make squares.

Arrange in a checkerboard pattern on dessert plates. Sprinkle with a little salt. Crumble some blue cheese over the melon. Serve with a small bowl or Chinese soupspoon of granité.

peach-basil compote ~
black sticky rice ~ coconut glaze

Daniel Skurnick, my past sous-chef, brought me this recipe, which came from his travels through Asia. Since Jean-Georges is also influenced by the flavors of Asia, it was a natural to incorporate this into the menu. It's a great combination of tastes and textures: The tender peaches contribute their sweet acidity; the rice has a nutty bite; and the coconut glaze contributes the fattiness that gives the dessert such a good mouthfeel.

Mix the black and white rices in a bowl. Cover with cold water by at least 1 inch and soak overnight in the refrigerator.

Line a bamboo steamer with a few layers of cheesecloth.

Drain and rinse the rice and spread it out in the steamer with the bai-toey leaf. Set the steamer over a pot of simmering water and steam until the black rice is chewy but not crunchy, 3 to 4 hours. Check on the water, and if it's running low, replenish it with boiling water.

Transfer the rice to a bowl, discard the bai-toey leaf, and stir in the sugar. Cover with plastic wrap and refrigerate until you're ready to serve.

Mix the potato starch with a couple of tablespoons of the coconut milk to make a smooth paste.

Put the remaining coconut milk in a small saucepan and stir in the paste and sugar. Bring to a boil over medium heat, stirring, and cook until thickened, about 2 minutes. Stir in the salt, transfer to a bowl, and cover with plastic wrap, pressing the plastic onto the glaze to prevent a skin from forming. Let cool before serving.

SERVES 4 TO 6 ON ITS OWN OR 8 TO 9 AS PART OF A FOURPLAY

MAKE IT SIMPLER
You could make the rice with white sticky rice only.

For the Rice
½ CUP BLACK STICKY RICE
   (SEE NOTE)
¾ CUP WHITE STICKY RICE
1 BAI-TOEY LEAF OR 2 FRESH
   KAFFIR LIME LEAVES
   (SEE NOTE)
⅔ CUP (130 G) SUGAR

NOTE: Black and white sticky rices are available in Thai markets and online from ImportFood.com. Look for bai-toey leaves, which have an earthy fragrance and flavor, at Asian markets and kaffir lime at better grocery stores.

For the Coconut Glaze
1 TABLESPOON (8 G) POTATO
   STARCH
1 CUP (250 G) CANNED COCONUT
   MILK
2 TABLESPOONS (25 G) SUGAR
¼ TEASPOON (1 G) COARSE SALT

CONTINUES . . .

For the Compote

3 RIPE PEACHES, PITTED AND CUT
INTO TINY DICE
FRESH THAI BASIL LEAVES,
THINLY SLICED
FRESH LIME JUICE
SUGAR

Toss the peaches with the basil, lime juice, and sugar to taste. Macerate for at least 10 minutes.

To Serve

WHITE SESAME SEEDS, TOASTED

Divide the peaches among small bowls or dessert plates, using a ring mold if desired to make a neat shape.

If the rice has hardened, microwave it for a minute or so to soften it.

Top the peaches with a layer of the rice. Spoon the coconut glaze evenly over the rice and sprinkle some sesame seeds on top.

summer peaches ~
farmer's cheese ~ candied pistachios

One summer, the peaches were so amazing that I didn't want to do anything to them. Unfortunately, you can't put a peach on a plate and send it out to a customer. So I chose ingredients—mellow cheeses, sweet and crunchy pistachios, and a mild balsamic vinegar glaze—that complemented the sweet raw peach.

Whisk the citric acid into the simple syrup.

Cut the peaches into 8 wedges each (don't peel them) and toss them in the syrup. Remove the peaches from the syrup and place on a tray or platter. Wrap tightly in plastic wrap and chill for at least 2 hours.

Put the vinegar in a small nonreactive saucepan and simmer gently until thick and syrupy, 10 minutes. Let cool before using.

Divide the peaches and cheese among dessert plates. Drizzle with a little of the balsamic glaze and garnish with the pistachios, some basil, and salt.

SERVES 4 TO 6 ON ITS OWN OR 8 TO 9 AS PART OF A FOURPLAY

For the Peaches
¼ TEASPOON CITRIC ACID
1 CUP (280 G) SIMPLE SYRUP (PAGE 184)
4 SUPER-RIPE PEACHES

For the Balsamic Glaze
½ CUP (110 G) WHITE BALSAMIC VINEGAR

To Serve
4 OUNCES (113 G) FARMER'S CHEESE
4 OUNCES (113 G) FRESH RICOTTA CHEESE
CANDIED PISTACHIOS (SEE PAGE 215)
MICRO BASIL (OR CHOPPED FRESH BASIL LEAVES)
FLEUR DE SEL

cherry-chocolate Linzer Tarts ~
Thai Basil Ice Cream

SERVES 8 TO 9

MAKE IT SIMPLER
You could use frozen cherries when making the jam, since they're pitted. And in a pinch, you could use a traditional store-bought jam.

I often find myself reflecting back on principal recipes and techniques when I'm changing the menu at Jean Georges, then reworking them with modern flavor combinations. The fresh jam in this recipe makes a traditional tart more seasonal. Thai basil has a distinct flavor, so in addition to striking a modern note, it holds up well against the more homey notes struck by the cherries.

For the Dough

¹/₂ POUND PLUS 1 TABLESPOON (241 G) UNSALTED BUTTER, SOFTENED

1 CUP PLUS 3 TABLESPOONS (125 G) CONFECTIONERS' SUGAR

¹/₂ TEASPOON (2 G) COARSE SALT

³/₄ CUP PLUS 2 TABLESPOONS (78 G) HAZELNUT FLOUR

2³/₄ CUPS (343 G) ALL-PURPOSE FLOUR

5 TABLESPOONS (31 G) UNSWEETENED COCOA POWDER (PREFERABLY Valrhona)

1¹/₄ TEASPOONS (2 G) GROUND CINNAMON

1 TEASPOON (2 G) GROUND CLOVES

Grated zest of half an orange

Grated zest of half a lemon

¹/₂ VANILLA BEAN, SPLIT AND SCRAPED

1 LARGE EGG, LIGHTLY BEATEN

1 LARGE EGG YOLK

Put the butter, confectioners' sugar, and salt in the bowl of a standing mixer fitted with the paddle. Beat just until combined.

Whisk the hazelnut flour, all-purpose flour, cocoa powder, cinnamon, cloves, orange and lemon zests, and vanilla seeds (rinse, dry, and save the pod for another use) together. Add to the butter and beat just until combined. Add the egg and yolk and beat until you have a smooth dough. Turn out onto a lightly floured work surface and divide in half. Shape each half into a brick and wrap in plastic. Chill for at least 30 minutes.

Roll one-half of the dough ¹/₈ inch thick on a lightly floured work surface (freeze the rest for another use). Transfer the dough to a baking sheet and chill for 30 minutes. Cut into 3¹/₂-inch circles and line eight to nine 2¹/₄-inch tart rings. Place the tarts on a baking sheet and chill for 30 minutes.

Heat the oven to 375°F or 350°F on convection.

Trim the excess dough from the tart shells. Line the shells with pieces of parchment and fill with dried beans or rice. Bake the tart shells until crisp, 5 to 6 minutes, rotating the pan halfway through baking. Let cool in the molds.

Put the chocolate in a small glass bowl. Microwave for 30 seconds.

Bring the cream to a boil in a small saucepan. Pour about one-third of the hot cream into the center of the chocolate and whisk, starting from the center and working out until combined. Add another third of the cream and whisk, again from the center out. Add the remaining cream and whisk until perfectly smooth. It will have the consistency of lightly whipped cream. Cover with plastic wrap, pressing it onto the surface of the ganache so a skin doesn't form, and keep at room temperature until needed.

Unmold the tart shells. Spread some ganache in the bottom of each shell and fill with the jam.

Spoon some ganache on the plate and set a tart on top. Add a spoonful of chocolate crumble to the plate and top with a scoop or quenelle of ice cream.

For the Ganache

3.5 OUNCES (100 G) BITTERSWEET
   CHOCOLATE (PREFERABLY
   VALRHONA LE NOIR AMER
   71% CACAO), CHOPPED
¾ CUP PLUS 2 TABLESPOONS
   (210 G) HEAVY CREAM

To Serve

CHERRY JAM (PAGE 251)
CHOCOLATE CRUMBLE (PAGE 213)
THAI BASIL ICE CREAM
   (PAGE 226)

autumn

Think of this as a vegetable tasting for dessert; it plays around with the earthy flavors of corn, beets, and sweet potatoes, with quince as the aromatic note.

serves 14 to 15

indian

summer

FOURPLAY

poached quinces ~ farmer's cheese ~ pedro ximenez granité

corn panna cotta ~ madeleine sponge cake ~ spiced walnuts

sweet potato cake ~ cranberry foam ~ flax seed tuiles

beet parfait ~ chocolate brittle gel ~ beet-raspberry fluid gel

poached quinces
~ farmer's cheese ~ pedro ximenez granité

I really like the combinations of flavors and textures that result when soft-curd cheeses are served with poached fruit. In this dessert, I add to that by layering on an icy granité and a crisp cracker.

I'm not giving you a yield here, since this is more of a combination of flavors than anything, and you can make as many as you like.

To Serve

POACHED QUINCES (PAGE 248)
PEDRO XIMENEZ GRANITÉ
    (PAGE 240)
FARMER'S CHEESE (I
    PARTICULARLY LIKE AYRSHIRE
    FARMER'S CHEESE FROM
    WESTFIELD FARM; SEE NOTE)
GRAHAM CRACKER TUILES
    (PAGE 206)

NOTE: Ayrshire farmer's cheese is available online at Chevre.com.

Cut the quinces into small dice. Spoon the granité into dessert bowls. Add the quinces and some farmer's cheese, and garnish with a few tuiles.

corn panna cotta
~ madeleine sponge cake ~ spiced walnuts

I've always considered corn a borderline fruit, so why not incorporate it into the pastry menu? Here I pair it with buttery Madeleine Sponge Cake, my adaptation of the classic seashell cake, with a shatteringly crisp sugar crust. And I pile on the garnishes: kettle corn and freeze-dried corn bring their own special crunch to the dessert, and they're easy because you can find them readymade in good grocery stores.

I use plastic tubes that I've had cut to my specifications when I make this panna cotta at the restaurant. You can, too, if you have access to a plastic supply shop; the tubes I use have a 1-inch diameter, and they're 18 inches long. But you can also make the panna cotta in cannoli forms or muffin tins (see Make It Simpler).

Line 14 to 15 cannoli forms with acetate. Wrap one end in plastic wrap and secure it with tape or rubber bands. Put the forms in the freezer.

Set up an ice bath in a large bowl.

Cut the kernels off the corncobs.

Put the butter and sugar in a skillet over medium-high heat. When the butter is melted, add the corn and the salt. Cook, stirring often, until the corn is completely tender but not browned, about 7 minutes.

Scrape the corn into a blender. Add the milk, and puree until very smooth. Strain through a fine strainer into a medium bowl (discard the solids) and set into the ice bath to cool.

Sprinkle the gelatin over the surface of the simple syrup. Let sit for at least 1 minute. Microwave for 45 seconds or heat gently in a saucepan until melted. Stir the gelatin into the corn puree.

CONTINUES . . .

SERVES 14 TO 15

MAKE IT SIMPLER
You could form the panna cotta in muffin tins lined with plastic wrap and cut the madeleine into circles instead of rectangles. And though you will have to come up with a different way of plating the dessert, you could even replace the Madeleine Sponge Cake with madeleines from a good bakery. But, please, make sure you sprinkle them with sugar and caramelize them.

For the Panna Cotta
6 EARS SWEET CORN
6 TABLESPOONS (85 G) UNSALTED BUTTER
1/4 CUP PLUS 2 TABLESPOONS (75 G) SUGAR
1 TABLESPOON (12 G) COARSE SALT
1 1/2 CUPS (350 G) WHOLE MILK
1 TABLESPOON POWDERED GELATIN (OR 13.5 G SHEET GELATIN; SEE PAGE 276)
7/8 CUP (240 G) SIMPLE SYRUP (PAGE 184)
1 1/4 CUPS (300 G) HEAVY CREAM

In a separate bowl, whip the cream to medium peaks. Fold it into the corn mixture, gently but thoroughly.

Fill a pastry bag with the panna cotta batter and pipe into the molds. Cover the open ends with plastic wrap and secure it. Freeze overnight or for up to 3 days.

To Serve

MADELEINE SPONGE CAKE
   (PAGE 193)
TURBINADO sugar
SPICED WALNUTS (PAGE 217)
HONEY
KETTLE corn (OPTIONAL)
FREEZE-DRIED CORN (OPTIONAL)

Heat the broiler. Cut the madeleine sponge into 1¼ x 3-inch fingers and place on a baking sheet. Sprinkle the tops with an even layer of turbinado sugar and caramelize the sugar under the broiler, watching carefully to make sure you don't scorch it. (Alternatively, you could caramelize the sugar with a culinary torch.) Set on dessert plates.

Unmold the panna cotta, pushing it out, and cut into 1-inch lengths. Place three pieces of panna cotta on each madeleine finger. Add a spiced walnut or two to the plate and garnish with a drizzle of honey and, if you want, some kettle corn and freeze-dried corn.

sweet potato cake ~ cranberry foam ~ flax seed tuiles

Here, I've created my version of sweet potato pie, but it's not as heavy and not as sweet. The cranberry foam gives a nice added pop of acidity.

Put the simple syrup and water in a saucepan and bring to a boil. Add the cranberries and bring back to a boil. Turn off the heat and leave the cranberries to plump for 30 minutes. Drain well.

Heat the oven to 425°F or 400°F on convection.

Prick the sweet potatoes in several places with the tip of a paring knife. Place on a piece of heavy-duty aluminum foil and bake until the potatoes are very tender and the juices that have seeped out have caramelized, about 1 hour. When the potatoes are cool enough to handle, peel and put through a food mill to make a puree. Put the puree in a saucepan and cook, stirring often, until the puree is very dry. Measure out 1½ cups.

Reduce the oven temperature to 375°F (350°F if you're using convection). Spray fourteen to fifteen 2 x 2-inch ring molds with cooking spray and coat the insides with sugar. Set them on a baking sheet lined with a Silpat or parchment.

CONTINUES . . .

SERVES 14 TO 15

For the Cranberry Filling
½ CUP (124 G) SIMPLE SYRUP (PAGE 184)
½ CUP (120 G) WATER
¾ CUP (100 G) DRIED CRANBERRIES

For the Cake
1 POUND SWEET POTATOES
¼ CUP (30 G) ALL-PURPOSE FLOUR
¾ TEASPOON (3 G) BAKING POWDER
⅛ TEASPOON (1 G) BAKING SODA
COARSE SALT
3 TABLESPOONS (45 G) HEAVY CREAM
5 LARGE EGG YOLKS
5 TABLESPOONS (75 G) UNSALTED BUTTER, MELTED
3 LARGE EGG WHITES
½ CUP (100 G) GRANULATED SUGAR
TURBINADO SUGAR

MAKE IT SIMPLER
Here's an alternative to the cranberry foam. Make the cranberry puree and mix it with an equal amount of heavy cream. Pour it into a soda siphon and charge it with a cream whipper charger (N_2O). Give it a good shake and try a squirt; if it's not carbonated enough for your liking, use a second charger. Make a variation of the Crispy Almond Phyllo (page 211) to stand in for the tuile; replace the almond flour with whole flax seeds.

Whisk the flour, baking powder, baking soda, and a pinch of salt together.

Put the heavy cream, egg yolks, and melted butter in a mixing bowl. Whisk until very smooth but not frothy. Whisk in the warm sweet potato puree. Whisk in the dry ingredients, beating just until smooth.

Put the egg whites in the bowl of a standing mixer fitted with the whisk. Turn it on to low, and beat the whites gently for 2 minutes, to start establishing a structure. The whites will look frothy but still a bit wet. Turn the speed up to medium and add 3 tablespoons of the granulated sugar. Continue to beat at medium speed until the whites have body and are just shy of having soft peaks. Add 3 more tablespoons of the sugar and continue beating until the whites have formed firm peaks. Add the remaining 2 tablespoons sugar and beat until the whites are glossy and smooth and almost stiff.

Fold one-quarter of the whites into the batter to lighten it. Fold in the remaining whites, gently but thoroughly.

Fill a pastry bag with the batter and pipe into the molds, filling them one-quarter of the way up. Make a layer of the cranberry filling, then pipe in more batter to fill the rings two-thirds full. Sprinkle the tops with turbinado sugar. Bake until a knife comes out clean, about 20 minutes, rotating the pan halfway through baking.

Let cool on a rack for a minute or so, then remove the rings. Let cool completely.

Set up an ice bath in a large bowl.

Put the cranberries and simple syrup in a saucepan. Bring to a boil over medium-high heat, then reduce the heat and simmer until the cranberries pop and have broken down a bit.

Scrape into a blender and make a smooth puree. Strain through a fine strainer into a medium bowl (discard the solids) and set into the ice bath, stirring often to chill completely.

Sprinkle the Versa-Whip and xanthan gum over the surface of the cranberry puree and whisk in slowly and thoroughly. Whisk until very light and airy, the consistency of shaving cream. Refrigerate, covered with plastic wrap, until you're ready to serve or for up to 5 hours.

Pit and chop the dates. Put them in a small saucepan with the water and bring to a boil over medium-high heat. Turn off the heat and let the dates sit for 10 minutes.

Put the dates and liquid in a blender and make a smooth puree. Strain through a fine strainer (discard the solids).

Smear a layer of the date puree across half a dessert plate. Set a sweet potato cake on the puree.

Whip the cranberry foam with a whisk to restore its consistency (it falls sometimes) and put a scoop of it next to the cake. Garnish with a tuile. Repeat for each serving.

For the Cranberry Foam

2⅔ CUPS (340 G) FRESH CRANBERRIES

¼ CUP PLUS 2 TABLESPOONS (100 G) SIMPLE SYRUP (PAGE 184)

2½ TEASPOONS (2.5 G) VERSA-WHIP 600K (SEE NOTE)

¼ TEASPOON (0.3 G) XANTHAN GUM

NOTE: Versa-Whip is a brand name for hydrolyzed soy protein, which acts as the emulsifier and whipping agent in this foam. You can buy it online from Terra Spice Company.

For the Date Puree

3½ OUNCES (100 G) FRESH DATES

1¼ CUPS (300 G) WATER

To Serve

FLAX SEED TUILES (PAGE 206)

beet parfait ~
chocolate brittle gel ~ beet-raspberry fluid gel

SERVES 14 TO 15

Beets and raspberries complement each other perfectly, covering sweet and acidic, earthy and bright flavors. The chocolate in this dessert is the secondary flavor, reinforcing the earthiness of the beets and bringing two additional textures to the plate.

For the Streusel

1½ CUPS PLUS 2 TABLESPOONS (200 G) ALL-PURPOSE FLOUR
¼ CUP (25 G) UNSWEETENED COCOA POWDER (PREFERABLY VALRHONA)
1 TEASPOON (2 G) GROUND CLOVES
2½ TEASPOONS (5 G) FRESHLY GROUND BLACK PEPPER
½ TEASPOON (2 G) COARSE SALT
8 TABLESPOONS (115 G) UNSALTED BUTTER, CUT INTO PIECES
½ CUP PLUS 1 TABLESPOON (115 G) SUGAR

Heat the oven to 375°F or 350°F on convection. Line a baking sheet with a Silpat or parchment and set fourteen to fifteen 1½-inch square molds on it.

Whisk the flour, cocoa powder, cloves, pepper, and salt together in the bowl of a standing mixer fitted with the paddle. Add the butter and sugar and mix on medium speed until crumbly.

Divide the streusel among the molds and press down so the streusel will hold a shape. Bake until crisp, about 6 minutes. Remove from the oven and unmold the streusel. Let cool.

For the Beet Juice

2 LARGE BEETS

Trim, peel, and chop the beets. Put through a juicer. You'll need the beet juice for the parfait and the beet-raspberry fluid gel.

MAKE IT SIMPLER
You could replace the chocolate brittle gel with chocolate ice cream. Scoop it, roll in Chocolate Crumble (page 213) or chocolate cookie crumbs, and refreeze. That way, you're bringing another layer of crunch to the plate.

For larger portions, you could use a 3¼-inch tart ring and for tasting portions you could use 2-inch ring molds in place of the 1½-inch square molds I use.

Line a baking sheet with a Silpat or parchment and set the 1½-inch square molds on it. Freeze while you make the parfait.

Put the 2 tablespoons heavy cream in a small bowl. Sprinkle the gelatin over the surface.

Combine the beet juice, sugar, egg yolks, and vanilla seeds and pod in a heatproof bowl set over simmering water. Cook, whisking pretty constantly, until the mixture reaches 175°F.

Microwave the gelatin for 30 seconds or heat gently in a saucepan until melted.

Strain the beet juice mixture into the bowl of a standing mixer fitted with the whisk. Add the gelatin and beat at medium-high speed until the sides of the bowl are cool.

In a separate bowl, beat the ½ cup heavy cream to medium peaks. Fold the cream into the beet mixture.

Fill a pastry bag with the parfait and pipe into the molds. Even off the tops. Cover with plastic wrap and freeze overnight.

Puree the raspberries in a food processor. Strain and measure out ½ cup (125 g).

Put the puree, beet juice, and agar in a saucepan and mix with an immersion blender. Bring to a boil over medium-high heat, then reduce the heat and simmer for 5 minutes. Pour into a baking dish and refrigerate until set.

Scrape the gel into a blender and blend on high until perfectly smooth and fluid. Store in the refrigerator until you're ready to serve or for up to 3 days.

For the Beet Parfait
½ CUP PLUS 2 TABLESPOONS (150 G) HEAVY CREAM
½ TEASPOON POWDERED GELATIN (OR 2.25 G SHEET GELATIN; SEE PAGE 276)
⅓ CUP (80 G) BEET JUICE
2 TABLESPOONS PLUS 2 TEASPOONS (35 G) SUGAR
3 LARGE EGG YOLKS
½ VANILLA BEAN, SPLIT AND SCRAPED

For the Beet-Raspberry Fluid Gel
12 OUNCES (340 G) FRESH RASPBERRIES
½ CUP (125 G) BEET JUICE
⅔ TEASPOONS (2.5 G) AGAR

CONTINUES . . .

For the Chocolate Brittle Gel

¼ CUP (50 G) SUGAR
¼ TEASPOON (1 G) AGAR
1 CUP PLUS 2 TEASPOONS (250 G)
    WHOLE MILK
2 OUNCES (57 G) BITTERSWEET
    CHOCOLATE (PREFERABLY
    VALRHONA MANJARI 64%
    CACAO), CHOPPED

Run a 9 x 12-inch rimmed baking sheet under cold water and shake off the excess. Line the damp pan neatly with plastic wrap.

Whisk the sugar and agar together in a small saucepan. Whisk in the milk.

Stirring constantly, bring the milk to a boil. Reduce the heat and simmer for 5 minutes, still stirring. Stir in the chocolate and emulsify with an immersion blender, keeping the blender under the surface so you avoid making bubbles. Pour into the baking sheet and refrigerate until set, about 2 hours.

To Serve

CACAO NIBS
MICRO BEET GREENS (OPTIONAL)
YOGURT POWDER (OPTIONAL; SEE
    NOTE)
BEET POWDER (OPTIONAL)

NOTE: Yogurt powder and beet powder are available from Terra Spice Company.

Use a spatula to smear some of the beet-raspberry fluid gel onto dessert plates.

Set a streusel on each plate, on the gel. Unmold a parfait, pushing it out, and set it on top of the streusel. Cover the top of the parfait with cacao nibs.

Cut the chocolate gel into ½ x 2-inch strips. Set one beside each parfait.

Garnish with a few greens, the yogurt powder, and beet powder if you want.

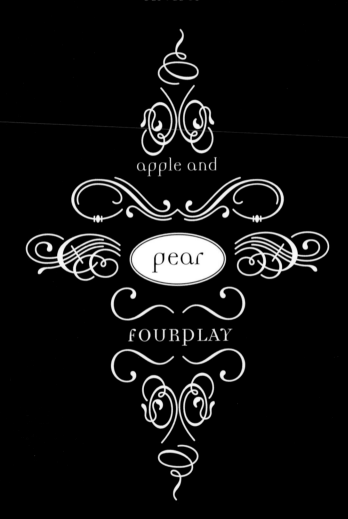

Apples and pears are standards in the autumn pastry kitchen, so the challenge is to find new ways to present these flavors. In this tasting, apples are turned into a mellow soup, a hot tempura snack, an icy sorbet, and a crisp chip—all with different textures and all revealing the distinct flavor of the apple used. Pears appear poached, frozen into a granité, sautéed in caramel, and turned into an elegant mousse.

serves 10

apple and

pear

FOURPLAY

apple soup ~ sweet potato gnocchi ~ apple tempura

green apple sorbet ~ apple chips

semolina pancakes ~ poached pears ~ pear-cumin granité

chocolate-pear cake

Apple soup ~
sweet potato gnocchi ~ Apple Tempura

SERVES 6 ON ITS OWN OR
10 AS PART OF A FOURPLAY

MAKE IT SIMPLER
You could serve the soup with
just the gnocchi or just the
tempura.

I go apple picking every year, and I'm always amazed by how easily you can taste the difference between varieties right off the tree. So when I work with apples, I try to capture those flavors.

This soup reminds me of mulled cider but lighter and fresher.

For the Soup
MAKES ABOUT 3½ CUPS
3 SMALL McINTOSH APPLES
1½ CUPS (360 G) WATER
1½ CUPS (360 G) APPLE CIDER
GRATED ZEST AND JUICE OF
  ¼ LEMON
⅔ CUP (130 G) SUGAR
1 VANILLA BEAN, SPLIT AND
  SCRAPED
1 CINNAMON STICK
2 BLACK PEPPERCORNS
½ NUTMEG, CRACKED
1 WHOLE CLOVE
1 STAR ANISE

Core and chop the apples. Put them in a large saucepan with the water, cider, lemon juice, and sugar. Tie the lemon zest, vanilla seeds and pod, cinnamon stick, peppercorns, nutmeg, clove, and star anise in a piece of cheesecloth and add to the pan. Bring to a simmer over medium heat and simmer until the apples break down, about 1 hour.

Remove the cheesecloth sachet and strain the soup through a fine strainer, pushing down on the solids. Line a strainer with at least 4 layers of cheesecloth and set over a bowl. Strain the soup again and put in the refrigerator overnight to clarify.

For the Cider Vinegar Gelée
¼ CUP (60 G) RICE VINEGAR OR
  CHAMPAGNE VINEGAR
3 TEASPOONS POWDERED GELATIN
  (OR 13.5 G SHEET GELATIN; SEE
  PAGE 276)
1½ CUPS (360 G) APPLE CIDER

Run a 9 x 12-inch rimmed baking sheet under water and shake off the excess. Line the damp pan neatly with plastic wrap.

Put the vinegar in a small bowl and sprinkle the gelatin over the surface. Let sit for at least 1 minute. Microwave for 30 seconds or heat gently in a saucepan until melted.

Stir the gelatin into the cider. Strain through a fine strainer. Pour into the baking sheet and refrigerate until set, about 4 hours.

Heat the oven to 375°F or 350°F on convection.

Tear off a piece of aluminum foil and make a bed of coarse salt in the center. Set the potato on the salt, wrap tightly, and roast until the potato is very soft, about 1½ hours. Unwrap. When the potato is cool enough to handle, peel it and put the flesh through a food mill.

Line a strainer with several layers of cheesecloth. Put the potato puree in the strainer, cover with cheesecloth, and set over a bowl. Put a weight on it and let sit for at least 1 hour to get rid of the excess liquid.

Taste the puree for salt. Put it in a bowl and make a well in the center. Add the flour, sugar, and 3 tablespoons of the egg. Mix together to make a smooth dough. Transfer to a pastry bag with a ½-inch opening (you do not need a tip).

Pour the soup into a saucepan and warm it. Cut the gelée into small cubes.

Bring a saucepan of water to a boil. Reduce the heat so you have an active simmer. Use one hand to pipe the gnocchi batter and your other hand to cut off ¾-inch lengths with a pair of scissors or a paring knife into the water. Cook, stirring gently, until the gnocchi rise to the surface. Remove with a slotted spoon and put in small bowls.

Ladle the warm soup over the gnocchi and garnish with a spoonful of crème fraîche and a few cubes of the gelée. Serve right away, with the tempura on the side.

For the Gnocchi
COARSE SALT
1 LARGE SWEET POTATO
SCANT ⅔ CUP (80 G) ALL-PURPOSE FLOUR
3 TABLESPOONS (37 G) SUGAR
1 LARGE EGG, BEATEN

To Serve
CRÈME FRAÎCHE
APPLE TEMPURA (PAGE 261)

green apple sorbet ~ apple chips

SERVES 10

Here is another example of presenting one flavor two ways, each reinforcing the other. The icy, refreshing sorbet captures all the bright freshness of Granny Smith apples; the chips present that fresh flavor in a completely different, shatteringly crisp form.

For the Apple Chips

MAKES ABOUT 40 CHIPS

1½ CUPS (420 G) SIMPLE SYRUP
    (PAGE 184)
1 TABLESPOON (14 G) FRESH
    LEMON JUICE
1 GRANNY SMITH APPLE

Heat the oven to 200°F. Line baking sheets with Silpats.

Bring the simple syrup to a boil. Add the lemon juice and turn off the heat.

Cut the apple in quarters vertically, then make another cut in each quarter to remove the core. Slice the apple as thin as possible on a vegetable slicer or mandoline. Immediately drop the slices into the hot syrup. Leave for 10 minutes, then remove, letting the syrup drip off. Lay out on the Silpats.

Slide the baking sheets into the oven and dry for 2½ to 3 hours, rotating the pans halfway through drying. To test, put one slice on the counter and let it cool for a few minutes. It should shatter when you break it. Let cool and store in an airtight container for up to 3 days.

To Serve

GREEN APPLE SORBET (PAGE 232)

Scoop the sorbet into dessert bowls and garnish with the apple chips.

semolina pancakes ~ poached pears ~ pear-cumin granité

This pancake recipe dates back to Jean-Georges's apprenticeship in Alsace. For me, the warm flavor of semolina combines well with the double whammy of pear in this dessert. Cumin brings out the rustic edge of all the ingredients. (See the photograph on pages 92-93.)

Put the cream, milk, and sugar in a small saucepan. Whisk in the semolina and add the butter. Bring to a boil over medium-high heat. Scrape into a bowl, cover with plastic wrap, and let sit for 10 minutes.

Put the egg whites and a pinch of cream of tartar in the bowl of a standing mixer fitted with the whisk attachment. Beat at medium-low speed until frothy. Increase the speed to medium and beat until the whites form soft peaks. Increase the speed to medium-high and beat until the whites form medium peaks.

Whisk the egg yolks into the semolina batter. Fold in one-quarter of the whites to lighten the batter, then fold in the remaining whites, gently but thoroughly. You can make the batter about 1 hour ahead of cooking. Store it, covered, in the refrigerator.

Heat a griddle over medium-high heat. When the griddle is hot, brush it with butter. If desired, place a few buttered 2¼-inch tart rings on the griddle, so you can make perfectly round pancakes. Fill each ring with batter and cook until the bottom is browned, 1½ to 2 minutes. Flip the pancake, ring and all, and cook until the second side is browned, another 2 minutes. Serve these immediately.

Cut the pears into perfect tiny dice.

Put a pancake on a plate with a pile of diced pears, a drizzle of the poaching liquid, and a small bowl of the granité.

SERVES 10

MAKE IT SIMPLER
Rather than poaching the pears, you could dice a super-ripe pear and serve that instead.

For the Pancakes
3 TABLESPOONS (45 G) HEAVY CREAM
SCANT ²/₃ CUP (145 G) WHOLE MILK
1½ TABLESPOONS (18 G) SUGAR
¼ CUP PLUS 2 TABLESPOONS (60 G) SEMOLINA FLOUR
5 TABLESPOONS (60 G) UNSALTED BUTTER, CUT INTO PIECES
3 LARGE EGGS, SEPARATED
CREAM OF TARTAR

To Serve
1 OR 2 POACHED PEARS (PAGE 247)
PEAR-CUMIN GRANITÉ (PAGE 241)

chocolate-pear cake

Rich texture is abundant in this multiflavored, multilayered dessert. The pears are presented in three different forms—caramelized, as a creamy mousse, and as a tender gelée—and each opens differently on the palate.

SERVES 10

For the Crunchy Pears

2 BOSC OR BARTLETT PEARS
$^1/_2$ CUP (100 G) SUGAR
COARSE SALT
2 TABLESPOONS (37 G) PRALINE
    PASTE (SEE PAGE 276)
$^1/_2$ OUNCE (18 G) BITTERSWEET
    CHOCOLATE (PREFERABLY
    VALRHONA CARAÏBE 66%
    CACAO), CHOPPED
$2^1/_2$ OUNCES (75 G) CHOCOLATE
    PEARLS (VALRHONA LES
    PERLES CROQUANTES)

Peel and core the pears. Cut them into medium dice.

Put the sugar and a pinch of salt into a heavy skillet and drizzle with a teaspoon or two of water. Turn the heat to high. Leave the pan alone until the sugar starts to color, then pick up the pan and roll the sugar in it so it colors evenly. Cook until the sugar is dark amber. Add the pears and cook until the caramel has softened and the pears are slightly tender. Scrape the pears into a strainer immediately and drain. Transfer to a bowl and toss with the praline paste and chocolate, then toss in the chocolate pearls.

For the Cakes

SPICED CHOCOLATE SPONGE CAKE
    (PAGE 190)
CHOCOLATE MOUSSE (PAGE 262)
PEAR MOUSSE (PAGE 255)

Line a baking sheet with parchment.

Use ten 2 x 2-inch ring molds to cut disks out of the spiced chocolate sponge cake, leaving the cake in the bottom of the molds. Set on the baking sheet.

Make the chocolate mousse. Pipe some mousse into each of the molds, filling them about half full. Use the back of a spoon or a small offset spatula to bring the mousse up the sides of the mold, all the way to the top, making a well. Refrigerate until the mousse has set, about 1 hour.

Put a spoonful of the crunchy pears into each mold, filling about two-thirds full. Refrigerate while you make the pear mousse.

Pipe the pear mousse into the molds, mounding it slightly. Refrigerate until the mousse has set, about 1 hour.

Rub the molds between your palms to release the mousse; push out the cakes. Set them on dessert plates. Cut the gelée up with a whisk to make irregular shapes and add a pile to each plate, along with a spoonful of the sauce. Lean a chocolate swirl against the cake if desired. For the photograph, I cut a special stencil, raked the sauce with a chocolate comb, and let the sauce set before removing the stencil.

To Serve
PEAR GELÉE (PAGE 254)
CHOCOLATE SAUCE (PAGE 268)
CHOCOLATE DÉCOR SWIRL
   (SEE PAGE 265; OPTIONAL)

As autumn progresses, I start thinking about holiday meals past and try to create desserts that are new and exciting, but that remind me of those meals. In this tasting, the Chestnut-Hazelnut Tarts remind me a bit of pecan pie, but the flaky pastry is the star. And the cake is reminiscent of pumpkin pie, with grown-up flavors.

serves 12

late

harvest

FOURPLAY

concord grape sorbet

chestnut-Hazelnut Tarts ~ chestnut sauce

frozen cranberry nougat ~ almond tuiles

pumpkin—pine nut cake ~ Armagnac prunes

concord grape sorbet

MAKES ABOUT 1½ QUARTS

We had Concords growing in the backyard when I was a kid, but I didn't like them. They were just too strong for my young palate. But I came to love this flavor and now I wait all year for the grapes to be in season so I can make this sorbet. It's my favorite thing to do with Concords. I always serve this sorbet on its own— pure and simple.

¾ CUP (180 G) WATER
½ CUP PLUS 2 TABLESPOONS
   (125 G) SUGAR
⅔ CUP (190 G) LIGHT CORN SYRUP
3½ POUNDS (1588 G) CONCORD
   GRAPES
JUICE OF HALF A LEMON
½ TEASPOON CITRIC ACID

Set up an ice bath in a large bowl.

Put the water, sugar, and corn syrup in a saucepan. Bring to a boil over medium-high heat, stirring to dissolve the sugar. Mix with an immersion blender. Pour into a medium bowl and set into the ice bath to chill down completely.

Stem the grapes and put them through a juicer.

Strain the juice and measure out 3⅓ cups. Add to the syrup with the lemon juice and citric acid.

Freeze immediately in an ice cream maker. Pack into a plastic container and freeze for at least 2 hours before serving.

chestnut-hazelnut tarts ~ chestnut sauce

The origin of this dessert is Tarte Vaudoise, a traditional European pastry. I've replaced the original heavy cream with crème fraîche and added different nut textures. It may look simple on the plate, but it's complex in flavor.

Put the milk, chestnut puree, crème fraîche, and salt in a blender. Blend until very smooth.

Scrape into a bowl, cover with plastic wrap, and refrigerate until you're ready to serve the dessert or for up to 2 days.

Divide the dough in half and roll each piece out into a rectangle about 9 x 14 inches and $1/16$ inch thick. Place the dough on parchment-lined baking sheets and refrigerate for 30 minutes. Cut the dough into $3\frac{1}{2}$-inch circles and line twelve $2\frac{1}{4}$-inch tart rings with the dough. Set on a Silpat- or parchment-lined baking sheet and refrigerate for at least 30 minutes.

Heat the oven to 425°F or 400°F on convection.

Whisk the crème fraîche, sugar, and flour together.

Trim the excess pastry and prick the shells—bottom and sides—with a fork. Put some chopped marrons glacés and hazelnuts in each shell and spoon in the crème fraîche mixture, filling the shells no more than one-quarter full. Dust lightly with cinnamon.

SERVES 12

For the Chestnut Sauce
$1/4$ CUP (60 G) WHOLE MILK, HEATED
SCANT $1/2$ CUP (110 G) CHESTNUT PUREE (PREFERABLY CLÉMENT FAUGIER; SEE NOTE)
SCANT 2 TABLESPOONS (25 G) CRÈME FRAÎCHE
$1/2$ TEASPOON (2 G) COARSE SALT

NOTE: Clément Faugier chestnut puree is available at specialty and gourmet markets and online from Amazon.

For the Tarts
$1/2$ RECIPE TART DOUGH (PAGE 181)
SCANT 1 CUP (200 G) CRÈME FRAÎCHE
$1/2$ CUP (100 G) SUGAR
$1/8$ TEASPOON (0.4 G) ALL-PURPOSE FLOUR
MARRONS GLACÉS (SEE NOTE), DRAINED AND CHOPPED
CHOPPED HAZELNUTS
GROUND CINNAMON

NOTE: Commercial crystallized chestnuts, marrons glacés, are available at specialty and gourmet markets.

CONTINUES . . .

Bake the tarts until the shells are golden brown and the filling is translucent, about 14 minutes. Rotate the baking sheet halfway through baking. The filling will bubble up and probably overflow and then subside as you bake the tarts. Let cool for a few minutes, then remove the tart rings. Slide the tarts back into the oven for 1 to 2 minutes, to crisp the outside of the pastry.

CHOPPED HAZELNUTS
MARRONS GLACÉS

To Serve Spoon some chestnut sauce on each plate. Top with a tart and garnish with hazelnuts and marrons glacés.

frozen cranberry nougat ~ almond tuiles

The technique here is traditional and French. The fresh and dried cranberries and the star anise are modern and provide bright hits of flavor in every bite.

You'll need two 6-cavity Flexipan savarin molds (the 2¾-inch size) if you want to match the shape of the dessert in the photograph. But you could also freeze the nougat in a baking sheet and cut pieces to serve.

Put the juice and star anise in a saucepan and bring to a boil over medium heat. Add the cranberries and reduce the heat to low. Poach gently until the cranberries are tender, but don't let them burst.

Chill, in the poaching liquid, before serving.

Heat the oven to 350°F or 325°F on convection.

Spread the pistachios and almonds out on a baking sheet and bake until the nuts are hot but not browned or toasted, about 7 minutes.

Meanwhile, put the sugar in a saucepan and mix with enough water to make a texture like wet sand. Cook over medium-high heat to 285°F. Add the hot nuts and stir until the sugar turns white. Scrape out onto a Silpat and let cool completely. Reserve about 2 tablespoons of the nuts for garnish. Break up the remaining nuts with your hands and put in a food processor. Pulse to coarsely chop the nuts.

Put the dried cranberries and Chambord in a glass bowl and microwave for 30 seconds or bring to a simmer in a small saucepan. Let cool completely. Drain well, reserving the Chambord. Chop the cranberries. Sprinkle the gelatin over the surface of the Chambord.

Put the egg whites and a pinch of cream of tartar in the bowl of a standing mixer fitted with the whisk. Start beating the whites at medium speed while you cook the honey.

For the Poached Cranberries
1½ CUPS (360 G) PURE CRANBERRY JUICE
¼ CUP (15 G) STAR ANISE
1½ CUPS (150 G) FRESH OR FROZEN CRANBERRIES

For the Frozen Nougat
SCANT ½ CUP (75 G) SHELLED UNSALTED PISTACHIOS
¼ CUP (25 G) SLIVERED ALMONDS
½ CUP (100 G) SUGAR
PACKED ⅓ CUP (50 G) DRIED CRANBERRIES
3 TABLESPOONS (45 G) CHAMBORD (BLACK RASPBERRY LIQUEUR)
¾ TEASPOON POWDERED GELATIN (OR 3.3 G SHEET GELATIN; SEE PAGE 276)
2 LARGE EGG WHITES
CREAM OF TARTAR
½ CUP (150 G) HONEY (PREFERABLY CRANBERRY HONEY)
2 CUPS (480 G) HEAVY CREAM

CONTINUES . . .

Put the honey in a large saucepan. Cook over medium-high heat to 250°F.

Microwave the gelatin and Chambord for 30 seconds or heat gently in a small saucepan until melted.

With the mixer still at medium speed (the egg whites should be holding whip marks, like whipped cream, at this point), pour the honey in a steady stream into the whites, avoiding the whisk and the sides of the bowl. Add the gelatin. Turn the speed to high and beat the whites until the sides of the bowl feel cool.

In a separate bowl, whip the cream to stiff peaks.

Fold the egg white mixture into the cream, then fold in the chopped nuts and macerated cranberries. Fill a pastry bag and pipe into twelve Flexipan savarin molds (2¾ inches). Level off the tops. Cover with parchment or plastic wrap and freeze overnight. Alternatively, you could spread the mixture in a 9 x 12-inch rimmed baking sheet lined with a Silpat or parchment and cut squares when you're ready to serve the dessert.

To Serve Unmold the frozen nougats and place one on top of a tuile on a dessert plate. Garnish with a spoonful of the poached cranberries, some of the poaching liquid, and the reserved nuts. Repeat for each serving.

ALMOND TUILES (PAGE 205)

pumpkin—pine nut cake ~ Armagnac prunes

Pumpkins and pine nuts are in the same boat in that both are easily influenced by other ingredients. I felt they needed each other in this dessert, which I created particularly for this book. In addition to flavor, the pine nuts provide structure in the cake and texture in the streusel.

Cut the prunes in half and put them in a bowl. Cover with boiling water and leave them to plump for 10 minutes. Drain well and place in a clean bowl. Mix the simple syrup and Armagnac together and pour over the prunes. Let macerate in the refrigerator for at least 4 hours but preferably overnight. Store the prunes in the maceration liquid.

Heat the oven to 375°F or 350°F on convection.

Cut the pumpkin in half and scoop out the seeds and fibers. Use a small sharp knife to score the flesh in a checkerboard pattern, cutting in about ½ inch. Rub each half with the butter, sprinkle with the brown sugar, and season with salt. Put the pumpkin on a baking sheet, cut-side up, and bake until very tender and browned, about 45 minutes.

When the pumpkin is cool enough to handle, peel it and put the flesh through a food mill.

Line a strainer with a few layers of cheesecloth. Scrape the pumpkin puree into the strainer, set it over a bowl, cover with cheesecloth, and weight it. Let the puree drain for at least 2 hours to remove the excess liquid.

CONTINUES . . .

SERVES 12

MAKE IT SIMPLER
You could use canned pumpkin puree.

For the Prunes
24 PITTED PRUNES
1 CUP (280 G) SIMPLE SYRUP
   (PAGE 184)
1 CUP (225 G) ARMAGNAC

For the Pumpkin Puree
1 SMALL CHEESE PUMPKIN
2 TABLESPOONS (28 G) UNSALTED
   BUTTER, SOFTENED
2 TABLESPOONS (26 G) DARK
   BROWN SUGAR
COARSE SALT

For the Streusel

GENEROUS ½ CUP (76 G) PINE
    NUTS
PACKED 2 TABLESPOONS (28 G)
    BROWN SUGAR
¼ CUP (50 G) GRANULATED SUGAR
COARSE SALT
4 TABLESPOONS (58 G) UNSALTED
    BUTTER, MELTED

Put the pine nuts, the sugars, and a pinch of salt in a food processor. Pulse to chop the nuts. Slowly add the butter, pulsing until you have pea-sized pieces. Transfer to a bowl and chill until ready to use.

For the Cake

5 TABLESPOONS (50 G) PINE NUTS
SCANT 1 CUP (120 G) ALL-PURPOSE
    FLOUR
1 CUP PLUS 2 TABLESPOONS (190 G)
    SEMOLINA FLOUR
½ TEASPOON (2 G) COARSE SALT
½ TEASPOON (2 G) BAKING
    POWDER
PACKED 5 TEASPOONS (25 G)
    BROWN SUGAR
⅓ CUP (65 G) GRANULATED SUGAR
5 TABLESPOONS (70 G) UNSALTED
    BUTTER, CUT INTO PIECES
2 LARGE EGGS
1 CUP (200 G) PUMPKIN PUREE
1 TABLESPOON (8 G)
    EXTRA-VIRGIN OLIVE OIL
GRATED ZEST OF HALF A LEMON
1 VANILLA BEAN, SPLIT AND
    SCRAPED

Heat the oven to 350°F or 325°F on convection. Line a baking sheet with a Silpat or parchment. Spray twelve 2 x 2-inch ring molds or 1½-inch square molds with cooking spray and set on the pan.

Put the pine nuts, all-purpose flour, semolina, salt, baking powder, and sugars in a food processor. Pulse and process until the pine nuts are ground. Add the butter and pulse until well mixed; the texture should be coarse.

Combine the eggs, pumpkin puree, olive oil, zest, and vanilla seeds (rinse, dry, and save the pod for another use) in a mixing bowl. Whisk until smooth. Add to the processor and process for 30 seconds.

Coarsely chop half of the drained prunes and fold into the batter. Fill the molds two-thirds full. Top with the streusel, filling the molds. Bake until a tester comes out clean and the streusel is browned, about 20 minutes, rotating the pan halfway through baking.

Let cool briefly, then remove the molds.

To Serve

Put the warm cakes on dessert plates and garnish with the remaining prunes and the maceration liquid.

winter

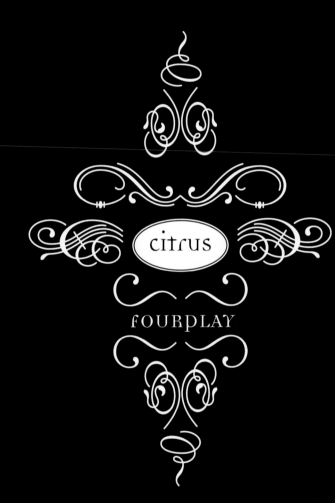

Winter may mean there are no more local stone fruits or berries in the markets, but this is the season for citrus. This tasting is an exercise in balance between sour and sweet, showcasing the bright flavors of citrus.

serves 8

citrus

FOURPLAY

citrus salad ~ calamansi noodles

lemongrass ice cream ~ dehydrated grapefruit ~ carbonated lime curd ~ crispy tangerine sticks

citrus-almond sponge cake ~ margarita semifreddo

meyer lemon tarts ~ chocolate crème chiboust ~ earl grey fluid gel

citrus salad ~ calamansi noodles

SERVES 4 ON ITS OWN OR
8 AS PART OF A FOURPLAY

MAKE IT SIMPLER
Instead of making noodles, you could pour the noodle base into glasses, let it set there, and then top with fruit and cream. Or combine it with gin for a killer "Jell-O" shot.

Calamansi is a limelike citrus from the Philippines with a distinct flavor. It's sweeter than a lime, but it retains that tartness you expect. For this dessert, I turn calamansi puree into "noodles" by setting it with gelatin and then weave the tangy, slippery noodles in and out of a salad made with blood oranges and clementines.

For the Noodles

¾ CUP (210 G) SIMPLE SYRUP
  (PAGE 184)
4 TEASPOONS POWDERED
  GELATIN (OR 18 G SHEET
  GELATIN; SEE PAGE 276)
GRATED ZEST OF HALF A LIME
2 CUPS (250 G) CALAMANSI PUREE
  (SEE PAGE 276), OR 1 CUP FRESH
  ORANGE JUICE, ½ CUP FRESH
  LEMON JUICE, AND ½ CUP
  FRESH LIME JUICE

Rinse a 9 x 12-inch rimmed baking sheet with water and shake off the excess. Line the damp pan neatly with plastic wrap.

Put the simple syrup in a glass bowl and sprinkle the gelatin over the surface. Let sit for at least 2 minutes to soften. Microwave for 1 minute or heat gently in a small saucepan until melted. Whisk the gelatin and the zest into the calamansi puree. Pour into the pan and chill until set, about 2 hours.

To Serve

1 THIN SLICE BRIOCHE
  (SEE PAGE 194)
OLIVE OIL
COARSE SALT
SUGAR
1 BLOOD ORANGE, SEGMENTED
  (SEE PAGE 115)
2 CLEMENTINES, SEGMENTED
  (SEE PAGE 115)
MICRO RED SHISO (OR THINLY
  SLICED FRESH RED SHISO
  LEAVES; OPTIONAL)
BLACK AND WHITE SESAME
  SEEDS, TOASTED

Cut the brioche into tiny dice and leave it on the counter for a few hours.

Heat the oven to 350°F or 325°F on convection.

Toss the brioche with a drizzle of olive oil and some salt and sugar. Spread out on a baking sheet and bake until lightly golden, about 10 minutes. Let cool.

Cut the calamansi into thin "noodles" with a sharp paring knife. Pick up a noodle by its end and lower it onto a dessert plate, adding citrus segments as you drape it so the noodle and citrus will be interwoven. Garnish with the shiso, sesame seeds, and brioche croutons. Repeat for each serving.

lemongrass ice cream ~ dehydrated grapefruit ~ carbonated lime curd ~ crispy tangerine sticks

This dessert is a delicate balancing act showcasing the diversity of citrus. Each element supplies a different taste and texture: the creamy ice cream, the chewy grapefruit, the crispy sticks, and the airy curd.

SERVES 4 ON ITS OWN OR
8 AS PART OF A FOURPLAY

MAKE IT SIMPLER
You could make Tangerine Meringues (page 117) instead of the sticks.

For the Dehydrated Grapefruit
2 RUBY RED GRAPEFRUITS
SUGAR FOR DREDGING

Heat the oven to 150°F. Line a baking sheet with a Silpat or parchment.

Cut off the top and bottom of each grapefruit with a thin, sharp knife, to the point where you expose the flesh. Set one cut end down on your work surface and cut off the peel and white pith. Just follow the shape of the fruit and then go back to trim off any bits of pith you've missed. Set a strainer over a bowl. Working over the strainer and holding the grapefruit in your hand, cut down next to one membrane, then up—along the other membrane that's holding the segment—and drop the segment into the strainer. Continue until you've freed all the segments.

Toss the grapefruit segments in sugar, carefully, so you don't break them. Shake off the excess.

Arrange the grapefruit segments on the baking sheet and dry in the oven until reduced by half in volume and just slightly moist and a bit sticky. Start checking at about 2 hours; drying time will depend on your oven and the moisture of the grapefruit. Alternatively, line dehydrator trays with acetate and spray with cooking spray. Set the dehydrator to 120°F. Arrange the grapefruit segments on the trays and dry for 6 hours. Store in a single layer in an airtight plastic container for up to 2 days.

CONTINUES . . .

For the Carbonated Lime Curd

4 LARGE EGG YOLKS
¼ CUP (50 G) SUGAR
¾ CUP PLUS 2 TABLESPOONS
   (210 G) FRESH LIME JUICE
2 TABLESPOONS WATER
1 TEASPOON POWDERED GELATIN
   (OR 4.5 G SHEET GELATIN; SEE
   PAGE 276)

Set up an ice bath in a large bowl.

Whisk the egg yolks and sugar together in a heatproof bowl until light. Whisk in the lime juice and set the bowl over a saucepan of simmering water. Cook, whisking and stirring often, until the curd reaches 180°F.

Meanwhile, put the 2 tablespoons water in a small bowl and sprinkle the gelatin over the surface. Let sit for at least 1 minute, then microwave for 30 seconds or heat gently in a small saucepan until melted. When the curd has reached 180°F, stir in the gelatin.

Strain into a medium bowl and mix with an immersion blender. Set into the ice bath to chill completely, then pour into a soda siphon, filling it two-thirds full (to leave room for the gasses). Screw on the top of the siphon and charge the curd with two cream whipper chargers (N_2O) and one soda charger (CO_2), shaking vigorously for at least 1 minute after each charge. Refrigerate until you're ready to serve or for up to 3 days.

To Serve

LEMONGRASS ICE CREAM
   (PAGE 227)
CRISPY TANGERINE STICKS
   (PAGE 260)

Layer the ice cream and grapefruit segments in the glass of your choice.

Cut the tangerine sticks into short lengths and stick several in the glasses. Shake the siphon and top with a squirt of the lime curd.

TANGERINE MERINGUES

These don't have the intense citrus kick of the tangerine sticks, but they do add a good texture to the dessert.

Heat the oven to 175°F.

Use a Microplane to grate the zest of 3 tangerines (or other small citrus). Put the zest on a piece of paper towel or a plate and microwave for 30 seconds. Fluff the zest. Repeat, microwaving for 30 seconds and fluffing, until the zest is completely dry. Grind the zest to a fine powder in a spice grinder.

Put 3 egg whites in the bowl of a standing mixer fitted with the whisk. Turn it on to low, and beat the whites gently for 2 minutes, to start establishing a structure. The whites will look frothy but still a bit wet. Turn the speed up to medium and add ¼ cup sugar. Continue to beat at medium speed until the whites have body and are just shy of having soft peaks. Add another ¼ cup sugar and continue beating. Continue beating until the whites have formed firm peaks. Add ¼ cup sugar and beat until the whites are glossy and smooth and almost stiff. Keep your eye on the whites, so you don't overbeat them.

Sift a scant ½ cup confectioners' sugar and a scant ¼ cup cornstarch together into a bowl. Whisk in the tangerine powder. Fold the dry ingredients into the egg whites, carefully but thoroughly.

Fill a pastry bag fitted with a medium plain round tip (#802 is perfect) with the meringue. Pipe long sticks onto parchment-lined baking sheets. Bake until crisp but with no hint of color, about 1 hour. Let cool and store in an airtight container for up to 3 days.

citrus-almond sponge cake ~ margarita semifreddo

SERVES 8 TO 9

As I'm a great fan of a true margarita, I thought it would be fun to take the components apart and rearrange them into a dessert. This makes a lot, but leftovers will keep for a month in the freezer.

I learned a version of this sponge cake, which is called biscuit mirliton, *at the Hôtel de Paris in Monte Carlo. I love it for its airy/cakey texture, which is like no other sponge. Perfumed with citrus zest, it is a great complement to the tangy semifreddo.*

The key to the sponge is baking just before serving. You'll need eight to nine 1-ounce aluminum timbale molds for the cake and twenty 2 x 2-inch ring molds for the semifreddo (see Note, page 120).

For the Margarita Semifreddo
¼ CUP (110 G) GOLD TEQUILA
½ CUP COINTREAU
2½ TEASPOONS (15 G) SIMPLE SYRUP (PAGE 184)
2 TABLESPOONS (4 G) FRESH LIME JUICE
GRATED ZEST OF 1 LIME
1 TEASPOON POWDERED GELATIN (OR 4.5 G SHEET GELATIN; SEE PAGE 276)
1 LARGE EGG
2 LARGE EGG YOLKS
⅓ CUP PLUS 2 TABLESPOONS (90 G) SUGAR
1 CUP (240 G) HEAVY CREAM

Put twenty 2 x 2-inch ring molds on a tray and put them in the freezer at least 1 hour before you start to make the semifreddo.

Stir the tequila, Cointreau, simple syrup, and lime juice and zest together to make the margarita base. Measure ⅔ cup (drink the rest).

Pour about 3 tablespoons of the margarita base into a small glass bowl and sprinkle the gelatin over the surface. Let sit for about 1 minute, then microwave for 45 seconds or heat gently in a small saucepan until melted.

Put the egg, egg yolks, and sugar in the bowl of a standing mixer. Set the bowl over a saucepan of simmering water—make sure the bottom of the bowl doesn't touch the water—and whisk until the sugar is melted and the mixture is hot. Whisk in the gelatin.

Move the bowl to the standing mixer fitted with the whisk and whisk at medium-high speed until the mixture is pale and light and the sides of the bowl are cool.

In a separate bowl, whip the cream to medium peaks.

Fold about half of the remaining margarita base into the eggs. Fold in half the cream, then repeat, folding in the remaining base and the cream, gently but thoroughly.

Fill a pastry bag and pipe the semifreddo into the ring molds (see Note), leaving about ⅓ inch of headroom. Cover with plastic wrap and freeze for at least 2 hours before serving.

Heat the oven to 375°F or 350°F on convection. Spray eight to nine 1-ounce aluminum timbale molds with cooking spray and coat them with sugar (vanilla sugar, page 185, would be best). Set the molds on a baking sheet.

In a small bowl, rub the sugar, orange and lemon zests, and vanilla seeds (rinse, dry, and save the pod for another use) together with your fingers.

Whisk the almond flour, cornstarch, and salt together.

Put the egg and egg yolk in the bowl of a standing mixer fitted with the whisk. Whisk at medium speed until frothy. Add the sugar mixture and beat at medium-high speed until light and doubled in volume. Add the dry ingredients gradually, scraping the sides of the bowl as needed. Increase the speed to high and beat until the batter regains its original volume, about 3 minutes. You can prepare the batter about 2 hours in advance. Cover the bowl with plastic wrap and refrigerate it right away.

If you've made the batter in advance, whisk it again on high speed for about a minute. Fill a pastry bag and pipe the batter into the molds, filling them about two-thirds full. Bake until puffed, golden, and firm, about 11 minutes. Rotate the pan halfway through baking.

Unmold the cakes right away. You'll need to nudge them out of the molds with a small knife. Serve them warm.

Mix the orange zest and sugar together in a small bowl. Dip the tops of the warm sponge cakes into the sugar and set them on small plates. Garnish with the candied kumquats and lemon zest. Unmold the margarita semifreddos by rubbing each mold briskly between your palms and then pushing the semifreddo out of the mold. Add them to the plates.

For the Sponge Cake

¼ CUP (50 G) SUGAR
GRATED ZEST OF HALF AN ORANGE
GRATED ZEST OF HALF A LEMON
½ VANILLA BEAN, SPLIT AND SCRAPED
½ CUP (50 G) ALMOND FLOUR
2 TEASPOONS (5 G) CORNSTARCH
½ TEASPOON (2 G) SALT
1 EXTRA-LARGE EGG
1 EXTRA-LARGE EGG YOLK

To Serve

GRATED ZEST OF HALF AN ORANGE
ABOUT ¼ CUP (50 G) SUGAR
CANDIED KUMQUATS (PAGE 258)
CANDIED LEMON ZEST (PAGE 258)

CONTINUES . . .

note: You can freeze this dessert in whatever size molds you like (just be sure it's something you can push the semifreddo out of). For tastings, I use small plastic molds for the semifreddo that I have cut to order at a plastics store on Canal Street. The tubes have a ¾-inch opening and they're cut in 1⅜-inch lengths. If you are freezing the semifreddo in plastic, make sure you line the molds with acetate first. Muffin tins lined with plastic wrap would also work.

Meyer Lemon Tarts ~
chocolate crème chiboust ~ Earl Grey fluid gel

Chocolate and lemon make an age-old combination; the tartness of lemon enhances the acidity of the cacao bean and cuts the fatty mouthfeel. Meyer lemons have a short window of availability, and they're coveted for their lemony-orangey flavor—which is particularly good when paired with chocolate. They're versatile, with as many uses in the savory kitchen as in the pastry kitchen.

SERVES 8

Put the water and tea in a small saucepan and bring to a simmer. Remove from the heat and infuse for 10 minutes. Strain, pressing on the solids, and measure; add water if necessary to make 1¼ cups. Refrigerate until cold.

Pour the tea into a blender and turn the blender on to low. Slowly sprinkle the agar into the vortex. When you've added all the agar, blend for 1 more minute.

Pour into a saucepan and bring to a boil. Reduce the heat and cook at an active simmer for 5 minutes, then pour into a baking dish. Refrigerate until set and chilled, at least 2 hours.

Put the gel back in the blender and blend until smooth and fluid. Store in an airtight container in the refrigerator for up to 2 days.

Grate the zest from the lemon and put it in a blender. Cut off the peel and pith, cut the lemon in half lengthwise, and remove the seeds. Chop the lemon and put it into the blender with the egg, egg yolk, vanilla sugar, and cream. Blend until very smooth. Strain into a pitcher or measuring cup. Skim off the foam and refrigerate until needed.

For the Earl Grey Fluid Gel
1⅓ CUPS (320 G) WATER
1 TABLESPOON EARL GREY TEA LEAVES
1½ TEASPOONS (3 G) AGAR

For the Meyer Lemon Custard
1 MEYER LEMON
1 LARGE EGG
1 LARGE EGG YOLK
5 TABLESPOONS (62 G) VANILLA SUGAR (PAGE 185)
½ CUP (120 G) HEAVY CREAM

CONTINUES . . .

For the Tarts

¹/₂ RECIPE SPICED CHOCOLATE
TART DOUGH (PAGE 182)

Roll the dough to ¹/₈ inch thick between two sheets of parchment. Refrigerate for 30 minutes.

Line a baking sheet with parchment.

Cut 3¹/₂-inch rounds from the dough and line eight 2¹/₄-inch tart rings with the dough, setting the rings on the sheet pan as you finish. Refrigerate for 30 minutes.

Heat the oven to 375°F or 350°F on convection.

Trim the excess dough. Line the dough with parchment and fill with dried beans (or rice or pastry weights) and bake until cooked through, about 10 minutes. Let the pastry shells cool and remove the beans and parchment.

Reduce the oven temperature to 250°F (225°F if you're using convection).

Pour the Meyer lemon custard into the tart shells. Bake until the custard is set, with just a slight jiggle in the center, 18 to 20 minutes. Let cool to room temperature.

To Serve

CHOCOLATE CRÈME CHIBOUST
(PAGE 263)
CONFECTIONERS' SUGAR
ALMOND PRALINE POWDER
(PAGE 216; OPTIONAL)
ALMOND PRALINE PASTE
(OPTIONAL)

Use a 2¹/₈-inch cutter to cut the chocolate crème chiboust into eight disks. Place them on a parchment-lined baking sheet and refrigerate.

Heat the oven to 400°F or 375°F on convection.

Set a chiboust disk on top of each tart. Bake until puffed, about 2 minutes.

Smear some Earl Grey gel onto a dessert plate. Dust a tart with confectioners' sugar and place it on the gel. Garnish the plate with some praline powder and praline paste, if you want. Repeat for each serving.

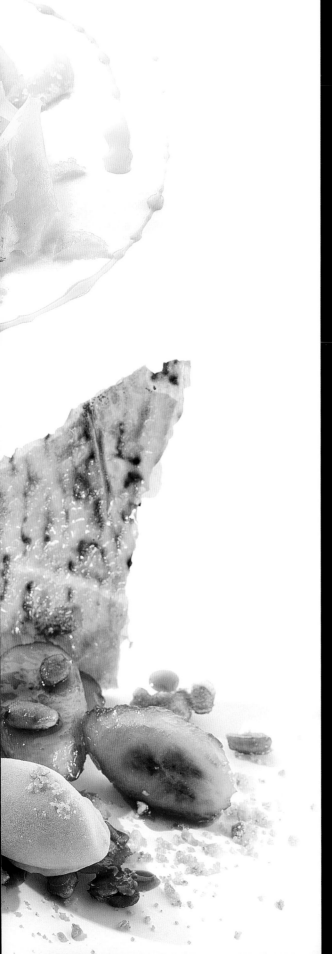

When I say exotic, I mean fruits that aren't local (which is always my preference) or that are imported. I use these flavors only in winter, partly because of their availability and partly to bring the taste of tropical islands to the dessert course in the dead of winter.

serves 10

exotic

FOURPLAY

mango Lhassi

coconut pain perdu ~ cream cheese ice cream ~ papaya-lime compote

flambéed bananas ~ rum and coke ice cream ~ peanut phyllo crisps

pineapple-polenta cake ~ pineapple-spice sauce

mango lhassi

SERVES 4 ON ITS OWN OR
10 AS PART OF A FOURPLAY

MAKE IT SIMPLER
I love the mixture of exotic fruit garnishes for this dessert, but you could use only one fruit.

I enjoy going out for Indian food and pairing a cool, calming lhassi with a heavily spiced meal. The more I thought about it, the more I wanted to develop one for my dessert menu. This one—which I worked out with my friend and onetime sous-chef Jason Casey—is creamy smooth and softly perfumed with rose water and cinnamon.

For the Lhassi
MAKES ABOUT 2 CUPS

1 CUP (250 G) MANGO PUREE
   (SEE PAGE 276)
½ CUP (115 G) PLAIN NONFAT
   YOGURT
¼ CUP PLUS 3 TABLESPOONS
   (105 G) SKIM MILK
1 TABLESPOON (20 G) ORANGE
   BLOSSOM HONEY
¾ TEASPOON (4 G) ROSE WATER
¼ TEASPOON (0.37 G) GROUND
   CINNAMON (PREFERABLY
   SAIGON)

Combine the mango puree, yogurt, milk, honey, rose water, and cinnamon in a blender and process until frothy. Transfer to a plastic container and store in the freezer for up to 2 hours so the lhassi will be icy cold when you serve it. Move it to the refrigerator about 10 minutes before serving.

To Serve

DICED MANGO
DICED PAPAYA
DICED KIWI FRUIT
PASSION FRUIT SEEDS
ICY COLD CARROT JUICE

Fill small glasses a little more than half full with the diced fruit and the passion fruit seeds. Top with the lhassi, leaving a little room for the carrot foam.

Put the carrot juice in a tall, narrow container and froth it with an immersion blender. Top each lhassi with foam and serve right away.

coconut pain perdu ~ cream cheese ice cream ~ papaya-lime compote

I like eating breakfast in the middle of the day and even for dinner, so why not turn a breakfast dish into dessert? This version of French toast is highlighted by seasonal exotic fruits—the acidity of papaya and lime taming the sweetness of the coconut.

Combine the coconut milk, cream, eggs, sugar, rum, and vanilla seeds (rinse, dry, and save the pod for another use) in a bowl and mix with an immersion blender. Cover with plastic wrap and refrigerate until needed.

Cut the brioche into 1-inch slices and trim the crusts. Cut the slices into 1 x 1 x 3-inch batons. Soak in the coconut custard for just 1 minute; you don't want to make the bread soggy.

Set the bread on a rack over a baking sheet and refrigerate until you're ready to serve the dessert.

Heat a griddle over medium heat. When the griddle's hot, brush it with clarified butter and cook the *pain perdu,* browning the batons on all sides, about 4 minutes.

Serve immediately, with the ice cream and compote and garnished with slices of papaya and a pinch or two of freeze-dried coconut, if desired.

SERVES 6 ON ITS OWN OR
10 AS PART OF A FOURPLAY

MAKE IT SIMPLER
You could buy a loaf of brioche instead of making the bread.

For the Coconut Custard
1 CUP (250 G) CANNED COCONUT
   MILK
½ CUP (120 G) HEAVY CREAM
3 EXTRA-LARGE EGGS
¾ CUP PLUS 2 TABLESPOONS
   (175 G) SUGAR
2 TABLESPOONS (30 G) MALIBU
   COCONUT RUM
½ VANILLA BEAN, SPLIT AND
   SCRAPED

For the Pain Perdu
BRIOCHE (PAGE 194)

To Serve
CLARIFIED BUTTER
CREAM CHEESE ICE CREAM
   (PAGE 223)
PAPAYA-LIME COMPOTE
   (PAGE 251)
SLICED PAPAYA
DRIED SHREDDED UNSWEETENED
   COCONUT (OPTIONAL)

flambéed bananas ~ rum and coke ice cream ~ peanut phyllo crisps

SERVES 6 ON ITS OWN OR
10 AS PART OF A FOURPLAY

I always thought it was a shame that you had to burn the alcohol off when you flambéed bananas, so I've reintroduced the rum in a different form—in ice cream. Peanut Phyllo Crisps add the crunch you need to play off the soft bananas and ice cream.

For the Bananas

6 TABLESPOONS (75 G) SUGAR

COARSE SALT

6 BABY BANANAS, HALVED
  LENGTHWISE OR SLICED ON
  AN ANGLE

4 TABLESPOONS (57 G) UNSALTED
  BUTTER, CUT INTO BITS

1/2 CUP (120 G) MYERS'S RUM

MAKE IT SIMPLER
Instead of making the ice cream, you could soften some store-bought vanilla ice cream, stir in some rum and some Coke, and refreeze it. And you could replace the candied peanuts and the phyllo with chopped honey-roasted peanuts and some crumbled cigarette cookies.

Set a large sauté pan over medium-high heat and get it good and hot. Sprinkle the sugar evenly over the pan and add a good pinch of salt. Cook, swirling the pan once the sugar has started to color, until the caramel is medium amber.

Add the bananas, cut side down, and scatter the butter around them. Cook, shaking the pan often, for about 1 1/2 minutes, until the bananas have browned. Turn them over and continue to cook, shaking the pan, for about 1 minute, to brown the other side.

Take the pan off the heat and pour in the rum. Return the pan to the heat, tip it to ignite the rum, and cook, shaking the pan and turning the bananas in the caramel, for about another minute, until the caramel has thickened and the bananas are just cooked through. No mushy bananas.

Put some candied peanuts on dessert plates and top with a scoop of ice cream. Add the bananas, a piece or two of the peanut phyllo, and some more peanuts. If you want, grind some of the nuts to a powder in a spice grinder to use as a garnish. Repeat for each serving.

To Serve

CANDIED PEANUTS (SEE PAGE 215)

RUM AND COKE ICE CREAM (PAGE 229)

PEANUT PHYLLO CRISPS (PAGE 212)

pineapple-polenta cake ~ pineapple-spice sauce

**SERVES 4 ON ITS OWN OR
10 AS PART OF A FOURPLAY**

Pineapple has a balance of sugar and acid that I really like. I wanted to capture that sweet-tart flavor in an upside-down cake, but in a refined one. So I've made a batter with cornmeal that gives the cake a great foundation and a terrific crumb.

For the Pineapple

¹/₂ CUP (100 G) SUGAR
COARSE SALT
¹/₂ RIPE PINEAPPLE

Wrap four 3¹/₄-inch or ten 2¹/₄-inch tart rings with aluminum foil to cover the bottoms, bringing the foil up around the outside of each ring, and place the rings on a baking sheet.

Put the sugar in a heavy skillet. Sprinkle with a tablespoon or two of cool water and a pinch of salt. Turn the heat to high. Leave the pan alone until the sugar starts to color, then pick up the pan and roll the sugar in it so it colors evenly. Cook until the caramel is dark amber. Immediately pour into the tart rings, carefully tilting them (hold on to the outer foil layer) to make an even layer on the bottom.

Cut the top and bottom off the pineapple. Cut off the peel and the eyes. Slice into vertical quarters and cut out the core. Cut one of the quarters into ¹/₂-inch-wide slices, then into pieces that will fit into the tart rings. Use one piece of pineapple for each of the smaller rings and two for the larger.

Heat the oven to 375°F or 350°F on convection.

Cut the butter into a few pieces and put it with the sugar into the bowl of a standing mixer fitted with the paddle. Beat at medium-high speed until light and fluffy. Beat in the egg and then the yolks, one at a time, scraping the bowl often.

Whisk the flour, cornmeal, baking powder, and salt together. Add to the wet ingredients and mix at low speed until you have a smooth batter, scraping the bowl as needed.

Fill a pastry bag with the batter and pipe over the pineapple, filling the rings three-quarters full. If you are making the larger tarts, pipe in some batter, add another layer of pineapple, then finish filling with batter. Bake until a tester comes out clean, about 8 minutes for the small cakes and 10 for the large, rotating the pan halfway through baking. Let cool briefly.

Run a knife around the cakes, then turn them over and peel off the aluminum and take off the rings.

Put a cake upside down on a dessert plate and garnish with some candied ginger, if desired, and sauce. Repeat for each serving.

For the Cake

4 TABLESPOONS (57 G) UNSALTED BUTTER, SOFTENED

7 TABLESPOONS (85 G) SUGAR

1 LARGE EGG

2 LARGE EGG YOLKS

$\frac{1}{3}$ CUP (42 G) ALL-PURPOSE FLOUR

$\frac{1}{4}$ CUP PLUS 2 TABLESPOONS (45 G) YELLOW CORNMEAL

$\frac{1}{4}$ TEASPOON (1 G) BAKING POWDER

$\frac{1}{4}$ TEASPOON (1 G) COARSE SALT

To Serve

CANDIED GINGER (OPTIONAL)

PINEAPPLE-SPICE SAUCE (PAGE 271)

Citrus is the building block in this tasting, contrasted with creamy textures and tastes—airy egg whites, lush ice cream, soft cheese, custardy white chocolate.

serves 12

grapefruit, tangerine, and

orange

FOURPLAY

Rose oeufs à la Neige ~ Tangerine-Campari granité ~ carbonated citrus curd

grapefruit gelée ~ honey-ginger ice cream

cheese doughnuts ~ lemon confit

white chocolate—vanilla cake ~ mandarin carpaccio

Rose Oeufs à la Neige ~ Tangerine-Campari Granité ~ Carbonated Citrus Curd

SERVES 6 TO 8 ON ITS OWN OR
12 AS PART OF A FOURPLAY

This dessert was the brainchild of Amanda Clarke, one of my cooks, who went on to become pastry chef at Jean-Georges's Perry Street Restaurant in New York. The floral notes of the rose, the bitter edge of the Campari, the sweet acids of the tangerine and citrus, all meld into a unique balance of flavor and texture.

For the Carbonated Citrus Curd
CITRUS CURD (PAGE 257)

Put the curd into a siphon and charge it with a cream whipper charger (N_2O). Shake vigorously for at least 1 minute. Test, and if the curd is too flat, charge it with a second charger, shaking vigorously for another minute. Refrigerate until you're ready to serve dessert.

For the Meringue
1 LARGE EGG WHITE
CREAM OF TARTAR
2 TABLESPOONS (25 G) SUGAR
¾ TEASPOON (4 G) ROSE WATER

Put the egg white and a pinch of cream of tartar in the bowl of a standing mixer fitted with the whisk. Turn it on to low, and whisk the white gently for 2 minutes, to start establishing a structure. The white will look frothy but still a bit wet. Turn the speed up to medium and add 1 tablespoon of the sugar. Continue to beat at medium speed until the white has body and is just shy of having soft peaks. Add the remaining 1 tablespoon sugar and continue beating until the white is glossy and smooth and almost stiff. Beat in the rose water.

To Serve
TANGERINE-CAMPARI GRANITÉ
(PAGE 239)
PETIT BEURRE CRUMBS (SEE
PAGE 200)
CRYSTALLIZED ROSE PETALS
(SEE PAGE 186)

Bring a saucepan of water to a simmer.

Drop heaping teaspoons of the meringue into the water and simmer gently until cooked through, 2 to 3 minutes. The meringues will double in size. Remove with a slotted spoon.

Spoon some granité into bowls or glasses. Squirt some curd around it and top with a meringue or two. Garnish with petit beurre crumbs and crumbled crystallized rose petals.

grapefruit gelée ~ Honey-ginger ice cream

SERVES 6 ON ITS OWN OR
12 AS PART OF A FOURPLAY

In this dessert, a grapefruit gelée gets poured over grapefruit segments, which brings a different flavor note out of the grapefruit. It's important to add the zest at the end to avoid bitterness. The combination of grapefruit and tarragon is one I really love, but I also wanted to add something spicy. Ginger is a natural, since it enlivens the herb flavors and is intense enough to carry through the ice cream, which gives this dessert its great mouthfeel.

For the Gelée

4 LARGE GRAPEFRUITS

1 TEASPOON POWDERED GELATIN
(OR 4.5 G SHEET GELATIN; SEE
PAGE 276)

$\frac{1}{2}$ VANILLA BEAN, SPLIT AND
SCRAPED

$\frac{1}{3}$ CUP (65 G) SUGAR

$2\frac{1}{4}$ TEASPOONS (7 G) POWDERED
APPLE PECTIN

Grate the zest from $1\frac{1}{2}$ of the grapefruits. Bring a saucepan of water to a boil. Add the zest and bring the water back to a boil. Drain. Repeat this blanching process two more times.

Juice enough of the grapefruits to make $2\frac{1}{2}$ cups juice. Section the remaining grapefruits (see page 115) and divide them among shallow dessert bowls.

Put $\frac{1}{4}$ cup of the grapefruit juice in a small glass bowl. Sprinkle the gelatin over the surface.

Put the remaining $2\frac{1}{4}$ cups grapefruit juice and the vanilla pod in a saucepan and bring to a simmer over medium-low heat. Whisk the sugar and pectin together and whisk into the juice. Simmer gently to reduce to $1\frac{1}{2}$ cups. Add the zest in the last few minutes of simmering.

Microwave the gelatin for 45 seconds or heat gently in a small saucepan until melted. Stir the gelatin into the reduced grapefruit juice along with the vanilla seeds. Strain and let cool to room temperature. Do not let set.

Pour in enough of the gelée to cover the grapefruit segments in their bowls halfway. Refrigerate until set or for up to 2 days.

To Serve

FRESH TARRAGON LEAVES

HONEY-GINGER ICE CREAM
(PAGE 226)

BRIOCHE CROUTONS (PAGE 197)

TARRAGON OIL (SEE PAGE 189)

Thinly slice the tarragon lengthwise.

Top the gelée with a scoop of the ice cream. Garnish with some tarragon, a few brioche croutons, and a drizzle of the oil.

cheese doughnuts ~ lemon confit

I'm a doughnut fanatic. I love eating them, and I love making them, but I'm always looking for a way to counter their tendency to be oversweet. Here, tangy cheese and the acid from kumquats and lemons are the answer.

Line a small rimmed baking sheet with plastic wrap.

Put the milk and vanilla pod and seeds in a saucepan and bring to a simmer.

Whisk the cornstarch and sugar together. Add to the yolks and whisk until smooth.

When the milk is simmering, slowly whisk about ½ cup into the yolks to temper them, then scrape the yolks into the saucepan and bring to a boil, whisking constantly. Strain onto the baking sheet and cover with plastic wrap, pressing it onto the surface of the pastry cream to prevent a skin from forming. Refrigerate until cold.

Measure 150 g of the pastry cream (reserve the rest for another use) and put it in a food processor. Add the ricotta and mascarpone and process until smooth. Transfer to a bowl and stir in the kumquats. Cover with plastic wrap and refrigerate until you're ready to make the doughnuts.

In a small bowl, crumble the yeast into the water (or sprinkle the dry yeast over the water). Whisk until dissolved. Add the sugar, milk powder, and flour and stir until smooth. Cover with plastic wrap and leave at room temperature until bubbling, about 45 minutes.

CONTINUES . . .

SERVES 6 OR MORE ON ITS OWN OR 12 OR MORE AS PART OF A FOURPLAY

For the Cheese Filling

1 CUP (240 G) MILK
½ VANILLA BEAN, SPLIT AND SCRAPED
2 TABLESPOONS (15 G) CORNSTARCH
1 TABLESPOON (12 G) SUGAR
2 LARGE EGG YOLKS
6 TABLESPOONS (75 G) FRESH RICOTTA CHEESE
6 TABLESPOONS (75 G) MASCARPONE
3 TABLESPOONS (50 G) CANDIED KUMQUATS (PAGE 258), DRAINED AND MINCED

For the Sponge

1 PACKED TABLESPOON (18 G) FRESH YEAST OR 1½ TEASPOONS INSTANT ACTIVE DRY YEAST
1 CUP (120 G) LUKEWARM WATER
1 TABLESPOON (12 G) SUGAR
½ CUP (40 G) NONFAT MILK POWDER
½ CUP (62 G) ALL-PURPOSE FLOUR

MAKE IT SIMPLER
You could substitute a good Seville orange marmalade for the candied kumquats in the filling, and lemon marmalade for the confit. Just make sure that they aren't too sweet.

For the Doughnuts

MAKES ABOUT 18 DOUGHNUTS

2 TABLESPOONS (28 G) UNSALTED
  BUTTER, SOFTENED
2 CUPS (250 G) ALL-PURPOSE
  FLOUR, PLUS ADDITIONAL IF
  NEEDED
1/2 CUP (100 G) SUGAR
1 LARGE EGG, WELL BEATEN
1 TEASPOON (4 G) COARSE SALT
GRATED ZEST OF 1 LEMON
1/2 TEASPOON (1.5 G) LEMON OIL

Mix the butter, flour, sugar, egg, salt, lemon zest, and lemon oil together in a large bowl until smooth. Add the yeast mixture and mix again until smooth. The dough should be barely firm enough to knead.

Turn the dough out onto a floured work surface and knead for 3 to 4 minutes, adding a little flour if necessary. Let the dough rest for a few minutes while you lightly oil a clean bowl (or spray it with cooking spray). Knead the dough again until smooth and elastic, another 3 minutes. Shape it into a ball, put it in the bowl, top side down, and turn the dough over. Cover with plastic wrap and refrigerate overnight.

Line a baking sheet with parchment and spray lightly with cooking spray.

Roll the dough out on a lightly floured work surface to 1/3 inch thick. Cut rounds with a 1 1/2-inch cutter.

Put the doughnuts on the baking sheet. Spray another piece of parchment and cover the doughnuts with the parchment, sprayed side down. Leave at room temperature until risen by half, then refrigerate until you're ready to serve (or let rise until doubled and fry right away).

For the Citrus Sugar

GRATED ZEST OF 1 ORANGE
GRATED ZEST OF 1 LEMON
GRATED ZEST OF 1 KEY LIME
  (OPTIONAL)
1/2 CUP (100 G) VANILLA SUGAR
  (PAGE 185)
1/2 CUP (100 G) GRANULATED
  SUGAR

Put the zests and sugars in a food processor and process for 15 seconds. Pour into a shallow bowl.

To Serve

CANOLA OIL FOR FRYING
LEMON CONFIT (PAGE 257)

Pour about 3 inches of oil into a wide saucepan and heat it to 365°F.

Fry the doughnuts a few at a time—don't crowd them—until golden, about 1 minute per side. Blot on paper towels and immediately dredge them in the citrus sugar.

Fill a pastry bag fitted with a medium round tip (#803 is perfect) with the cheese filling. Push the tip into the warm doughnuts and pipe in the filling.

Serve the warm doughnuts on top of some lemon confit.

white chocolate–vanilla cake ~ mandarin carpaccio

SERVES 6 ON ITS OWN OR
12 AS PART OF A FOURPLAY

MAKE IT SIMPLER
You can replace the carpaccio with a simple citrus salad. Segment a variety of oranges (see page 115), such as navels, clementines, tangelos, and Cara Cara, and collect the resulting juice in a cup. Warm a couple of tablespoons of honey and stir it into the juice. Pour over the segments and refrigerate until very cold.

For all the years I've been working with Jean-Georges, I've had his legendary molten chocolate cake on the dessert menu. Finally, I decided I had to do something to make the cake my own, so I took it apart and put it back together with white chocolate and a good hit of vanilla. This cake isn't molten; it's much more a lush, custardy soufflé.

I love combining citrus with chocolate, hot with cold. The frozen mandarin orange refreshes and cleanses the palate.

For the
White Chocolate–Vanilla Cake
6½ OUNCES (184 G) WHITE
   CHOCOLATE (PREFERABLY
   VALRHONA), CHOPPED
4 LARGE EGG WHITES
1 VANILLA BEAN, SPLIT AND
   SCRAPED
CREAM OF TARTAR
7 TABLESPOONS PLUS 1½
   TEASPOONS (91 G) SUGAR
GENEROUS 1 TABLESPOON (10 G)
   ALL-PURPOSE FLOUR
6 LARGE EGG YOLKS
9 TABLESPOONS (5 G) UNSALTED
   BUTTER, MELTED

Heat the oven to 275°F or 250°F on convection. Set six 6-ounce ramekins or twelve 2½-inch square molds on a baking sheet and spray them with cooking spray, rotating the tray so you can spray all sides of the ramekins.

Melt the chocolate in a glass bowl in 30-second spurts in the microwave, or melt in a double boiler. After each spurt, let the chocolate sit for a minute or so, then stir it with a heatproof rubber scraper. Let the chocolate cool to 115°F.

Meanwhile, combine the egg whites, vanilla seeds (rinse, dry, and save the pod for another use), and cream of tartar in the bowl of a standing mixer fitted with the whisk. Turn it on to low, and beat the whites gently for 2 minutes, to start establishing a structure. The whites will look frothy but still a bit wet. Turn the speed up to medium and add 3 tablespoons of the sugar. Continue to beat at medium speed until the whites have body and are just shy of having soft peaks. Add 3 more tablespoons of the sugar and continue beating until the whites have formed firm peaks. Add the remaining 1 tablespoon sugar and beat until the whites are glossy and smooth and almost stiff. Keep your eye on the whites, so you don't overbeat them.

While you whip the whites, sift the flour and the 1½ teaspoons sugar together onto a piece of waxed paper. Beat the yolks with a whisk in a medium bowl until they are satiny smooth, then whisk in the flour and sugar. You're not trying to aerate here; just get the yolks smooth again.

Scrape the chocolate into a large mixing bowl and check to make sure it's at temperature. If it has cooled below 115°F, heat up the melted butter, using that to play with the chocolate temperature. Whisk the chocolate and butter together. Right after you add the remaining tablespoon of sugar to the whites, whisk the egg yolks into the chocolate. Chances are, this will look a little grainy, and the butter may separate. It will come together with the whites.

Scoop out a little less than one-quarter of the whites with a big rubber scraper and fold them into the chocolate to lighten it. Add the rest of the egg whites and fold in quickly and thoroughly.

Transfer the batter to a pastry bag and pipe into the ramekins, filling them just more than halfway. Slide the sheet into the oven and bake for 12 minutes, rotating the pan halfway through baking. The cakes are done when they are doubled in size and feel just set when you touch them. Any air bubbles that have risen to the top will have burst.

Let cool, still on the baking sheet, on a rack. The cakes will fall, and quickly. When the cakes have cooled, cover them all with plastic wrap and keep them at room temperature until you're ready to serve.

Heat the oven to 350°F or 325°F on convection. Uncover the cakes and slip them into the oven for about 5 minutes, just until warmed through and rerisen slightly. The cakes should also take on a little bit of color. Invert the cakes onto dessert plates.

Unwrap the carpaccio and push it partway out of the tube. Cut thin slices and set one slice next to each cake. Shower the cake with confectioners' sugar and garnish with some micro shiso if you want.

To Serve

MANDARIN CARPACCIO
   (PAGE 259)
CONFECTIONERS' SUGAR
MICRO SHISO (OR THINLY SLICED
   FRESH SHISO; OPTIONAL)

chocolate

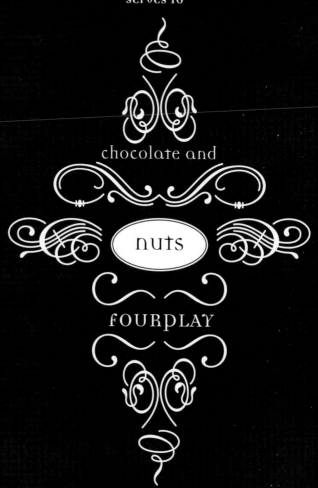

No matter what other tastings I have on the menu, chocolate is always the #1 bestselling dessert. Maybe it's because it's people's safe bet or comfort zone. This combination focuses on the luxurious. There's a simple soup with a rich cream topping. Jean-Georges's celebrated molten cake. Dessert panini with a layer of crunchy filling. And a truly elegant chocolate-peanut cake.

serves 16

chocolate and

nuts

FOURPLAY

chocolate soup ~ devon foam ~ chocolate-covered cocoa puffs

Jean-Georges's warm chocolate cake ~ vanilla bean ice cream ~ chocolate crumble

chocolate-olive panini ~ balsamic vinaigrette

chocolate-peanut cake ~ bitter chocolate sorbet ~ peanut caramel

chocolate soup ~ Devon Foam ~ chocolate-covered cocoa puffs

SERVES 8 ON ITS OWN OR
16 AS PART OF A FOURPLAY

When I was growing up, chocolate milk was a treat, and the chocolate milk that ended up in a bowl of Cocoa Puffs when I had those for breakfast was the biggest treat of all. This soup is chocolate milk made cool and grown up, with quality ingredients and a contrast of textures. It reminds me of home.

For the Cocoa Puffs

8 OUNCES (227 G) MILK
CHOCOLATE (PREFERABLY
VALRHONA JIVARA 40% CACAO),
CHOPPED
1 CUP COCOA PUFFS

Melt the chocolate in a glass bowl in the microwave in 30-second bursts, stirring between each burst, or melt in a double boiler. Roll the Cocoa Puffs in the chocolate, coating them completely. Lift them out with a fork, letting the excess chocolate drip off, and place on a parchment-lined baking sheet to set. Store in a cool place.

For the Chocolate Soup

MAKES ABOUT 4½ CUPS

4 CUPS (960 G) WHOLE MILK
4 TEASPOONS (7 G) JUNIPER
BERRIES, CRUSHED IN A
MORTAR OR COARSELY GROUND
IN A SPICE GRINDER
9 OUNCES (255 G) BITTERSWEET
CHOCOLATE (PREFERABLY
VALRHONA ARAGUANI 72%
CACAO), FINELY CHOPPED

Put 1 cup of the milk in a small saucepan with the juniper berries. Bring to a boil, then turn off the heat and let the juniper infuse for 25 minutes. Have the chopped chocolate ready in a heatproof bowl, and, remember, the finer you've chopped the chocolate, the better.

Bring the milk back to a boil, then strain into a measuring cup. Add some of the remaining 3 cups milk, if needed, to make 1 cup. Pour the hot milk over the chocolate, let it sit for a moment, then whisk to melt the chocolate and make an emulsion.

Pour in the rest of the cold milk, and froth the soup with an immersion blender. Transfer to a pitcher and refrigerate until you're ready to serve.

Whisk the heavy cream and Devon cream together in a bowl until thick. Whisk in the milk, then froth with an immersion blender (add additional milk if you need to). Transfer to a pitcher and refrigerate until you're ready to serve.

For the Devon Foam

²/₃ CUP (160 G) HEAVY CREAM

¹/₂ CUP (200 G) DEVON CREAM (SEE NOTE)

¹/₂ CUP (120 G) WHOLE MILK, PLUS ADDITIONAL IF NEEDED

NOTE: Devon cream is available at gourmet markets and specialty stores.

Thin the chocolate soup with some cold milk if it's too thick to sip, and froth it again with an immersion blender.

Divide the soup among sixteen small glasses (for tasting portions) or among eight coffee cups. Drop in a few of the Cocoa Puffs, then spoon on a layer of the Devon foam. Top with a few more Cocoa Puffs.

To Serve

WHOLE MILK, IF NEEDED

jean-georges's warm chocolate cake ~
vanilla bean ice cream ~ chocolate crumble

SERVES 8 ON ITS OWN OR
16 AS PART OF A FOURPLAY

Just about every restaurant around has a version of molten chocolate cake on the menu, and many claim to be the original, but the cake that Jean-Georges developed at Lafayette Restaurant in New York is the most delicious, the one with the greatest contrast in textures. It's the only dessert that stays on the menu year-round at Jean Georges. (The photograph is on pages 144–145.)

For the Cake

18 TABLESPOONS (255 G)
    UNSALTED BUTTER, CUT INTO
    PIECES
8½ OUNCES (250 G) BITTERSWEET
    CHOCOLATE (PREFERABLY
    GUITTARD QUETZALCOATL
    72% CACAO), CHOPPED
5 LARGE EGG YOLKS
5 LARGE EGGS
½ CUP PLUS 2 TABLESPOONS
    (125 G) SUGAR
⅓ CUP PLUS 1 TABLESPOON (50 G)
    ALL-PURPOSE FLOUR

Butter eight 4-ounce ramekins or sixteen 2-ounce molds and dust them lightly with flour. Set the ramekins on a baking sheet.

Put the butter and chocolate in a glass bowl and melt in the microwave, using 30-second bursts. Stir until smooth.

Put the egg yolks and eggs in the bowl of a standing mixer fitted with the whisk. Beat at medium speed until frothy. Pour in the sugar and increase the speed to medium-high. Continue to beat until the eggs have tripled in volume.

Scrape the butter and chocolate into the eggs. Beat until well mixed, scraping the bowl once or twice. Sift the flour over the batter and fold it in gently.

Put the batter in a pastry bag and pipe into the ramekins. Cover with plastic wrap and refrigerate until you're ready to serve the dessert or for up to 8 hours.

To Serve

CHOCOLATE SAUCE (PAGE 268)
CHOCOLATE CRUMBLE (PAGE 213)
VANILLA BEAN ICE CREAM
    (PAGE 220)
CRYSTALLIZED VANILLA (PAGE
    186; OPTIONAL)
CONFECTIONERS' SUGAR
    (OPTIONAL)

Take the cakes out of the refrigerator to bring them to room temperature. Heat the oven to 475°F or 450°F on convection.

Slide the baking sheet into the oven and bake the cakes until the sides and tops are set, about 4 minutes for small cakes or 6 to 7 minutes for large ones. The centers will still be very soft.

Invert the ramekins onto dessert plates. Leave for about 10 seconds, then lift off the ramekins. Spoon a little chocolate sauce around each cake. Make a small pile of chocolate crumble to the side, and top with a scoop of ice cream. Garnish the ice cream with crystallized vanilla and the cake with confectioners' sugar, if you want. Serve immediately.

chocolate-olive panini ~ balsamic vinaigrette

Late-night eating is one of those things that's pretty much a fact of a chef's life. Really late-night eating. And I often end up with friends at 'ino and 'inoteca, where they make the greatest panini in New York. One very late night, my cooks and I thought it would be fun to create a sandwich for the dessert menu. Here's the result. The combination of chocolate with the tangy olives is addictive.

Rinse the olives and drain well.

Cut the olives in half lengthwise and put them in a small saucepan with the simple syrup. Bring to a simmer over medium-high heat. Remove from the heat and let cool to room temperature.

Heat the oven to 150°F. Line a baking sheet with a Silpat.

Drain the olives and toss them in sugar to coat lightly. Lay them out on the Silpat and dry in the oven for about 3 hours. The olives should still be meaty but not crisp. You could also set the olives on acetate-lined dehydrator trays and dry for 4 hours at 135°F.

Store in an airtight container for up to 3 days.

Line a 9 x 12-inch rimmed baking sheet with parchment.

Melt the gianduja in 30-second bursts in the microwave, letting it sit for about 1 minute and stirring between bursts. Stir in the feuilletine and olives. Spread the paste out evenly in the baking sheet. Cover with another sheet of parchment and flatten to make sure it's completely even. Refrigerate until cold and set.

SERVES 8 ON ITS OWN OR
16 AS PART OF A FOURPLAY

MAKE IT SIMPLER
If you don't want to make Chocolate Brioche, you could make the panini with some nice black bread.

For the Candied Olives
1 CUP (100 G) PITTED BLACK OLIVES IN BRINE (SUCH AS KALAMATA, GAETA, OR NIÇOISE)
1½ CUPS (420 G) SIMPLE SYRUP (PAGE 184)
SUGAR

For the Crispy Olive Gianduja
10½ OUNCES (300 G) GIANDUJA PASTE (SEE NOTE)
2½ OUNCES (75 G) FEUILLETINE (SEE NOTE)
1¾ OUNCES (50 G) CANDIED OLIVES, CHOPPED

NOTE: Gianduja paste and feuilletine are both available online from L'Epicerie. You could also buy cigarette cookies from a gourmet store and crush them as a substitute for the feuilletine.

CONTINUES . . .

For the Balsamic Vinaigrette

3 TABLESPOONS (40 G) AGED
    (25-YEAR) BALSAMIC VINEGAR
$^1\!/_3$ CUP (80 G) WATER
$^1\!/_4$ TEASPOON (0.35 G) XANTHAN
    GUM
COARSE SALT
SUGAR
$^1\!/_4$ CUP (45 G) EXTRA-VIRGIN OLIVE
    OIL

Stir the vinegar and water together.

Combine the xanthan gum with a pinch of salt and a pinch of sugar and whisk slowly into the vinegar and water; make sure there are no lumps. Whisk in the olive oil.

Store in a jar for up to 3 days.

To Serve

UNSALTED BUTTER, SOFTENED
8 VERY THIN SLICES CHOCOLATE
    BRIOCHE (PAGE 196), CRUSTS
    REMOVED
4 OUNCES (113 G) FONTINA VAL
    D'AOSTA, SHREDDED
MICRO ARUGULA (OR THINLY
    SLICED ARUGULA; OPTIONAL)

Heat a panini press or an electric grill.

Butter the brioche slices lightly on one side each and place half of the slices, buttered side down, on the counter.

Cut the crispy olive gianduja into squares the size of your bread. Place a square of gianduja on the bread, cover with a layer of shredded cheese, and top with another piece of bread, buttered side up.

Cook in the panini press until the gianduja is soft and the cheese has started to melt, about 90 seconds.

Cut the panini in half or, if serving as a part of a fourplay, in quarters. Serve the panini with a drizzle of the vinaigrette, some arugula, if desired, and some broken pieces of candied olives.

chocolate-peanut cake ~
Bitter chocolate sorbet ~ peanut caramel

Ever since I ate my first Reese's Peanut Butter Cup, I've been a fan of chocolate and peanut butter, and I have a lot of fun taking that flavor combination to new levels. This dessert has many textures and flavor dimensions and is a winner in more ways than one. I entered this recipe in a Peanut Advisory Board competition, and it came away with first prize.

This is one of my most complicated desserts. Make sure to read through the entire recipe before beginning. Freeze any leftovers: they will be fine for about one month, and you can eat them like frozen Snickers bars.

Line a 9 x 12-inch rimmed baking sheet with parchment.

Put the peanut butter and praline paste in a food processor and pulse to combine, scraping the bowl.

Melt the chocolate in a glass bowl in the microwave—use 30-second bursts—or melt in a double boiler and add to the food processor. Pulse to combine. Scrape into a bowl. Fold in the feuilletine thoroughly, but try not to break the pieces too much.

Turn the mixture out into the baking sheet and use an offset spatula to spread it evenly into the pan. Cover with another piece of parchment and freeze until needed.

CONTINUES . . .

SERVES 8 ON ITS OWN OR
16 AS PART OF A FOURPLAY

For the Chocolate-Peanut Praline
½ CUP (125 G) SMOOTH PEANUT
   BUTTER
4⅓ OUNCES (124 G) HAZELNUT
   PRALINE PASTE (SEE NOTE)
2 OUNCES (56 G) WHITE
   CHOCOLATE (PREFERABLY
   VALRHONA), CHOPPED
4 OUNCES (116 G) FEUILLETINE
   (SEE NOTE)

NOTE: You can purchase the praline paste online from L'Epicerie. Feuilletine is also available online from L'Epicerie. You could also buy cigarette cookies from a gourmet store and crush them as a substitute for the feuilletine.

For the Hazelnut-Peanut Sponge

1/4 CUP (25 G) HAZELNUT FLOUR
1/4 CUP (25 G) PEANUT FLOUR
4 TEASPOONS (12 G) ALL-PURPOSE
    FLOUR
4 LARGE EGG WHITES
CREAM OF TARTAR
1/2 CUP PLUS 2 TABLESPOONS
    (125 G) SUGAR
3 TO 4 TABLESPOONS (32 G)
    COARSELY CHOPPED
    HAZELNUTS AND PEANUTS

Heat the oven to 375°F or 350°F on convection. Line a 9 x 12-inch rimmed baking sheet with parchment.

Whisk the hazelnut flour, peanut flour, and all-purpose flour together in a bowl. Sift two times to aerate.

Put the egg whites and a tiny pinch of cream of tartar in the bowl of a standing mixer fitted with the whisk. Turn it on to low, and whisk the whites gently for 2 minutes, to start establishing a structure. The whites will look frothy but still a bit wet. Turn the speed up to medium and add one-third of the sugar. Continue to beat at medium speed until the whites have body and are just shy of having soft peaks. Add another one-third of the sugar and continue beating until the whites have formed soft peaks. Add the remaining sugar and beat until the whites are glossy and smooth and almost stiff. Keep your eye on the whites, so you don't overbeat them.

Sift the dry ingredients over the egg whites and fold them in. Spread the mixture evenly into the pan. Scatter the chopped nuts on top, covering the surface lightly but evenly. Bake until lightly browned and springy, about 10 minutes, rotating the pan halfway through baking. Remove from the pan immediately and let cool on the counter.

Remove the parchment paper and transfer the cake to a clean 9 x 12-inch rimmed baking sheet lined with parchment.

For the Chocolate-Peanut Ganache

5 3/4 OUNCES (162 G) MILK
    CHOCOLATE (PREFERABLY
    VALRHONA JIVARA 40% CACAO),
    FINELY CHOPPED
1 CUP (240 G) HEAVY CREAM
1/4 TEASPOON (1 G) COARSE SALT
1/2 CUP (125 G) SMOOTH PEANUT
    BUTTER

Put the chocolate in a glass bowl. Melt it partially in the microwave, giving it one 30-second burst.

Put the cream in a small saucepan with the salt and bring to a boil over medium-high heat. Add the peanut butter and whisk until smooth.

Pour one-third of the cream mixture into the center of the chocolate and stir from the center out toward the edges. Pour in another one-third of the cream mixture and continue to stir from the center out. Pour in the remaining cream mixture and stir, from the center out, until the ganache is completely smooth.

Pour a thin layer of the ganache—use about one-quarter of it—over the cake on the baking sheet and spread it evenly.

Take the praline out of the freezer and peel off the top piece of parchment. Invert the praline over the ganache and press down firmly all over with your palms to make sure you don't have any air bubbles between the layers and that the praline will stick to the ganache. Peel off the bottom piece of parchment. Spread the remaining chocolate-peanut ganache evenly over the praline and refrigerate until it sets, about 30 minutes.

Put 2 tablespoons of the cream in a small glass bowl and micro-wave for 30 seconds.

Melt the chocolate in a glass bowl in the microwave, in 30-second bursts, stirring between bursts. Let cool to 122°F.

Whip the remaining cream to soft peaks.

Put the sugar and salt in a very small saucepan and moisten it with enough water to make it the consistency of wet sand. Cook over medium-high heat, swirling the sugar in the pan once it begins to take on color, until it is a rich, dark amber. Pour in the warm cream and stir until smooth.

Meanwhile, put the yolks in the bowl of a standing mixer fitted with the whisk. Beat until light. With the mixer on medium, pour the caramel into the yolks, avoiding the whisk and the sides of the bowl. Beat at high speed until cool.

Fold about half the whipped cream into the chocolate. Micro-wave for 10 seconds. Fold in the yolk mixture little by little, incorporating it completely before adding more. Fold in the remaining whipped cream.

Spread the mousse evenly over the ganache layer on the baking sheet. Using a pointed cake trowel, comb the mousse to create ridges. Freeze overnight.

Remove the cake from the pan and dust it lightly with cocoa powder. Cut into pieces to serve on its own, or cut into strips with a very sharp knife and then cut the strips on an angle. Garnish each piece of cake with a little gold leaf, if desired, and serve with the caramel, sorbet, chocolate décor, and praline powder, if desired.

note: In the restaurant, I spray the cake with a mixture of equal parts melted chocolate and cocoa butter, using a Wagner paint sprayer.

For the Caramel-Chocolate Mousse

1 CUP PLUS 3 TABLESPOONS (285 G) HEAVY CREAM

3 OUNCES (84 G) BITTERSWEET CHOCOLATE (PREFERABLY VALRHONA LE NOIR GASTRONOMIE 61% CACAO), CHOPPED

2 TABLESPOONS (25 G) SUGAR

1/4 TEASPOON (1 G) COARSE SALT

2 LARGE EGGS YOLK

To Serve

UNSWEETENED COCOA POWDER

GOLD LEAF (OPTIONAL)

PEANUT CARAMEL (PAGE 216)

BITTER CHOCOLATE SORBET (PAGE 231)

CHOCOLATE DÉCOR SWIRLS (PAGE 265; OPTIONAL)

ALMOND PRALINE POWDER (PAGE 216; OPTIONAL)

This tasting shows off how versatile chocolate can be when carrying flavors as varied as the heat from chiles and the acid of passion fruit. It's a mix of crisp and creamy textures and ideal for the winter months—which is when I turn to exotic fruits.

serves 8

exotic

chocolate

FOURPLAY

chocolate-chipotle soup ~ milk chocolate—coconut foam

malted-chocolate rice pudding ~ crispy rice crackers

chocolate-filled passion soufflé tarts

milk chocolate mousse ~ flambéed bananas
~ hazelnut caramel sauce

chocolate-chipotle soup ~
milk chocolate—coconut foam

SERVES 4 TO 6 ON ITS OWN OR
8 AS PART OF A FOURPLAY

Working in a restaurant affords me the opportunity to learn the food cultures of many of my colleagues, who often bring home cooking to share for lunch. When that home cooking is Mexican, the dishes are sometimes flavored with chipotles or another chile, and I've come to crave that little kiss of heat, even in dessert. The gentle kick in the chocolate soup is tamed by the soothing chocolate-coconut foam.

For the
Milk Chocolate-Coconut Foam
5 OUNCES (150 G) WHOLE MILK
    CHOCOLATE (PREFERABLY
    VALRHONA JIVARA 40% CACOA),
    CHOPPED
1 (14-OUNCE) CAN COCONUT MILK

Put the chocolate in a glass bowl and melt in the microwave, using 30-second bursts and stirring after each burst, or melt in a double boiler.

Bring the coconut milk to a simmer in a saucepan. Add the chocolate and emulsify with an immersion blender. Refrigerate until cool, then emulsify again with an immersion blender. Pour into a whipped cream maker and charge with a cream whipper charger (N_2O). Shake vigorously. Refrigerate until needed or for up to 2 days.

For the Soup
MAKES ABOUT 3½ CUPS
SCANT ¼ OUNCE (6 G) CHIPOTLE
    CHILES
ABOUT 3¼ CUPS (780 G) MILK
5 OUNCES (150 G) MILK
    CHOCOLATE (PREFERABLY
    VALRHONA JIVARA 40% CACAO),
    CHOPPED

Heat a small skillet, preferably cast iron, over medium-high heat. When the skillet is hot, add the chiles, and toast them for about 90 seconds, turning them once. Let the chiles cool, then remove the seeds and chop.

Put the chiles in a small saucepan with 1½ cups of the milk. Bring to a simmer, then turn off the heat and infuse for 20 minutes. Mix with an immersion blender to pulverize the chiles. Strain through a fine strainer into a measuring cup and add enough milk to make 3 cups. Pour the milk into a clean saucepan and bring to a boil.

Put the chocolate in a heatproof bowl. Pour about one-third of the milk into the center and stir from the inside of the bowl out. Continue adding milk gradually as the chocolate melts. Mix with an immersion blender.

Fill a small glass or a cup about two-thirds full with the soup and top with the foam. Garnish with some croutons and toasted coconut. Repeat for each serving.

For the photograph, I held the glass on its side while I added the foam.

To Serve

CHOCOLATE BRIOCHE CROUTONS
    (SEE PAGE 195)
SHREDDED UNSWEETENED
    COCONUT, TOASTED

malted-chocolate rice pudding ~
crispy rice crackers

SERVES 4 TO 6 ON ITS OWN OR
8 AS PART OF A FOURPLAY

MAKE IT SIMPLER
If you don't want to make the rice crackers, serve the rice pudding with Cocoa Booty or with Pirate's Booty dusted with cocoa powder.

Growing up, the one thing I wanted when I went to the movies was a box of Whoppers, those malted milk balls. When I was looking around for a flavor to add to a chocolate rice pudding, I remembered that taste.

For the Pudding Base

1 CUP (190 G) ARBORIO RICE
2½ CUPS (600 G) WHOLE MILK
1 CUP (150 G) MALT POWDER
    (SEE NOTE)
6 TABLESPOONS (75 G) SUGAR
1 VANILLA BEAN, SPLIT AND
    SCRAPED
2½ OUNCES (75 G) UNSWEETENED
    CHOCOLATE (PREFERABLY
    VALRHONA CACAO PASTE),
    FINELY CHOPPED

Note: Malt powder is a sweetener derived from barley and should not be confused with malted milk powder. It's available online from Terra Spice Company.

Bring a large saucepan of water to a boil.

Rinse the rice and add it to the water. Cook for 8 minutes and drain. The rice should be about half cooked.

Meanwhile, put the milk, malt powder, sugar, and vanilla pod and seeds in a saucepan and bring to a boil over medium-high heat, stirring often. Add the rice and reduce the heat. Simmer until the rice is tender, 9 to 10 minutes.

Melt the chocolate in a glass bowl in the microwave in 30-second bursts, stirring after each burst, or melt in a double boiler. Stir into the rice.

Spread the rice out in a baking dish and cover with plastic wrap, pressing the plastic onto the surface. Refrigerate until cold.

Discard the vanilla pod. Measure out 625 g of the pudding base and put it in a large bowl.

Put the milk and 1 tablespoon of the sugar in a saucepan. Bring to a simmer over medium heat.

Whisk the yolks with the remaining 3 tablespoons sugar in a medium bowl. When the milk is simmering, slowly whisk about ½ cup into the yolks to temper them, then scrape the yolks into the saucepan and cook, stirring pretty much constantly, until the mixture reaches 180°F. Keep an eye on the color of the foam on the surface; when it turns the same color as the mixture, you're very close to the right temperature. Stir in the chocolate and mix with an immersion blender. Strain over the rice and mix well.

Whip the cream to medium peaks. Fold it into the pudding with the nibs. Divide the pudding among dessert bowls and refrigerate until chilled, at least 2 hours.

Garnish each pudding with a rice cracker.

For the Pudding

½ CUP (120 G) WHOLE MILK
4 TABLESPOONS (50 G) SUGAR
2 LARGE EGG YOLKS
1¾ OUNCES (50 G) BITTERSWEET
    CHOCOLATE (PREFERABLY
    VALRHONA ARAGUANI 72%
    CACAO), CHOPPED
¾ CUP PLUS 2 TABLESPOONS
    (210 G) HEAVY CREAM
GENEROUS ⅓ CUP (40 G) CACAO
    NIBS

To Serve

CRISPY RICE CRACKERS
    (PAGE 210)

chocolate-filled passion soufflé tarts

These little desserts are all about contrast. Picture a spongy soufflé with a creamy center, sitting in a crisp pastry shell. Then there's the sensation of the two different kinds of chocolate playing off the bright, acidic taste of the passion fruit.

Experiment with the flavors of the soufflé if you want, but keep it acidic. Try it with a puree of red currant, black currant, or raspberry.

MAKE IT SIMPLER
Replace the chocolate cream with mini candy bars. Use something creamy, like 3 Musketeers or Milky Way. Omit the pastry and bake the filled soufflés in ramekins that have been brushed with softened butter and coated with sugar.

For the Dough
½ RECIPE CHOCOLATE TART DOUGH (PAGE 182)

Spray eight mini brioche molds (3 inches across the top) lightly but evenly with cooking spray.

Roll the dough out on a lightly floured work surface to ¼ inch thick. Cut out a 6-inch circle of dough and fit it into one of the molds to make sure you've got the correct size. (These molds vary in size, and there's no point in cutting out all the pieces until you're sure you've got it right.) Cut the rest of the dough and line the rest of the molds with it. Set the molds on a baking sheet and refrigerate for at least 1 hour.

Stack the scraps and reshape them into a brick. Wrap tightly in plastic and refrigerate or freeze for another use.

Heat the oven to 375°F or 350°F on convection. Prick the pastry shells all over with a fork, then line them with parchment (or cut-down coffee filters) and fill with dried beans (or rice or pastry weights). Bake until the pastry is crisp, about 16 minutes, rotating the pan halfway through baking.

Lift the parchment and beans out right away and let the shells cool completely on a rack.

For the Chocolate Cream
2 OUNCES (62 G) BITTERSWEET CHOCOLATE (PREFERABLY VALRHONA MANJARI 64% CACAO), FINELY CHOPPED
½ CUP (120 G) HEAVY CREAM

Put the chocolate in a heatproof bowl.

Bring the cream to a boil in a small saucepan. Pour the cream over the chocolate and leave it alone for about 1 minute. Stir with a heatproof rubber scraper until the chocolate is completely melted. Cover with plastic wrap and refrigerate for at least 1 hour or up to 3 days.

Mix the xanthan gum and sugar together. Whisk into the passion fruit puree, a few grains at a time, taking care that it doesn't clump. Refrigerate for 20 minutes, then stir in the passion fruit seeds. Refrigerate, covered, until you're ready to serve.

Put the egg whites and a pinch of cream of tartar in the bowl of a standing mixer fitted with the whisk. Turn it on to low, and beat the whites gently for 2 minutes, to start establishing a structure. The whites will look frothy but still a bit wet. Turn the speed up to medium and add 2 teaspoons of the sugar. Continue to beat at medium speed until the whites have body and are just shy of having soft peaks. Add 2 more teaspoons of the sugar and continue beating until the whites have formed firm peaks. Add the remaining 2 teaspoons sugar and beat until the whites are glossy and smooth and almost stiff. Keep your eye on the whites, so you don't overbeat them.

Whisk the yolk into the passion fruit puree in a wide bowl. Fold in a spoonful of the whites to lighten the puree. Then add the rest of the whites and fold in quickly and lightly, spinning the bowl as you fold.

CONTINUES . . .

For the Passion Glaze

½ TEASPOON (1.5 G) XANTHAN GUM
1 TEASPOON (4 G) SUGAR
1 CUP (250 G) PASSION FRUIT PUREE
SEEDS FROM 1 PASSION FRUIT

For the Passion Soufflé

2 LARGE EGG WHITES
CREAM OF TARTAR
6 TEASPOONS (75 G) SUGAR
1 LARGE EGG YOLK
2 TABLESPOONS (30 G) PASSION FRUIT PUREE (SEE PAGE 276)

CONFECTIONERS' SUGAR
(OPTIONAL)

To Serve Heat the oven to 375°F or 350°F on convection.

Set the chocolate tart shells on a baking sheet.

Fill a pastry bag with the chocolate cream and pipe a plug of cream into the center of each shell. Fill a second pastry bag with the passion soufflé and pipe into the shells, covering the chocolate cream center completely.

Bake for 6 to 7 minutes, until the soufflés have risen and browned lightly. Rotate the pan halfway through baking.

Transfer to dessert plates and sprinkle with confectioners' sugar, if you want. Spoon the passion glaze over the tart or serve it on the side.

NOTE: You can assemble the tarts and freeze them for later baking, if you want. Don't cover the baking sheet with plastic wrap until the soufflé mix has frozen, though; otherwise, you'll make a mess of your tarts. You'll need to bake them for another 1 to 2 minutes.

milk chocolate mousse ~ flambéed bananas ~ hazelnut caramel sauce

François Payard, with whom I worked at Daniel and at his own pastry shop, believes in signature desserts. His banana tartlet is one of those signatures, with crunchy cashews and creamy white chocolate mousse paired with rum-sautéed bananas.

In this tribute to his dessert, I borrowed the structure and changed the flavors to creamy milk chocolate paired with a salty hazelnut caramel.

Line a baking sheet with parchment and put eight 3-inch tart rings on it.

Whisk the butter and cocoa powder together until smooth.

Lay a sheet of phyllo on your work surface and brush it with the chocolate butter. Sprinkle with 1 tablespoon of the hazelnut flour. Cover with another sheet of phyllo, brush with chocolate butter, and sprinkle with another tablespoon of the hazelnut flour. Cover with another sheet of phyllo and brush with chocolate butter. Roll the phyllo with a rolling pin to compress the layers. Cut out 4 rounds with a 4-inch cutter and line four of the tart rings with the phyllo. Take your time doing this so you make tight corners and don't crack the phyllo. Repeat with the remaining 3 sheets of phyllo. Freeze the shells, on the baking sheet, for at least 1 hour or, well wrapped, for up to 1 month. The freezing helps guarantee that the shells won't slump when you bake them.

CONTINUES . . .

SERVES 8

For the Phyllo Shells
5 TABLESPOONS (71 G) UNSALTED
   BUTTER, MELTED
3 TABLESPOONS (18 G)
   UNSWEETENED COCOA POWDER
   (PREFERABLY VALRHONA)
6 (9 X 13-INCH) PHYLLO SHEETS,
   DEFROSTED
4 TABLESPOONS (25 G) HAZELNUT
   FLOUR

MAKE IT SIMPLER
You can replace the chocolate mousse with ice cream. Let the ice cream soften, then pack it into 3-inch ring molds set on a baking sheet lined with parchment. Even off the tops with a spatula and refreeze the ice cream. Fill the phyllo right before serving.

Instead of making the Hazelnut Caramel Sauce, warm up some store-bought caramel sauce and fold in toasted hazelnuts. Or fold in honey-roasted peanuts, cashews, or pecans. But don't forget the salt.

Heat the oven to 375°F or 350°F on convection. Line the pastry with parchment and fill with dried beans (or rice or pastry weights). Bake the shells until crisp, about 12 minutes. Lift the parchment and beans out right away and let the shells cool completely on a rack. Lift off the rings when you're ready to put the dessert together.

For the Chocolate Mousse

8 OUNCES (225 G) MILK
    CHOCOLATE (PREFERABLY
    VALRHONA JIVARA 40% CACAO),
    CHOPPED
1 CUP (240 G) HEAVY CREAM

Line a 9 x 12-inch rimmed baking sheet with parchment.

Melt the chocolate in a glass bowl in the microwave in 30-second spurts, or melt in a double boiler. After each spurt, let the chocolate sit for a minute or so, then stir it with a heatproof rubber scraper. Let the chocolate cool to 120° to 115°F. The temperature is important here. If the chocolate is too hot or too cold, the mousse will be grainy or sludgy.

Meanwhile, pour the cream into the bowl of a standing mixer fitted with the whisk. Whisk on medium speed to very soft peaks. You want the cream to hold a loose shape.

Scrape the chocolate into a large wide bowl and pour in all the cream. Fold together quickly, spinning the bowl as you fold, and keeping the mousse light and frothy.

Pour the mousse into the baking sheet and spread it out evenly with an offset spatula. Freeze for about 20 minutes.

Lay a piece of parchment on top of the mousse. Set another baking sheet on top. Holding the two sheets together, invert. Lift up the top sheet and peel away the original parchment. Cut out 3-inch rounds of the mousse and return the sheet to the freezer for another 20 to 30 minutes, to set the mousse completely and make sure the rounds have nice clean edges before you try to lift them. Once the mousse has set, you can transfer the rounds to a tray with an offset spatula and refrigerate until you're ready to serve or for up to 2 days.

Heat the oven to 375°F or 350°F on convection.

Set the chocolate phyllo shells on a baking sheet. Fill each with a couple of tablespoons of hazelnut caramel sauce. Add two banana halves, trimming them so they fit, to the shell. Slide the baking sheet into the oven and heat through, until warm to the touch, about 5 minutes.

Transfer the shells to dessert plates, top each with a round of mousse, and serve. If you want, you can dust the mousse with cocoa powder, drizzle the plate with the caramel from the bananas, spoon on more hazelnut caramel, or spoon on some chocolate sauce.

To Serve

Hazelnut Caramel Sauce
  (page 270)
Flambéed Bananas
  (see page 128)
Unsweetened cocoa powder
  (preferably Valrhona;
  optional)
Chocolate Sauce (page 268;
  optional)

There is a lot of experimentation going on in today's pastr kitchens, and I continue to learn and work with new techniques that allow me to create exciting textures. But the bottom line for me is that the dessert has to be delicious. These are some of the most technically challeng recipes in the book, but they are also some of the most satisfying in flavor and texture.

serves 8

modern

chocolate

FOURPLAY

two chocolate consommés

warm crispy-creamy chocolate "doughnuts"

chocolate spaetzle ~ balsamic ice cream ~ strawberry so

bitter chocolate custard ~ pistachio-chocolate crunc

~ espresso bubbles

two chocolate consommés

SERVES 4 ON ITS OWN OR
8 AS PART OF A FOURPLAY

I've been exploring new ways to make chocolate soups. In particular, I wanted to find a way to remove the fat and keep a full, deep chocolate flavor, and I thought it would be interesting to contrast cold white chocolate with warm dark chocolate. I've succeeded in this recipe, which is a play on temperatures, textures, and techniques.

A scale is essential for this recipe. You will also need a hotel pan and a perforated hotel pan, both half size. You can get these online from BigTray. The technique of clarifying the soup base by freezing and slow defrosting comes from Wylie Dufresne of wd-50 in Manhattan and Heston Blumenthal of The Fat Duck in England.

**For the White Chocolate
Consommé**

MAKES ABOUT 2 CUPS

10 G SHEET GELATIN
1,333 G WATER
500 G WHITE CHOCOLATE
    (PREFERABLY VALRHONA),
    CHOPPED
0.4 G GELLAN F (LOW ACYL)
0.5 G CALCIUM LACTATE

Day 1: Set up an ice bath in a large bowl.

Soften the gelatin in a bowl of cold water. Squeeze out the water and set the gelatin aside in a strainer.

Bring the 1,333 g water to a simmer in a saucepan over medium-high heat. Add the chocolate and whisk until it comes to a boil. Remove from the heat and whisk in the gelatin. Mix with an immersion blender and pour into a medium bowl. Set into the ice bath to chill down quickly. Once cool, pour into a half-size hotel pan and freeze overnight.

Day 2: Early in the day, line a half-size perforated hotel pan with several layers of cheesecloth. Unmold the frozen block into it (in the restaurant, we use a blowtorch on the back of the pan to release the consommé quickly; at home you could set the pan into a sink of hot water) and set the perforated pan into the hotel pan. Cover with plastic wrap and refrigerate for 36 hours.

Day 3: Set up an ice bath in a large bowl. Line a strainer with several layers of cheesecloth and pass the flavored water from the bottom of the hotel pan through it. Discard all the solids. Weigh 500 g of the flavored water. Pour the flavored water into a blender and add the gellan F a few grains at a time. Pour into a saucepan and heat to 190°F. Return to the blender and add the calcium lactate a few grains at a time. Pour into a medium bowl and set into the ice bath. Stir constantly until cooled and set. Refrigerate until you're ready to serve.

Day 1: Set up an ice bath in a large bowl.

Soften the gelatin in a bowl of cold water. Squeeze out the water and set the gelatin aside in a strainer.

Bring the 1,920 g water to a simmer in a saucepan over medium-high heat. Add the chocolate and whisk until it comes to a boil. Remove from the heat and whisk in the gelatin. Mix with an immersion blender and pour into a medium bowl. Set into the ice bath to chill down quickly. Once cool, pour into a half-size hotel pan and freeze overnight.

Day 2: Early in the day, line a half-size perforated hotel pan with several layers of cheesecloth. Unmold the frozen block into it and set the perforated pan over the hotel pan. Cover with plastic wrap and refrigerate for 36 hours.

Day 3: Set up an ice bath in a large bowl. Line a strainer with several layers of cheesecloth and pass the flavored water from the bottom of the hotel pan through it. Discard all the solids. Weigh 500 g of the flavored water. Pour the flavored water into a blender and add the gellan F and gellan LT 100 a few grains at a time. Pour into a saucepan and heat to 190°F. Return to the blender and add the calcium lactate a few grains at a time, then add the glucose. Pour into a medium bowl and set into the ice bath. Stir constantly until cooled and set. Refrigerate until you're ready to serve.

Shear the consommés—you're slicing through the gels—with an immersion blender, keeping the blender under the surface to avoid making air bubbles. (In the restaurant, we remove any resulting air bubbles in the Cryovac machine.)

Put the dark chocolate consommé in a saucepan and bring it to just under a simmer over low heat. Don't heat it more than this, or the consommé will set.

Fill each glass about one-third full with the dark chocolate consommé. Float the white chocolate consommé on top (pour it slowly over the back of a spoon). Garnish with a few chocolate pearls.

Leftovers will keep for 2 days in the refrigerator.

For the Dark Chocolate Consommé

MAKES ABOUT 2 CUPS

15 G SHEET GELATIN

1,920 G WATER

500 G BITTERSWEET CHOCOLATE (PREFERABLY VALRHONA ARAGUANI 72% CACAO), CHOPPED

0.5 G GELLAN F (LOW ACYL)

0.1 G GELLAN LT 100 (HIGH ACYL)

0.6 G CALCIUM LACTATE

150 G GLUCOSE

To Serve

CHOCOLATE PEARLS (VALRHONA LES PERLES CROQUANTES)

warm crispy-creamy chocolate "doughnuts"

SERVES 4 ON ITS OWN OR
8 AS PART OF A FOURPLAY

Industrial technology is making its way more and more into the pastry kitchen and allowing us to create new textures. Here, the "doughnuts" are made with a creamy ganache. The alginate and lactate work to maintain the shape of the doughnuts, and the Methocel prevents the ganache from running while they fry. The result is a warm creamy ganache encased in a super-crisp panko coating.

Having a scale is essential for this recipe.

For the Alginate Base

144 G COLD WATER
3 G SODIUM ALGINATE

Put the water in a blender. Turn it on to medium speed. Add the sodium alginate a few grains at a time so it won't clump. Once it's all in, blend on high speed for 1 minute.

For the Doughnuts

MAKES 30 MINI DOUGHNUTS

87 G HEAVY CREAM
65 G WATER
12 G SUGAR
9 G METHOCEL A16-SG
146 G BITTERSWEET CHOCOLATE
    (PREFERABLY VALRHONA
    MANJARI 64% CACAO),
    CHOPPED
143 G ALGINATE BASE
1.5 G COARSE SALT

Put the cream and water in a small saucepan and bring to a boil over medium-high heat.

Mix the sugar and Methocel A16-SG and whisk into the hot liquid. Transfer to a blender and blend on high speed for 1 minute.

Put the chocolate in a glass bowl and microwave for 30 seconds. Pour about one-third of the hot liquid into the center and stir from the center out. Repeat, pouring in another one-third of the liquid and stirring. Add the remaining liquid and stir to make an emulsion. Stir in the alginate base and a pinch of salt. Mix until completely homogenous.

Transfer the batter to a pastry bag and pipe into mini savarin molds. Alternatively, you could spread the batter into a 9 x 12-inch rimmed baking sheet. Freeze overnight.

For the Calcium Bath

1,000 G WATER
20 G CALCIUM LACTATE

Bring the water to a simmer. Whisk in the calcium and pour into a blender. Blend on high for 1 minute. Pour into a hotel pan (or a roasting pan) and refrigerate overnight.

Drop the frozen doughnuts into the calcium bath. (If you've frozen the batter in a sheet pan, use a 1¾-inch cutter to cut out rounds.) Let soak for 5 minutes. Remove and let dry completely on a baking sheet lined with paper towels.

Put the panko in a food processor with the salt and pulse a few times to make semi-fine crumbs. Transfer to a shallow bowl.

Beat the egg and egg yolk together in a bowl. Add the flour and whisk until smooth.

Dip each doughnut into the egg wash, then into the panko. Place on a rack, set the rack over a pan, and refrigerate overnight to dry.

Heat at least 3 inches of canola oil in a large, deep saucepan to 375°F. Fry the doughnuts, a few at a time, until the coating is golden, 2 to 3 minutes. Drain on paper towels, sprinkle with fleur de sel, and serve immediately.

Note: You can freeze the doughnuts at any point in the process, but it may make the most sense to freeze them after you've breaded them.

Keep any doughnuts that you don't plan to fry immediately on a rack set over a pan (don't cover them). Freeze for 2 hours, then transfer the frozen doughnuts to a freezer bag. They will keep for about 1 month. Don't defrost before frying.

To Finish the Doughnuts (see Note)
100 G PANKO
0.5 G COARSE SALT
1 LARGE EGG
1 LARGE EGG YOLK
12 G ALL-PURPOSE FLOUR

To Serve
CANOLA OIL FOR FRYING
FLEUR DE SEL

chocolate spaetzle ~
Balsamic ice cream ~ strawberry sorbet

I've always wanted to create some interesting chocolate texture to pair with strawberries, and one night during a brainstorming session, Michal Shelkowitz—one of my cooks—suggested spaetzle. After much manipulation, we figured out how to make it something great and new and a cool contrast to the berries.

For the Chocolate Spaetzle

2 OUNCES (57 G) BITTERSWEET
   CHOCOLATE (PREFERABLY
   VALRHONA GUANAJA 70%
   CACAO), CHOPPED
1 CUP PLUS 2 TABLESPOONS (241 G)
   CRÈME FRAÎCHE
2 LARGE EGGS
2 VANILLA BEANS, SPLIT AND
   SCRAPED
¾ CUP PLUS 3 TABLESPOONS (89 G)
   UNSWEETENED COCOA POWDER
   (PREFERABLY VALRHONA)
1½ CUPS PLUS 1 TABLESPOON
   (195 G) ALL-PURPOSE FLOUR
5 TEASPOONS (16 G) SALT
2 TABLESPOONS PLUS 1 TEASPOON
   (29 G) SUGAR
OLIVE OIL

Melt the chocolate in a glass bowl in the microwave, using 30-second bursts, stirring between each burst, or melt in a double boiler. Let cool to 155°F.

Put the crème fraîche, eggs, and vanilla seeds (rinse, dry, and save the pods for another use) in a blender and puree.

With the blender running, add the chocolate, and puree until smooth and emulsified.

Put the cocoa powder, flour, salt, and sugar in a bowl and whisk together. Make a well in the center and pour in the wet ingredients. Stir together, working from the center out. Cover with plastic wrap and let the batter rest at room temperature for 30 minutes.

Bring a pot of water to a boil, then lower the temperature so the water is at an active simmer.

Working in batches, fill a spaetzle maker or potato ricer with the batter and press into the boiling water. Stir. When the spaetzle rise to the surface, cook for 1 minute. Remove with a slotted spoon, shaking to drain well. Toss in a bowl with a pinch of salt and just enough olive oil to coat the spaetzle lightly. They can stay at room temperature for up to 1 hour. Otherwise, cover with plastic wrap and refrigerate.

Put the strawberries in a bowl and cover with simple syrup. Leave at room temperature to macerate for at least 30 minutes.

Combine equal amounts of the ice cream and sorbet in a bowl. Mix together just enough to combine and make swirls. Return to the freezer.

When you are ready to serve, heat a skillet over medium-high heat. Working in batches, cook the spaetzle to heat them through and crisp them slightly.

Drain the strawberries and warm them in a separate skillet.

Put the berries in dessert bowls. Top with the spaetzle and a scoop of the ice cream/sorbet. Break up a meringue or two and add it to each bowl.

For the Strawberries

$\frac{1}{2}$ PINT (227 G) FRESH STRAWBERRIES, HULLED AND HALVED

SIMPLE SYRUP (PAGE 184)

To Serve

BALSAMIC ICE CREAM (PAGE 225)
STRAWBERRY SORBET (PAGE 236)
CHOCOLATE MERINGUES (PAGE 209)

Bitter chocolate custard ~
pistachio-chocolate crunch ~ espresso bubbles

SERVES 8

I've always liked the classic combination of chocolate and coffee and have been searching for a unique way to pair the two. In this dessert, the custard is dense and rich, so I wanted the coffee to be light. By using lecithin, I can turn coffee into a cloud.

For the Pistachio-Chocolate Crunch

2¼ OUNCES (62 G) BITTERSWEET CHOCOLATE (PREFERABLY VALRHONA ARAGUANI 72% CACAO), CHOPPED

2¼ OUNCES (62 G) PISTACHIO PRALINE PASTE

3½ OUNCES (100 G) FEUILLETINE

Melt the chocolate and praline separately in glass bowls in the microwave, using 30-second bursts. Stir together until smooth, then fold in the feuilletine.

Roll the mixture between two sheets of parchment to a little less than ¼ inch thick. Clean up the edges and slide onto a baking sheet. Freeze for at least 2 hours.

Note: You can replace the feuilletine with crushed cigarette cookies, which you'll find at gourmet markets.

For the Bitter Chocolate Custard

4¾ OUNCES (137 G) BITTERSWEET CHOCOLATE (PREFERABLY VALRHONA GUANAJA 70% CACAO), CHOPPED

¾ CUP PLUS 2 TABLESPOONS (210 G) WHOLE MILK

¾ TEASPOON POWDERED GELATIN (OR 3.3 G SHEET GELATIN; SEE PAGE 276)

¾ CUP PLUS 2 TABLESPOONS (210 G) HEAVY CREAM

½ VANILLA BEAN, SPLIT AND SCRAPED

½ TEASPOON (2 G) COARSE SALT

3 LARGE EGGS

⅓ CUP (65 G) SUGAR

2 TEASPOONS (3 G) ORANGE OIL

Set up an ice bath in a large bowl.

Put the chocolate in a glass bowl and microwave for 30 seconds. It won't be completely melted.

Spoon 3 tablespoons of the milk into a small glass bowl. Sprinkle the gelatin over the surface and set aside.

Put the remaining ½ cup plus 3 tablespoons milk, the cream, the vanilla pod and seeds, and salt in a saucepan. Bring to a simmer over medium heat.

Whisk the eggs and sugar in a medium bowl until pale yellow. When the milk mixture is simmering, slowly add about 1 cup to the eggs and whisk for about a minute to temper them (keep the pan off the heat while you do this). Scrape the eggs back into the saucepan and cook, stirring pretty much constantly, until the mixture reaches 180°F. Keep an eye on the color of the foam on the surface; when it turns the same color as the mixture, you're very close to the right temperature.

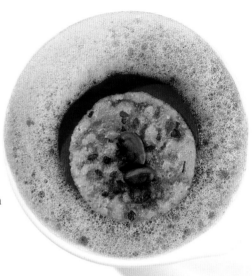

Microwave the milk and gelatin for 30 seconds or heat gently in a small saucepan until melted. Whisk into the mixture.

Pour one-third of the mixture over the chocolate and stir from the center out. Pour in another one-third, stirring again from the center out. Pour in the remaining mixture; stir from the center out until smooth. Add the orange oil and mix with an immersion blender. Strain into a medium bowl and set into the ice bath. Cover with plastic wrap placed directly on the surface. Let cool completely.

Line eight 2¼-inch tart rings with acetate or parchment, making a collar, and place on a baking sheet.

Cut eight 2¼-inch disks of devil's food cake and place in the bottom of the molds. Cut 2-inch disks of the pistachio-chocolate crunch and set on top of the cake. Fill a pastry bag with the bitter chocolate custard and pipe into the molds, filling them to the top of the collar. Even off the tops. Refrigerate until set, about 2 hours or up to 2 days.

Put the espresso, lecithin, sugar, and butter in a small saucepan and bring to a boil over high heat. Keep warm until you're ready to serve.

Aerate the espresso with an immersion blender until very bubbly.

Spoon a generous amount of the espresso bubbles into each dessert bowl. Unmold the desserts carefully. Set a pistachio tuile on top of each dessert, then place the dessert in the center of the bubbles and garnish with some cacao nibs and pistachios, if you want. Alternatively, you could serve the bubbles next to the desserts.

To Assemble
DEVIL'S FOOD CAKE (PAGE 192)
PISTACHIO-CHOCOLATE CRUNCH

For the Espresso Bubbles
1 CUP (240 G) ESPRESSO
½ TEASPOON (1.2 G) LECITHIN
1 TABLESPOON (12 G) SUGAR
½ TEASPOON (3 G) UNSALTED
    BUTTER

To Serve
PISTACHIO TUILES (PAGE 207)
CACAO NIBS (OPTIONAL)
SHELLED UNSALTED PISTACHIOS
    (OPTIONAL)

building blocks

some

basic

RECIPES

pâte brisée

MAKES ENOUGH FOR
SIXTEEN 2¼-INCH TARTS OR
TWO 9-INCH TARTS

This is an all-round great tart dough. It's my adaptation of a dough I learned from Thomas Haas when he was the executive pastry chef at Daniel. The pastry's not too sweet, so it's versatile. You can use it for everything from berry tarts to quiche.

Put the flour in the refrigerator for about 30 minutes before you start making this pastry. Chilled flour will make the flakiest dough.

2 CUPS (250 G) ALL-PURPOSE
 FLOUR
1 TABLESPOON (12 G) SUGAR
½ TEASPOON (2 G) COARSE SALT
9 TABLESPOONS (125 G) COLD
 UNSALTED BUTTER, CUT INTO
 PIECES
1 LARGE EGG
2 TABLESPOONS PLUS 1 TEASPOON
 (39 G) ICE WATER

Put the flour, sugar, and salt into a food processor and pulse a few times to combine. Add the butter and process until you have some pea-sized lumps left.

Beat the egg and water together lightly and add to the processor. Process only until the dough comes together.

Turn out onto a lightly floured work surface and divide in half. Form each half into a small brick, wrap in plastic, and refrigerate for at least 1 hour before rolling.

This dough will keep for several days in the refrigerator and for 2 months in the freezer. Defrost before rolling.

NOTE: I find that you get the best texture from this pastry when you use a food processor. But you could make it the old-fashioned way, cutting in the butter by hand with two knives.

Tart Dough

This adaptation of Pâte Brisée (page 180) uses milk rather than water to make a richer pastry.

Put the flour, sugar, salt, and baking powder in a food processor and pulse to combine. Add the butter to the processor. Pulse until the mixture is crumbly. Add ½ cup of the milk and pulse again, until the dough starts to come together.

Turn the dough out into a bowl and gather it into a ball. If the dough is still a bit dry, add a little more milk, tossing the dough with your fingers. You may not need all the milk.

Shape the dough into a brick, wrap in plastic, and refrigerate for at least 1 hour before using. The dough will keep for about 3 days in the refrigerator and for several months in the freezer. Defrost before rolling.

MAKES ENOUGH FOR
TWENTY-FOUR 2¼-INCH TARTS
OR THREE 9-INCH TARTS

SCANT 3½ CUPS (432 G) ALL-
 PURPOSE FLOUR
4 TEASPOONS (16 G) SUGAR
1 TEASPOON (4 G) COARSE SALT
1 TEASPOON (4 G) BAKING POWDER
12 TABLESPOONS (168 G) COLD
 UNSALTED BUTTER, CUT INTO
 PIECES
ABOUT 1 CUP (240 G) WHOLE MILK

BLIND-BAKING

Most of the tart shells in this book are blind-baked—that is, baked without a filling and cooled. The result is crisp pastry. In a restaurant kitchen, we bake a lot of tart shells, so there are a couple of tricks I can share.

I'm always looking for a quick and easy way to weight the dough when blind-baking. Parchment paper and dried beans work well for large tarts: Cut a circle of parchment a couple of inches larger than your mold and then cut into the circle at 1-inch inter-vals to fit the paper into the dough-lined mold. Fill with beans, which you can reuse infinitely, and you're ready to go. However, parchment is a little too stiff to fit easily into small tart rings, so often I'll cut down small coffee filters—the ones with flat bottoms—and fill them with rice. You could use muffin tin liners just as easily. But more often than not, I'll use disposable 4-ounce aluminum molds or baking cups filled with rice for 2¼-inch tarts. Wrap them in aluminum foil so you can use them over and over.

I always glaze tart shells after they're baked. It seals the pastry, helps make sure it won't get soggy, and gives it a great look.

As soon as the pastry comes out of the oven, remove the weight, brush the tart shell with egg wash (an egg and an egg yolk beaten with a pinch of salt), and put it back in the oven for another minute. Then let the tart shells cool before filling.

chocolate tart dough

MAKES ENOUGH FOR
SIXTEEN 2¼-INCH TARTS OR
THREE 9-INCH TARTS

Because this pastry is good at maintaining its shape and with-standing humidity, it's the dough I turn to for blind-baking. It's ideal for tarts with custard or light pastry cream fillings—or even Chocolate Crème Chiboust (see page 263). Sometimes I roll this pastry out flat, bake it until crisp, and then process it to use as a crumble under ice cream.

10 TABLESPOONS (141 G) COLD
UNSALTED BUTTER, CUT INTO
PIECES
¾ CUP (150 G) SUGAR
COARSE SALT
1 LARGE EGG
1 LARGE EGG WHITE
2½ CUPS (310 G) ALL-PURPOSE
FLOUR
½ CUP (50 G) UNSWEETENED
COCOA POWDER (PREFERABLY
VALRHONA)
1 TEASPOON (4 G) BAKING POWDER

Put the butter in the bowl of a standing mixer fitted with the paddle along with the sugar and a pinch of salt. Beat until pale.

In a separate bowl, whisk the egg and egg white together. Add gradually to the butter, scraping the bowl often and beating until smooth.

Whisk the flour, cocoa powder, and baking powder together. Add to the wet ingredients and mix on low speed only until blended.

Dump the dough onto a lightly floured work surface and divide in half. Shape each half into a small brick, wrap in plastic, and refrigerate for at least 1 hour before rolling. The dough will keep for several days in the refrigerator and for 2 months in the freezer. Defrost before rolling.

spiced chocolate tart dough

Add ½ teaspoon (0.5 g) ground allspice and ⅛ teaspoon (0.2 g) ground cinnamon to the bowl when you are beating the butter and sugar.

chocolate glazing ganache

Keep this on hand to glaze birthday cakes and for plate decoration. Warmed, it makes a nice hot fudge sauce.

Put the cream, milk, sugar, and corn syrup in a saucepan and bring to a boil over medium-high heat.

Put the chocolate into a large heatproof bowl and pour in the hot liquid. Stir with a rubber spatula until smooth. Add the butter a piece at a time, stirring until it's incorporated before adding the next piece.

If not using immediately, transfer the ganache to a smaller bowl and cover with plastic wrap, pressing the plastic onto the surface of the ganache. Refrigerate for up to 3 days. Warm in the microwave before using.

MAKES ABOUT 2½ CUPS

1½ CUPS (360 G) HEAVY CREAM
¼ CUP (60 G) WHOLE MILK
½ CUP PLUS 2 TABLESPOONS (125 G) SUGAR
¼ CUP PLUS 3 TABLESPOONS (125 G) LIGHT CORN SYRUP
11 OUNCES (312 G) BITTERSWEET CHOCOLATE (PREFERABLY VALRHONA CARAÏBE 66% CACAO), FINELY CHOPPED
9 TABLESPOONS (125 G) UNSALTED BUTTER, VERY SOFT, CUT INTO PIECES

vanilla whipped cream

MAKES ABOUT 1½ CUPS

The tang of crème fraîche works as a balancing agent in this vanilla-speckled cream, making it a great contrast to sweet things like fruit.

½ CUP (120 G) HEAVY CREAM
½ CUP PLUS 1 TABLESPOON (120 G) CRÈME FRAÎCHE
SCANT ½ CUP (50 G) CONFECTIONERS' SUGAR
1 VANILLA BEAN, SPLIT AND SCRAPED

Chill or freeze the bowl of a standing mixer.

Combine the cream, crème fraîche, sugar, and vanilla seeds (rinse, dry, and save the pod for another use) in the chilled bowl. Use the whisk to whip the cream to stiff peaks.

You can make the whipped cream in advance and refrigerate it for several hours. Whisk it again before serving.

simple syrup

MAKES ABOUT 2½ CUPS

This is an important building block in so many dessert recipes. Since the sugar has been dissolved, you can add sweetness to delicate fruits such as berries or citrus without heating them, thus keeping their flavors fresh and pure. This keeps practically forever in the refrigerator.

2 CUPS (400 G) SUGAR
2 CUPS (480 G) WATER

Combine the sugar and water in a small saucepan. Bring to a boil over medium heat, cooking until the sugar is completely dissolved.

Transfer to a heatproof jar and let cool completely before using. Store in the refrigerator.

invert sugar

MAKES ABOUT 1¾ CUPS

When sucrose—which is table sugar—is treated with an enzyme or acid, it breaks down into its component parts: fructose and glucose. When invert sugar is made commercially, the enzyme used is invertase, but you can easily make invert sugar at home, using lemon juice. Like simple syrup, it lasts for months in the refrigerator.

I use invert sugar in ice creams, sorbets, and other frozen desserts for two main reasons: It creates a smoother texture and softer mouth-feel, and it prevents water from crystallizing, so the ice creams won't crystallize or be dense and rock hard.

2¼ CUPS (450 G) SUGAR
1 CUP LESS 1 TABLESPOON (225 G) WATER
2 TEASPOONS (10 G) FRESH LEMON JUICE

Combine the sugar, water, and lemon juice in a small saucepan. Bring almost to a boil over high heat. Reduce the heat and cook at an active simmer for 30 minutes. If you taste the mixture at this point (carefully, because it is very hot), there should be no hint of acidity.

Transfer to a heatproof jar and let cool completely before using. Store in the refrigerator.

vanilla sugar

MAKES 1 CUP

I use a lot of vanilla beans in the restaurant, and I always reuse the pods, rinsing and drying them before storing. Sometimes they become a garnish (see page 186), but often I use them to make this perfumed sugar.

DRIED POD FROM 1 SCRAPED VANILLA BEAN
1 CUP (200 G) SUGAR

Chop the vanilla pod and put it in a spice grinder with ¼ cup of the sugar. Grind to a fine powder. Mix well with the remaining ¾ cup sugar and store in a jar. You can use it right away, but it will be better if you let it sit for a few days.

crystallized vanilla

I make this garnish with the vanilla pods I have left in the restaurant from other desserts. I'm not giving quantities here, since it will all depend on how many vanilla pods you have on hand. (The photograph is on page 178.)

DRIED PODS FROM SCRAPED VANILLA BEANS
SIMPLE SYRUP (PAGE 184)
SUGAR

Cut the pods into 2-inch lengths, then lengthwise again into very thin strips.

Put the vanilla in a small saucepan and cover with simple syrup by about an inch. Bring to a simmer and cook gently for 5 minutes. Turn off the heat and let sit for 8 hours or so.

Drain the vanilla and dredge in sugar. Lay out on a baking sheet lined with a Silpat or parchment and slide into a cold oven. Leave overnight to dry completely. Store in an airtight container.

crystallized herbs

I'm not giving quantities here, since you can make as much as you like. Crystallized herbs bring a bright, sweet herb flavor to the plate when you use them as a garnish. You can follow the same procedure with rose petals, too; just make sure they are unsprayed, or pesticide-free.

FRESH HERB LEAVES, SUCH AS MINT OR CILANTRO, OR
    FRESH LEMON THYME SPRIGS
SIMPLE SYRUP (PAGE 184)
SUGAR

Dip the herbs in simple syrup. Let the excess drip off, then place the herbs on paper towels.

Dust lightly with sugar and place on a Silpat-lined baking sheet. Place in a cold oven to dry overnight (you could also use a home dehydrator, if you have one).

Store in an airtight container.

NOTE: In the restaurant, I store these with silica packets (see page 280) to keep them fresh for more than a day.

herb oil

MAKES ABOUT ¼ CUP

Use this technique to make infused oils with any soft herbs, such as tarragon, basil, and mint.

I use herb oil as a garnish whenever I want an intense, concentrated herb flavor in a dessert. Think about serving strawberries and ice cream with a drizzle of black peppermint oil. Or drizzle some tarragon oil on a salad of tender lettuce and shrimp.

PACKED ½ CUP (25 G) FRESH HERB
  LEAVES
⅓ CUP (55 G) GRAPESEED OIL

Set up a bowl of ice water.

Bring a pot of water to a boil. Add the herbs and blanch for 30 seconds. Drain and immediately plunge the herbs in the ice water. Drain again and squeeze out all the water.

Put the herbs in a blender with the oil and blend to a smooth puree. Leave, covered, at room temperature for 1 hour to infuse.

Strain through several layers of cheesecloth and store the oil, covered, in the refrigerator for up to 3 days.

cakes

AND BRIOCHE

spiced chocolate sponge cake

This cake forms the base for the Chocolate-Pear Cake on page 98. You could also use it as the start of a birthday cake. Or cut it into cubes and skewer it with fruit and berries for a dessert kebab.

For the Spice Mix

1¼ TEASPOONS (2.5 G) FRESHLY
    GRATED NUTMEG
2 TABLESPOONS (12 G) GROUND
    CINNAMON
3½ TEASPOONS (7 G) GROUND
    CORIANDER
3½ TEASPOONS (7 G) GROUND
    CLOVES
1 TEASPOON (2 G) GROUND
    ANISEED
4 TEASPOONS (5 G) GROUND
    GINGER

Mix the spices together and store for up to 4 months in a glass jar out of the light.

For the Cake

1 OUNCE (31 G) UNSWEETENED
    CHOCOLATE (PREFERABLY
    VALRHONA CACAO PASTE),
    FINELY CHOPPED
2 TABLESPOONS (31 G) UNSALTED
    BUTTER
¼ CUP (30 G) ALL-PURPOSE FLOUR
1 TABLESPOON (7 G)
    UNSWEETENED COCOA POWDER
    (PREFERABLY VALRHONA)
2 TABLESPOONS (6 G) SPICE MIX
3 OUNCES (93 G) ALMOND PASTE
⅓ CUP (40 G) CONFECTIONERS'
    SUGAR
4 LARGE EGG YOLKS
1 LARGE EGG
4 LARGE EGG WHITES
CREAM OF TARTAR
3 TABLESPOONS PLUS 1 TEASPOON
    (40 G) GRANULATED SUGAR

Heat the oven to 375°F or 350°F on convection. Line a 9 x 12-inch rimmed baking sheet with a Silpat or parchment.

Put the chocolate and butter into a glass bowl and melt in the microwave in 30-second bursts, stirring between each burst, or melt in a double boiler. Stir until smooth.

Whisk the flour, cocoa powder, and spice mix together.

Crumble the almond paste into the bowl of a standing mixer fitted with the paddle. Add the confectioners' sugar. Start mixing at low speed until combined, then increase the speed to medium and beat until the mixture resembles fine crumbs. Add the egg yolks one by one, beating each yolk in thoroughly and scraping the sides and bottom of the bowl often. Take care to make sure you have no lumps. Add the egg and beat in thoroughly. Scrape the bowl again. Add about one-third of the batter to the melted chocolate and butter and whisk until smooth. Scrape back into the bowl and beat until smooth. Scrape the batter into a large, wide bowl and use a rubber spatula to fold in the dry ingredients.

Put the egg whites into the clean bowl of a standing mixer fitted with the whisk. Add a tiny pinch of cream of tartar. Turn the mixer on to low, and beat the whites gently for 2 minutes, to start establishing a structure. The whites will look frothy but still a bit wet. Turn the speed up to medium and add 1 tablespoon of the granulated sugar. Continue to beat at medium speed until the whites have body and are just shy of having soft peaks. Add another 1 tablespoon of the granulated sugar and continue beating until the whites have formed firm peaks. Add the remaining 1 tablespoon plus 1 teaspoon granulated sugar and beat until the whites are glossy and smooth and almost stiff.

Fold one-quarter of the whites into the batter to lighten it. Fold in the rest of the whites, gently but thoroughly.

Scrape the batter out into the baking sheet. Smooth it out evenly with an offset spatula.

Bake until a tester comes out clean, about 10 minutes, rotating the pan halfway through baking. As soon as you take the cake out of the oven, run a knife around the edges to release the cake. Slip a knife or offset spatula under the cake so you can grab the Silpat or parchment, and slide the cake out onto the counter to cool.

devil's food cake

MAKES ONE 12 X 18-INCH
SHEET CAKE
(OR ONE 9 X 3-INCH ROUND)

This recipe came from Maya Eyler, a cook who worked for me at Daniel. I don't remember the story behind it, but I think it was a family recipe—which makes sense. It's an old-style cake, using mayonnaise to ensure moistness.

I make it as a sheet cake and use it as a component in several desserts. Baked in a cake pan for a little longer and layered with ganache or frosting, it could become a birthday cake, though.

2 LARGE EGGS

1 CUP PLUS 2 TABLESPOONS (225 G) SUGAR

1 TEASPOON (2 G) VANILLA EXTRACT

¾ CUP (160 G) MAYONNAISE

1½ CUPS (187 G) ALL-PURPOSE FLOUR

½ CUP (50 G) UNSWEETENED COCOA POWDER (PREFERABLY VALRHONA), SIFTED

¾ TEASPOON (4 G) BAKING SODA

¼ TEASPOON (1 G) BAKING POWDER

½ TEASPOON (2 G) COARSE SALT

¾ CUP (180 G) WATER

Heat the oven to 375°F or 350°F on convection. Line a 12 x 18-inch rimmed baking sheet with a Silpat or parchment.

Put the eggs in the bowl of a standing mixer fitted with the whisk. Beat at medium-high speed, adding the sugar gradually. Beat until light and fluffy. Add the vanilla extract and mayonnaise and beat to combine.

Whisk the flour, cocoa powder, baking soda, baking powder, and salt together.

Using a rubber spatula, fold and stir the dry ingredients into the egg mixture in batches, alternating with the water and beginning and ending with the flour mixture.

Scrape the batter into the pan and spread it out evenly. Give the pan a rap or two on the counter to release any air bubbles. Bake until a tester comes out clean, about 10 minutes, rotating the pan halfway through baking. Let cool.

Run a knife around the edge of the pan to release the cake before turning it out.

madeleine sponge cake

One of the first things I learned to make at Restaurant Daniel was a madeleine, and I fell for the buttery, citrusy flavor. I wanted to find a way to use the little cake as part of a plated dessert, without making the classic seashell form. So I worked on the recipe, adapting it until I captured the texture and flavor of a fresh-baked madeleine in a sponge cake baked in a sheet pan.

Heat the oven to 400°F or 375°F on convection. Line a 9 x 12-inch rimmed baking sheet with a Silpat or parchment and spray it lightly with cooking spray.

Whisk the flour, salt, and baking powder together.

Put the sugar, zest, and eggs in the bowl of a standing mixer fitted with the paddle and beat at medium-high speed until light and fluffy. Add the milk and beat to combine. Scrape down the sides of the bowl. Add the dry ingredients and mix until smooth. Add the lemon juice, butter, and honey one by one, mixing until combined and scraping the bowl after each addition. Beat at high speed until the batter is light.

Spread the batter evenly into the baking pan. Bake until the cake just starts to color, 6 to 10 minutes, rotating the pan halfway through baking.

Let cool.

1¾ CUPS PLUS 1 TABLESPOON (226 G) ALL-PURPOSE FLOUR
2 TEASPOONS (8 G) COARSE SALT
2¼ TEASPOONS (9 G) BAKING POWDER
1 CUP PLUS 2 TABLESPOONS (225 G) SUGAR
GRATED ZEST OF 2 LEMONS
4 LARGE EGGS
2 TABLESPOONS (30 G) WHOLE MILK
JUICE OF 3 LEMONS
6 TABLESPOONS (85 G) UNSALTED BUTTER, MELTED
SCANT ½ CUP (140 G) HONEY

Brioche

MAKES ONE 9 X 5-INCH LOAF

This bread is a staple in the pastry kitchen and it has many uses—from French toast to croutons. The direct mixing method and overnight rise is a technique I picked up over the years. Brioche freezes beautifully.

2¼ CUPS (281 G) ALL-PURPOSE FLOUR

1½ TEASPOONS (5 G) ACTIVE DRY YEAST OR 2 PACKED TEASPOONS (12 G) FRESH YEAST

½ CUP LESS 2 TABLESPOONS (90 G) MILK

2 EXTRA-LARGE EGGS, LIGHTLY BEATEN

12 TABLESPOONS (170 G) UNSALTED BUTTER, SOFTENED AND CUT INTO PIECES

2 TABLESPOONS (25 G) SUGAR

2½ TEASPOONS (10 G) COARSE SALT

Put the flour and yeast in the bowl of a standing mixer fitted with the paddle. (If you are using fresh yeast, crumble it into the flour and continue to crumble until the mixture resembles fine crumbs.) Add the milk and eggs and beat at medium speed until you have a smooth dough. Add the butter a few pieces at a time and beat at medium speed until completely incorporated.

Change to the dough hook. Add the sugar and salt and mix on low until combined. Increase the speed to medium-high and knead the dough until glossy and very elastic, 12 to 15 minutes. The dough should be almost thin enough to see through when stretched; if the dough breaks instead of stretching, keep kneading.

Spray a bowl with cooking spray. Scrape the dough into the bowl, then turn the dough over. Cover tightly with plastic wrap and refrigerate overnight.

Spray a 9 x 5-inch loaf pan with cooking spray.

Flatten the dough into an 8 x 12-inch rectangle. Roll the dough tightly, starting with a short side and pressing down firmly as you roll. As you reach the far end, flatten it with the heel of your hand, then finish rolling. Place the dough, seam side down, in the loaf pan. Cover with plastic wrap and let rise until doubled, about 2 hours.

Thirty minutes before the dough has completely risen, heat the oven to 350°F or 325°F on convection.

Uncover the brioche and bake for 30 minutes. Reduce the oven temperature to 325°F (300°F if you're using convection) and bake for another 30 to 45 minutes, until the crust is crisp and the loaf sounds hollow when you rap on the bottom. Remove the brioche from the pan and let cool on a rack.

BRIOCHE CROUTONS

Croutons aren't just for the savory kitchen. I make them with plain Brioche (page 194) and with Chocolate Brioche (page 196) and use them as a crunchy component in many desserts.

I store brioche in the freezer, not just because it keeps it fresh, but because it's easier to cut thin, even slices from a loaf when it is frozen. I recommend you do the same.

Cut ⅓-inch slices of plain or chocolate brioche. Trim the crusts and discard. Cut the slices into ⅓-inch dice. Spread the bread cubes out on a baking sheet and leave them on the counter overnight to dry.

Heat the oven to 325°F or 300°F on convection. Line a small rimmed baking sheet with parchment.

Toss the bread cubes with a teaspoon or two of oil, then with sugar and coarse salt to taste. Spread out again on the baking sheet. Bake, stirring carefully and often, until golden, about 10 minutes. Let cool completely and then store in an airtight container for up to 3 days.

chocolate brioche

This bread gets put to so many uses in my kitchen, from pressed sandwiches to croutons (which could go on a cool sundae). You could use it for French toast or as the base of a chocolate bread pudding. Or just slather it with butter and jam for breakfast. I recommend keeping some of this bread on hand in the freezer.

1¾ CUPS PLUS 2 TABLESPOONS (232 G) ALL-PURPOSE FLOUR

1¼ TEASPOONS (4.5 G) ACTIVE DRY YEAST OR SCANT 2 PACKED TEASPOONS (10 G) FRESH YEAST

⅓ CUP (80 G) MILK

2 LARGE EGGS, LIGHTLY BEATEN

12 TABLESPOOONS (170 G) UNSALTED BUTTER, SOFTENED AND CUT INTO PIECES

5 TEASPOONS (20 G) SUGAR

⅓ CUP PLUS 2 TABLESPOONS (42 G) UNSWEETENED COCOA POWDER (PREFERABLY VALRHONA)

2 TEASPOONS (8 G) COARSE SALT

Put the flour and yeast in the bowl of a standing mixer fitted with the paddle. (If you are using fresh yeast, crumble it into the flour and continue to crumble until the mixture resembles fine crumbs.) Add the milk and eggs and beat at medium speed until you have a smooth dough. Add the butter a few pieces at a time and beat at medium speed until completely incorporated.

Whisk the sugar, cocoa powder, and salt together.

Change to the dough hook. Add the dry ingredients to the bowl and mix at low speed until incorporated. Increase the speed to medium-high and knead the dough until glossy and very elastic, about 25 minutes. The dough should be almost thin enough to see through when stretched; if the dough breaks instead of stretching, keep kneading.

Spray a bowl with cooking spray. Scrape the dough into the bowl, then turn the dough over. Cover tightly with plastic wrap and refrigerate overnight.

Spray a 9 x 5-inch loaf pan with cooking spray.

Flatten the dough into an 8 x 12-inch rectangle. Roll the dough tightly, starting with a short side and pressing down firmly as you roll. As you reach the far end, flatten it with the heel of your hand, then finish rolling. Place the dough, seam side down, in the loaf pan. Cover with plastic wrap and let rise until doubled, about 2 hours.

Thirty minutes before the dough has completely risen, heat the oven to 350°F or 325°F on convection.

Uncover the brioche and bake for 30 minutes. Reduce the oven temperature to 325°F (300°F if you're using convection) and bake for another 30 to 45 minutes, until the crust is crisp and the loaf sounds hollow when you rap on the bottom. Remove the brioche from the pan and let cool on a rack.

If you are making this for the Chocolate-Olive Panini on page 149, wrap the brioche with aluminum foil, then put it in a sealable plastic bag and freeze it. That way, you'll be able to cut the very thin slices you need.

cookies

tuiles

AND TEXTURES

petit beurre cookies or crumbs

*I love this cookie for its buttery, fragile tenderness, but I also like
to make crumbs from it because they're such a great texture in a
layered dessert (like the Rose Oeufs à la Neige on page 134).*

*The cookies are best served the day they're baked. I've written
the recipe so you freeze half the dough and have it waiting for
another day.*

For the Dough

½ POUND (227 G) PLUS 3 TO 5
  TABLESPOONS (40 TO 70 G)
  UNSALTED BUTTER, SOFTENED
2¼ CUPS (287 G) ALL-PURPOSE
  FLOUR
¾ CUP (90 G) CONFECTIONERS'
  SUGAR
1 CUP PLUS 2 TABLESPOONS (109 G)
  ALMOND FLOUR
1 TEASPOON (2 G) VANILLA
  EXTRACT

Cut the ½ pound butter into pieces and put it in the bowl of a
standing mixer fitted with the paddle. Beat until light. Add the
flour, confectioners' sugar, almond flour, and vanilla extract.
Mix until the dough comes together. Turn the dough out onto a
lightly floured counter and divide it in half. Form each half into
a brick and wrap in plastic. Refrigerate one packet for at least
1 hour and freeze the other for up to 3 months.

Heat the oven to 350°F or 325°F on convection.

Remove the dough from the refrigerator and roll it between
two sheets of parchment to ⅛ inch thick. Lift it up onto a baking
sheet, peel off the top parchment, and clean up the edges. Bake
until golden, 19 to 21 minutes, rotating the pan halfway through
baking. Let cool completely.

Crumble the cookie and put it back in the clean bowl of a
standing mixer fitted with the paddle. Mix for a minute or so to
make smaller crumbs. Add the 3 tablespoons butter and mix. If
the dough doesn't come together, add 1 or 2 tablespoons butter, a
tablespoon at a time, mixing until you have a dough you can roll.

Roll the dough between two pieces of parchment to ¼ inch
thick. Freeze for 1 hour.

If you're making crumbs, carefully peel off the top piece of
parchment. Bake until golden, about 15 minutes, rotating the
pan halfway through baking. Let cool, then crumble and store in
an airtight container for up to 2 days.

If you're making cookies, carefully peel off the top piece of parchment. Cut the frozen dough with a 1½-inch cutter. The cookies will be too delicate to move, so instead remove the excess dough from the parchment. Slide the parchment onto a baking sheet.

Beat the egg and yolk together until smooth. Brush onto the cookies. Mix the salt and sugar together and sprinkle over the cookies.

Bake until a rich golden brown, about 15 minutes, rotating the pan halfway through baking. Let cool. The cookies will be very delicate, so don't move them around. Leave them on the pan until you serve them.

NOTE: To bake the frozen dough, you must first defrost it in the refrigerator, before proceeding with the recipe.

For Cookies

1 LARGE EGG

1 LARGE EGG YOLK

1 TEASPOON (4 G) FLEUR DE SEL OR COARSE PINK SALT

1 TEASPOON (4 G) DEMERARA SUGAR

salt butter shortbread

MAKES ABOUT FORTY
2-INCH COOKIES

This cookie, called sablé Breton, is a classic French recipe from Brittany. I've learned many versions, and this is my favorite. I love the sandy texture, something between a crisp cookie and a sponge. The dough is also a great foil for different spices and salts.

14 TABLESPOONS (198 G)
    UNSALTED BUTTER, SOFTENED
6 LARGE EGG YOLKS
1 CUP (200 G) SUGAR
2¼ CUPS (281 G) ALL-PURPOSE
    FLOUR
1 TABLESPOON (12 G) BAKING
    POWDER
1 TEASPOON (4 G) COARSE SALT

Cut the butter into pieces and put it in the bowl of a standing mixer fitted with the paddle. Beat at medium-high speed until fluffy.

In a separate bowl, whisk the egg yolks and sugar until pale and thick. Add to the butter and beat until combined.

Whisk the flour, baking powder, and salt together. Add to the wet ingredients and beat on low just to combine. Don't overmix.

Dump the dough onto a lightly floured work surface and divide in half. Shape each half into a brick and wrap in plastic. Refrigerate one package for at least 1 hour and freeze the other for up to 3 months.

Remove the dough from the refrigerator and roll it on a lightly floured work surface to ¼ inch thick. Transfer to a baking sheet and refrigerate for 30 minutes. Use a 2-inch cutter to cut the cookies, and place them on a Silpat- or parchment-lined baking sheet. Refrigerate for another 30 minutes.

Meanwhile, heat the oven to 375°F or 350°F on convection.

Bake the cookies until they are just beginning to color, 8 to 10 minutes. For the best-looking cookies, cut them again with the 2-inch cutter while they are still hot. Let cool.

These are best served the day they're made.

NOTE: To bake the frozen dough, you must first defrost it in the refrigerator, before proceeding with the recipe.

chocolate salt butter shortbread

The high fat content in this dough makes for very rich cookies. It's great when you want to add crunch to a creamy dessert like panna cotta. Or you might break the cookies into pieces and make a parfait with fruit and whipped cream.

I make these as round cookies, too, brushed with an egg wash and sprinkled with sugar and coarse salt before baking. Follow the method below, using a round cutter; don't weight round cookies with a Silpat.

Cut the butter into pieces and put it in the bowl of a standing mixer fitted with the paddle. Beat at medium-high speed until fluffy.

In a separate bowl, whisk the egg yolks until frothy. Keep whisking as you pour in the sugar. Whisk until light and fluffy. Add to the butter and beat until combined.

Put the flour, baking powder, and cocoa powder in a bowl with a pinch of salt. Whisk to combine. Sift into the wet ingredients and mix on low speed only until blended.

Dump the dough onto a lightly floured work surface and divide in half. Shape each half into a brick. The dough will be very soft. Wrap the dough in plastic and refrigerate one package for at least 1 hour before rolling. Freeze the other for up to 2 months.

Roll the pastry between two sheets of parchment into a 12-inch square. The pastry should be $^1/_{16}$ inch thick. Slide onto a baking sheet and refrigerate for 30 minutes.

Cut the pastry into 12 2$^1/_2$-inch squares and separate them on the parchment, giving them room to spread. Refrigerate while you heat the oven.

Heat the oven to 375°F or 350°F on convection.

Lay a Silpat (top-side down) on the pastry to weight it. Bake until the pastry is cooked, about 12 minutes, longer if you're not using convection. Let cool.

MAKES ABOUT TWENTY-FOUR
2½-INCH SQUARES

14 TABLESPOONS (198 G) UNSALTED BUTTER, SOFTENED
6 LARGE EGG YOLKS
1 CUP (200 G) SUGAR
2¼ CUPS (280 G) ALL-PURPOSE FLOUR
2 TEASPOONS (8 G) BAKING POWDER
4 TEASPOONS (8 G) UNSWEETENED COCOA POWDER (PREFERABLY VALRHONA)
COARSE SALT

graham cracker sablé cookies

MAKES ABOUT SIXTEEN
2½-INCH COOKIES

Graham cracker crusts are never crispy enough for me, and I'm not a fan of soggy crusts. I developed this crunchy cookie to serve as a bed for my Key Lime Parfait (page 26).

It will garnish any ice cream, and it could be the start of a terrific s'more. Because it's not overly sweet, you could also serve it with cheese.

6 TABLESPOONS (85 G) UNSALTED
   BUTTER, MELTED
1¼ CUPS PLUS 3 TABLESPOONS
   (142 G) GRAHAM CRACKER
   CRUMBS
¼ CUP (50 G) SUGAR
6 TABLESPOONS (47 G) ALL-
   PURPOSE FLOUR
2 LARGE EGGS, LIGHTLY BEATEN

Combine the butter, graham cracker crumbs, and sugar in the bowl of a standing mixer fitted with the paddle. Beat at medium speed until crumbly. Add the flour and eggs and mix on low speed just until blended.

Dump the dough onto a floured work surface and shape it into a brick. Wrap in plastic and refrigerate for at least 1 hour.

Heat the oven to 375°F or 350°F on convection. Line a baking sheet with a Silpat or parchment.

Roll the dough between two sheets of parchment to ⅛ inch thick. Cut with a 2½-inch cutter and place on the baking sheet. Reroll the scraps and cut out a few more rounds.

Bake until golden, 12 to 13 minutes. Let cool.

almond tuiles

This crisp, sweet almond cookie looks beautiful and has tremendous flavor and a perfect layering texture. What's great about the batter is that you can freeze it or keep it in the refrigerator and just pull it out when you're ready to bake.

MAKES ABOUT 24 COOKIES

Heat the oven to 350°F or 325°F on convection. Line a baking sheet with a Silpat or use a nonstick baking sheet.

Put the water, honey, and butter in a small saucepan and cook over low heat until the butter is melted.

Whisk the confectioners' sugar and flour together. Pour in the wet ingredients and stir until smooth. Stir in the nuts.

Use a small ice cream scoop (1-tablespoon capacity) to scoop up 1 tablespoon of the batter. Level off the top and drop onto the Silpat, leaving about 2 inches between each tuile (you should fit 6 on the baking sheet). Bake in batches until golden, about 14 minutes, rotating the pan halfway through baking. Let cool completely on the Silpat.

4 TEASPOONS (22 G) WATER
GENEROUS 1 TABLESPOON (22 G) HONEY
2 TABLESPOONS PLUS 2 TEASPOONS (37 G) UNSALTED BUTTER
SCANT $\frac{2}{3}$ CUP (75 G) CONFECTIONERS' SUGAR
2 TABLESPOONS (15 G) ALL-PURPOSE FLOUR
$5\frac{1}{3}$ OUNCES (150 G) SLICED ALMONDS, CHOPPED

flax seed tuiles

MAKES ABOUT 30 PIECES

This is the most visual of all my tuiles, shimmering and translucent. The sugars lend texture as well as carry the delicate flavor of the flax seeds.

$^1/_3$ CUP (110 G) FONDANT (SEE PAGE 275)
$^1/_4$ CUP (72 G) LIGHT CORN SYRUP
SCANT 1 TABLESPOON (12 G) UNSALTED BUTTER
2 TABLESPOONS (20 G) FLAX SEEDS, TOASTED

Line a baking sheet with a Silpat.

Put the fondant, corn syrup, and butter in a saucepan. Bring to a boil over medium-high heat. Reduce the heat and cook at an active simmer until the mixture starts to color. Pour onto the Silpat and let cool. Break into pieces and store in an airtight container.

When you are ready to finish the tuiles, heat the oven to 375°F or 350°F on convection. Line a 12 x 18-inch baking sheet with a Silpat.

Working in small batches, grind the fondant mixture to a powder in a spice grinder. Sift the powder evenly over the Silpat and sprinkle with the flax seeds. Bake until the sugar melts, 3 to 5 minutes. You don't want the sugar to take on any color.

Let cool on a rack, then flip over onto a piece of parchment. Break into jagged abstract pieces. Store any leftovers layered between pieces of parchment in an airtight container.

graham cracker tuiles

MAKES ABOUT 30 PIECES

I love the flavor of graham crackers, but I have always thought the crackers are too thick. So I grind them, rebind them, and make them thin and very crisp.

$1^1/_4$ CUPS (125 G) GRAHAM CRACKER CRUMBS
$^1/_4$ TEASPOON (1 G) COARSE SALT
$^1/_3$ CUP (80 G) SIMPLE SYRUP (PAGE 184)

Heat the oven to 375°F or 350°F on convection. Line a baking sheet with a Silpat or parchment.

Stir the graham cracker crumbs, salt, and simple syrup together until well combined. Dump the mixture onto the Silpat and pat it out. Cover with a piece of parchment and roll to a little less than $^1/_8$ inch thick. Carefully peel off the parchment and clean up the edges to prevent burning.

Bake until golden brown, 13 to 15 minutes. Let cool on a rack.

Break into small shards and store in an airtight container.

pistachio tuiles

Try making this sweet, delicate cookie with any nut. It's a terrific garnish for ice creams or chocolate desserts.

Combine the fondant and corn syrup in a saucepan and cook over medium heat until a light caramel color. Stir in the pistachios and scrape out onto a Silpat or parchment. Let cool completely.

Heat the oven to 325°F or 300°F on convection.

Break the pistachio mixture into small pieces. Working in small batches, process to a very fine powder in a spice grinder.

Line a baking sheet with a Silpat and set a 2¼-inch round stencil (see Note) on top. Sprinkle a thin, even layer of the powder into the stencil. Lift the stencil up and repeat.

Bake until golden brown, about 10 minutes. Let cool completely and store, layered between pieces of parchment, in an airtight container.

Note: You can make a stencil with the lid from a yogurt container. Cut off most of the lip, leaving a piece to use as a tab. Trace a 2¼-inch circle in the center of the lid and cut it out with a sharp knife.

If you aren't making these for the Bitter Chocolate Custard dessert on page 174, you can just sprinkle the powder in a thin, even layer on a Silpat, bake, and let cool. Then you can cut or break the tuile into abstract shapes.

MAKES ABOUT THIRTY
2¼-INCH COOKIES

¾ CUP (250 G) FONDANT (SEE
    PAGE 275)
3 TABLESPOONS (50 G) LIGHT CORN
    SYRUP
GENEROUS ⅓ CUP (50 G) SHELLED
    UNSALTED PISTACHIOS

sesame tuiles

One of the most important things I learned from Thomas Haas when I worked with him at Daniel was the significance of texture in desserts. I also learned this recipe from him. This tuile is super-crispy. The sesame seeds toast as the tuile bakes, which brings out their nuttiness, and the sugar caramelizes, bringing in a slightly bitter edge.

SCANT ¼ CUP (55 G) MILK

11 TABLESPOONS (160 G) UNSALTED BUTTER, CUT INTO PIECES

¾ CUP PLUS 1 TABLESPOON (160 G) SUGAR

3 TABLESPOONS (50 G) LIGHT CORN SYRUP

2 CUPS (260 G) WHITE SESAME SEEDS

½ CUP (70 G) BLACK SESAME SEEDS

Put the milk, butter, sugar, and corn syrup in a saucepan and bring to a simmer over medium heat. Stir in the sesame seeds.

Transfer to a bowl, cover with plastic, and refrigerate overnight.

Heat the oven to 375°F or 350°F on convection.

Roll the dough into small balls, about 1 inch in diameter, and place on a Silpat- or parchment-lined baking sheet or nonstick baking sheet, leaving at least 2 inches between the tuiles because they will spread. Bake until golden, about 10 minutes, rotating the pan halfway through baking.

Let cool completely. Store leftovers between sheets of parchment in an airtight container.

chocolate meringues

Meringues are a staple in the pastry kitchen because they can carry so many different flavors. Here, cocoa powder and cacao nibs are combined to create tremendous chocolate flavor.

Heat the oven to 150°F.

Line a 9 x 12-inch rimmed baking sheet with parchment and using a pen, trace twenty-four 2-inch circles onto the paper. Turn the parchment over, so the ink won't bleed into the meringues.

Put the egg whites and a tiny bit of cream of tartar in the bowl of a standing mixer fitted with the whisk. Turn the mixer on to low, and beat the whites gently for 2 minutes, to start establishing a structure. The whites will look frothy but still a bit wet. Turn the speed up to medium and add 2 tablespoons of the granulated sugar. Continue to beat at medium speed until the whites have body and are just shy of having soft peaks. Add 2 more tablespoons of the sugar and continue beating until the whites have formed firm peaks. Add the remaining 1 tablespoon sugar and beat until the whites are glossy and smooth and almost stiff. Keep your eye on the whites, so you don't overbeat them.

Sift the cocoa powder and confectioners' sugar over the whites and sprinkle on the nibs. Fold in gently but thoroughly.

Transfer the meringue to a pastry bag fitted with a small plain round tip (#803 is perfect) and pipe out neat concentric circles from the outside in, using the circles you drew as a guide. Bake the meringues until crisp, about 1 hour, rotating the pan halfway through baking. Let cool completely and store in an airtight container.

coconut meringues

Replace the cocoa powder and cacao nibs with 6 tablespoons shredded unsweetened coconut.

MAKES TWENTY-FOUR 2-INCH CIRCLES

2 LARGE EGG WHITES
CREAM OF TARTAR
5 TABLESPOONS (62 G) GRANULATED SUGAR
2 TABLESPOONS (12 G) UNSWEETENED COCOA POWDER (PREFERABLY VALRHONA)
2 TABLESPOONS (16 G) CONFECTIONERS' SUGAR
4 TEASPOONS (8 G) CACAO NIBS

crispy rice crackers

So much of recipe development is taking an ingredient and manipulating its texture without diluting the flavor. This is a good example. I have always liked the texture of puffed-rice cakes but not the flavor, which seems bland to me. So I've developed a cracker that highlights the nutty flavor of rice.

1 CUP (100 G) ARBORIO RICE
5 CUPS (1,200 G) WATER
CANOLA OIL FOR FRYING
COARSE SALT

Heat the oven to 150°F. Line a 9 x 12-inch rimmed baking sheet with a Silpat.

Put the rice and water in a saucepan and bring to a boil over high heat. Reduce the heat and simmer until the rice is very tender and starting to get mushy, about 20 minutes.

Drain the rice and put it in a food processor. Pulse a few times to make a very coarse puree, but make sure it retains some texture.

Scrape the rice out onto the Silpat and spread it out evenly, filling the baking sheet. Put it in the oven to dry completely, about 3 hours.

Pour about 3 inches of oil into a large saucepan and heat to 365°F. Break off pieces of the dried rice and fry, a few pieces at a time, until crisp and golden, about 2 minutes. Drain and sprinkle with salt.

These are best served right away, but you can store leftovers, once cool, in an airtight container, between layers of parchment, for up to 2 days.

crispy almond phyllo

I love the texture that shatteringly crisp phyllo—brushed with butter and sprinkled with almond flour—adds to desserts. You can easily manipulate the flavors by using different nut flours or even instant espresso powder or dried coconut between the layers.

Heat the oven to 375°F or 350°F on convection.

Melt the butter in a small saucepan (or in a cup in the microwave) and stir in the honey.

Lay one sheet of the phyllo on a piece of parchment and brush with the honey butter. Sprinkle with 2 tablespoons of the almond flour. Top with another sheet of the phyllo. Brush again with the honey butter and sprinkle with the remaining 2 tablespoons almond flour. Top with the remaining sheet of phyllo and brush very lightly with the honey butter.

Place a piece of parchment on top of the phyllo and roll to compress the layers.

Transfer to a baking sheet, top with another baking sheet to keep the phyllo weighted, and bake until golden brown, 10 to 12 minutes, rotating the pan halfway through baking. Remove the top baking sheet and parchment. Let cool completely, break into shards, and store, layered between sheets of parchment, in an airtight container for up to 2 days.

2 TABLESPOONS (28 G) UNSALTED BUTTER
2 TABLESPOONS (14 G) HONEY
3 (9 X 13-INCH) SHEETS PHYLLO, DEFROSTED
¼ CUP (25 G) ALMOND FLOUR

peanut phyllo crisps

MAKES ABOUT 30 PIECES

This riff on Crispy Almond Phyllo (page 211)—caramelized with confectioners' sugar and with peanuts as the nut flavor—is a great example of how versatile this technique of layering phyllo and nuts is. These crisps have a great nutty flavor and crunchy texture to pair with something soft or creamy.

¼ CUP PLUS 1 TABLESPOON (38 G) CONFECTIONERS' SUGAR
¼ CUP (25 G) PEANUT FLOUR
COARSE SALT
3 (9 X 13-INCH) SHEETS PHYLLO, DEFROSTED
2 TABLESPOONS (28 G) UNSALTED BUTTER, MELTED

Place a rack in the top position of the oven. Heat the oven to 350°F or 325°F on convection.

Mix the ¼ cup confectioners' sugar and the peanut flour together with a pinch of salt.

Place one sheet of the phyllo on a piece of parchment. Brush it with the butter and sprinkle with ¼ cup of the sugar and peanut flour mix. Place another sheet of the phyllo on top. Brush with the butter and sprinkle with the remaining ¼ cup sugar and nut flour. Place the remaining sheet of phyllo on top and brush with the butter. Place a piece of parchment on top of the phyllo and roll to compress the layers.

Slide onto a baking sheet and place another baking sheet on top. Bake until lightly golden, about 10 minutes, rotating the pan halfway through baking. Reserve on the stove and remove the top baking sheet and parchment.

Increase the oven temperature to 500°F or 475°F on convection.

Sift the 1 tablespoon confectioners' sugar evenly over the phyllo. Bake until the sugar caramelizes, about 2½ minutes, rotating the pan halfway through baking.

Let cool completely. Break into shards and store, layered between sheets of parchment, in an airtight container for up to 2 days.

chocolate crumble

When I was a young cook, every restaurant I worked in used a tuile to present ice cream. The tuiles kept the ice cream from sliding around on the plate; but while they were pretty, they didn't impart any flavor. So I started making crumbles and streusels to set underneath ice creams. They have the added bonus of reinforcing flavors and adding texture.

I lay quenelles of ice cream on a pile of these intense chocolate crumbs, but you could easily sprinkle the crumble over a scoop of ice cream.

Heat the oven to 375°F or 350°F on convection. Line a baking sheet with a Silpat or parchment.

Cut the butter into pieces and put it in the bowl of a standing mixer fitted with the paddle. Whisk the cocoa powder, flour, sugar, and salt together and add to the bowl. Mix at medium speed until well combined, dark brown, and in big crumbs.

Spread out on the baking sheet, breaking up the biggest crumbs and leaving room for spreading. Bake until crisp, about 20 minutes, rotating the pan halfway through baking. Let cool.

When the crumble is cool, put it in a food processor and process to fine, even crumbs. Store in an airtight container for up to 1 week.

MAKES ABOUT 3 CUPS

6½ TABLESPOONS (94 G)
   UNSALTED BUTTER, SOFTENED
⅓ CUP (30 G) UNSWEETENED
   COCOA POWDER (PREFERABLY
   VALRHONA)
¾ CUP (94 G) ALL-PURPOSE FLOUR
7 TABLESPOONS (87 G) SUGAR
¼ TEASPOON (1 G) COARSE SALT

graham streusel

This recipe makes more than you will need for the Rhubarb-Flan Tarts on page 40, but you can use it for any fruit cobbler or crisp or crumble. I love those kinds of desserts.

7 TABLESPOONS (99 G) UNSALTED
   BUTTER, SOFTENED
SCANT ½ CUP (94 G) SUGAR
½ TEASPOON GRATED LEMON
   ZEST
GENEROUS ¼ TEASPOON (1.5 G)
   COARSE SALT
¾ CUP (94 G) ALL-PURPOSE FLOUR
1 CUP LESS 1 TABLESPOON (94 G)
   GRAHAM CRACKER CRUMBS
¼ TEASPOON (1 G) BAKING
   POWDER

Put the butter, sugar, lemon zest, and salt in the bowl of a standing mixer fitted with the paddle. Beat at medium speed until creamy.

Whisk the flour, graham cracker crumbs, and baking powder together. Add to the butter mixture and beat at medium-low speed just until crumbly, scraping the bowl a couple of times.

Transfer to an airtight container and store in the freezer until you're ready to use it or for up to 2 months.

candied nuts

MAKES ABOUT 1 CUP

I often put these nuts under ice cream, but they make a great bar snack, too.

5 OUNCES (142 G) NUTS SUCH AS HONEY-ROASTED
    PEANUTS, SLIVERED ALMONDS, OR WHOLE
    BLANCHED HAZELNUTS
2 TABLESPOONS (34 G) LIGHT CORN SYRUP
COARSE SALT

Heat the oven to 350°F or 325°F on convection. Line a baking sheet with a Silpat or parchment.

Toss the nuts with the corn syrup and a big pinch of salt, making sure all the nuts are coated. Spread out on the Silpat. Bake, tossing and stirring often with a rubber spatula, until the nuts are golden, about 15 minutes.

Let cool completely and store in an airtight container for up to 1 week.

candied pistachios

MAKES ABOUT 1½ CUPS

These elegant nuts are a great accent to summer fruits.

If you can find the longer, thinner pistachios from Sicily, use them for this recipe—or any time you're eating pistachios. They have the best flavor.

9 OUNCES (250 G) SHELLED UNSALTED PISTACHIOS
2 TABLESPOONS (16 G) CONFECTIONERS' SUGAR
3 TABLESPOONS (45 G) WATER
5 TABLESPOONS (62 G) GRANULATED SUGAR
½ TEASPOON (3.5 G) LIGHT CORN SYRUP
½ TEASPOON (2 G) COARSE SALT

Heat the oven to 350°F or 325°F on convection.

Spread the pistachios out on a rimmed baking sheet and bake until the nuts are hot but not browned or toasted, about 7 minutes.

Dump the nuts into a bowl and toss with the confectioners' sugar.

Line a baking sheet with a Silpat or parchment.

Meanwhile, put the water, granulated sugar, and corn syrup in a small saucepan. Bring to a boil over medium-high heat and cook to 285°F. Add the nuts and salt and cook, stirring constantly, until the sugar turns white. Scrape out onto the Silpat. Working fast, use a couple of forks to separate the nuts while the sugar is still hot.

Let cool completely and store in an airtight container for up to 1 week.

peanut caramel

MAKES ABOUT 2½ CUPS

What I like most about this caramel is the balance the salt provides; you taste caramel, not sugar. The key to making this is cooking the honey long enough so it just crosses from being sweet to bitter.

You could use this as a crunchy topping for ice cream. Or pour it into a ring mold when you make it and use it as a layer in a cake.

⅔ CUP (200 G) HONEY
¼ TEASPOON (1 G) COARSE SALT
2⅔ TABLESPOONS (37 G) UNSALTED BUTTER
½ CUP (120 G) HEAVY CREAM
5¼ OUNCES (150 G) UNSALTED PEANUTS, CHOPPED
    AND TOASTED
5¼ OUNCES (150 G) HAZELNUTS, CHOPPED AND
    TOASTED
MILK, IF NEEDED

Line a baking sheet with a Silpat.

Put the honey and salt in a saucepan over medium heat. Cook, swirling the pan, until the honey caramelizes and turns dark amber. Stir in the butter. Add the cream and cook, stirring, until smooth. Stir in the nuts. If the caramel is very thick—too thick to stir—thin it with a little milk.

Scrape out onto the Silpat and use two forks to break the caramel up into small pieces while it's still warm. Let cool completely. Store in an airtight container for up to 1 week.

Almond praline powder

MAKES ABOUT ¾ CUP

This nutty powder is a great garnish. I use powders like this whenever I want to add flavor to a dessert without adding heaviness.

My buddy and fellow pastry chef Sam Mason developed this as peanut butter powder when he was working at the restaurant wd-50 in New York. He shared the technique with me, and I've adapted it to make a praline powder perfumed with citrus.

½ CUP (125 G) PRALINE PASTE
1 CUP (16 G) TAPIOCA MALTODEXTRIN
⅛ TEASPOON (0.5 G) COARSE SALT
¼ TEASPOON (0.8 G) ORANGE OIL
¼ TEASPOON (0.8 G) LEMON OIL
GRATED ZEST OF ¼ ORANGE
GRATED ZEST OF ¼ LEMON

Put the praline paste, tapioca maltodextrin, salt, orange oil, lemon oil, and zests in a food processor. Process, scraping the sides and bottom of the processor several times, until the mixture forms a powder. Store in an airtight container for up to 3 days.

spiced walnuts

I like serving these with Corn Panna Cotta (page 83), but they're also delicious with cheese and perfect to put out with beer for Sunday football.

Combine all the spices with the salt in a spice grinder and grind to a fine powder. Sift, then store for up to 3 months in a glass jar out of the light.

For the Spice Mix

3 CINNAMON STICKS, BROKEN INTO PIECES
6 ALLSPICE BERRIES
1¼ TEASPOONS (5 G) BLACK PEPPERCORNS
4 WHOLE CLOVES
17 CARDAMOM SEEDS
2 STAR ANISE
⅛ TEASPOON (0.4 G) GROUND MACE
⅛ TEASPOON (0.5 G) COARSE SALT

For the Walnuts

3 TABLESPOONS (42 G) UNSALTED BUTTER
4 OUNCES (113 G) WALNUT HALVES
1 TABLESPOON (6 G) SPICE MIX

Melt the butter in a skillet over medium heat. When the butter foams, add the nuts and cook, stirring often, until the nuts are fragrant and toasted, about 3 minutes.

Scrape into a strainer so all the excess butter can drip off. Transfer to a bowl and toss the nuts with the spice mix.

Let cool completely and store in an airtight container for up to 3 days.

ice creams

sorbets

AND GRANITÉS

vanilla bean ice cream

MAKES ABOUT 1 QUART

1½ CUPS (360 G) WHOLE MILK

1½ CUPS (360 G) HEAVY CREAM

1½ VANILLA BEANS, SPLIT AND
   SCRAPED

2 TABLESPOONS (34 G) LIGHT CORN
   SYRUP

8 LARGE EGG YOLKS

4 TEASPOONS (20 G) INVERT
   SUGAR (PAGE 185)

¾ CUP (150 G) GRANULATED
   SUGAR

This is it: pure vanilla flavor in a nice, creamy ice cream.

Set up an ice bath in a large bowl.

Put the milk, cream, vanilla pods and seeds, and corn syrup in a saucepan and bring to a simmer over medium-high heat.

Whisk the yolks with the invert sugar and granulated sugar in a medium bowl. When the milk mixture is simmering, slowly whisk about 1 cup into the yolks for about 1 minute to temper them (keep the pan off the heat while you do this). Then scrape the yolks into the saucepan and cook, stirring pretty much constantly, until the mixture reaches 180°F. Keep an eye on the color of the foam on the surface; when it turns the same color as the mixture, you're very close to the right temperature.

Strain into a medium bowl and set into the ice bath. Pull the vanilla pods out of the strainer and return them to the ice cream base. Chill completely, stirring often. Then cover with plastic wrap and refrigerate overnight for the flavors to mature.

Remove the vanilla pods (rinse, dry, and save them for another use). Mix thoroughly with an immersion blender, then freeze in an ice cream maker. Pack into a plastic container and freeze for at least 2 hours before serving.

white chocolate ice cream

*This very rich ice cream, with the lush mouthfeel of white choco-
late, may be one of my sweetest recipes. Try serving it with ripe
peaches and a drizzle of tarragon oil or basil oil (see page 187).*

*You should be aware that this ice cream can take a long time to
freeze in a home ice cream maker, and that it will need to cure in
the freezer overnight before serving.*

Set up an ice bath in a large bowl. Put the chocolate in a
medium bowl.

Put the milk and ¼ cup of the sugar in a saucepan. Bring to a
simmer over medium heat.

Whisk the eggs with the remaining ½ cup sugar in a medium
bowl. When the milk is simmering, slowly whisk about 1 cup into
the eggs for about 1 minute to temper them (keep the pan off the
heat while you do this). Then scrape the eggs into the saucepan
and cook, stirring pretty much constantly, until the mixture
reaches 180°F. Keep an eye on the color of the foam on the
surface; when it turns the same color as the mixture, you're very
close to the right temperature.

Strain over the chocolate and leave for about 1 minute. Then
mix thoroughly with an immersion blender. Set into the ice bath
and chill completely, stirring often.

Freeze in an ice cream maker, then transfer to a plastic
container and freeze overnight before serving.

12 OUNCES (340 G) WHITE
    CHOCOLATE (PREFERABLY
    VALRHONA), FINELY CHOPPED
3 CUPS (720 G) WHOLE MILK
¾ CUP (150 G) SUGAR
3 LARGE EGGS

coconut ice cream

MAKES ABOUT 1 QUART

1½ CUPS PLUS 1 TABLESPOON
(372 G) WHOLE MILK

¾ CUP PLUS 2 TABLESPOONS
(210 G) HEAVY CREAM

½ CUP PLUS 1 TABLESPOON (45 G)
NONFAT MILK POWDER

2 TABLESPOONS (30 G) INVERT
SUGAR (PAGE 185)

4 TEASPOONS (24 G) LIGHT CORN
SYRUP

¼ CUP PLUS 3 TABLESPOONS (90 G)
GRANULATED SUGAR

¾ CUP PLUS 2 TABLESPOONS
(225 G) CANNED COCONUT MILK

One bite of this ice cream, and you're transported to a beach in the Caribbean.

Set up an ice bath in a large bowl.

Put the milk, cream, milk powder, invert sugar, corn syrup, and granulated sugar in a saucepan and bring to a simmer over medium-high heat, stirring to dissolve the milk powder and sugar. Bring to a boil. Mix with an immersion blender and pour into a medium bowl. Set into the ice bath and chill completely, stirring often. Add the coconut milk and mix thoroughly with the immersion blender. Cover with plastic wrap and refrigerate overnight for the flavors to mature.

Freeze in an ice cream maker. Pack into a plastic container and freeze for at least 2 hours before serving.

SOME TIPS FOR MAKING
ICE CREAM AND SORBETS

⊚ Make the base the day before for all the infused ice creams and sorbets. That way the flavors have a chance to ripen and develop in the refrigerator overnight.

⊚ Make sure the base is very cold before you start churning it in your ice cream maker.

⊚ For best results, churn the ice cream or sorbet the morning you plan to serve it. These ice creams and sorbets should cure in the freezer for at least 2 hours before serving, but they will be at their best when they've had a few more hours in the freezer.

⊚ Move the ice creams and sorbets to the refrigerator 10 minutes before serving, so they soften a little before you scoop them.

cream cheese ice cream

Rafael Gonzalez, a Cuban sous-chef at Jean Georges, thought I was prejudiced against Cuban flavor combinations. To prove him wrong, I made this ice cream to pair with Coconut Pain Perdu (page 127) and Papaya-Lime Compote (page 251). It's got that faintly sour edge of cream cheese, which never seems to over-power other flavors, and a great mouthfeel.

Set up an ice bath in a large bowl.

Put the milk, milk powder, sugar, and corn syrup in a saucepan and whisk until smooth. Bring to a boil over medium-high heat.

Put the cream cheese in a medium bowl and pour in the hot milk mixture. Mix with an immersion blender until smooth. Add the lemon juice and mix again. Strain into a medium bowl and set into the ice bath. Chill completely, stirring often.

Freeze in an ice cream maker. Pack into a plastic container and freeze for at least 2 hours before serving.

MAKES ABOUT 1 QUART

1¼ CUPS (300 G) WHOLE MILK
½ CUP (40 G) NONFAT MILK
   POWDER
½ CUP (100 G) SUGAR
GENEROUS 2 TABLESPOONS (37 G)
   LIGHT CORN SYRUP
16 OUNCES (453 G) CREAM CHEESE,
   CUT INTO PIECES
JUICE OF 1 LEMON

Honey-ginger ice cream

The first thing I do when I feel a sore throat coming on is make some hot honey and ginger tea. And the more I thought about those flavors, the more I thought they would make a great ice cream. They do.

6 TABLESPOONS (120 G) HONEY

2 CUPS (480 G) WHOLE MILK

1/2 CUP (120 G) HEAVY CREAM

2 OUNCES (60 G) FRESH GINGER, PEELED AND THINLY SLICED

1 VANILLA BEAN, SPLIT AND SCRAPED

2 TABLESPOONS PLUS 1 TEASPOON (40 G) LIGHT CORN SYRUP

5 TABLESPOONS (25 G) NONFAT MILK POWDER

4 LARGE EGG YOLKS

Set up an ice bath in a large bowl.

Put the honey in a saucepan. Cook over medium-high heat, swirling the pan once the honey begins to boil, until the honey caramelizes to a rich amber.

Meanwhile, put the milk, cream, ginger, and vanilla pod and seeds in another saucepan. Bring to a boil.

Pour the milk into the honey—carefully, because it will sputter and boil up—and whisk to dissolve the honey. Remove from the heat, cover, and infuse for 15 minutes.

Strain the honey-milk mixture into a clean saucepan (rinse and dry the vanilla pod and save it for another use) and whisk in the corn syrup and milk powder. Bring to a simmer over medium heat.

Whisk the yolks in a medium bowl. When the honey-milk mixture is simmering, slowly whisk about 1 cup into the yolks for about 1 minute to temper them (keep the pan off the heat while you do this). Then scrape the yolks into the saucepan and cook, stirring pretty much constantly, until the mixture reaches 180°F. Keep an eye on the color of the foam on the surface; when it turns the same color as the mixture, you're very close to the right temperature. Strain the mixture into a medium bowl, set into the ice bath, and mix thoroughly with an immersion blender. Chill completely, stirring often. Then cover with plastic wrap and refrigerate overnight for the flavors to mature.

Mix again with the immersion blender, then freeze in an ice cream maker. Pack into a plastic container and freeze for at least 2 hours before serving.

balsamic ice cream

François Payard loves the combination of balsamic vinegar and strawberries and serves it every season. I wanted to tie the flavors together but in a different way, so I came up with this ice cream, which I pair with Strawberry Sorbet (page 236). You could just serve this with Slow-Roasted Strawberries (page 245), of course.

Set up an ice bath in a large bowl.

Put the milk in a small saucepan and bring to a simmer over medium-high heat.

Whisk the yolks with the granulated sugar and invert sugar in a medium bowl. When the milk is simmering, slowly whisk about 1 cup into the yolks for about 1 minute to temper them (keep the pan off the heat while you do this). Then scrape the yolks into the saucepan and cook, stirring pretty much constantly, until the mixture reaches 180°F. Keep an eye on the color of the foam on the surface; when it turns the same color as the mixture, you're very close to the right temperature.

Remove from the heat and add the cream and balsamic vinegar. Mix thoroughly with an immersion blender. Push through a fine strainer into a medium bowl and set into the ice bath. Chill completely, stirring often. Then cover with plastic wrap and refrigerate overnight for the flavors to mature.

Mix again with an immersion blender, then freeze in an ice cream maker. Pack into a plastic container and freeze for at least 2 hours before serving.

MAKES ABOUT 3 CUPS

2 CUPS (480 G) MILK
5 LARGE EGG YOLKS
²/₃ CUP (130 G) GRANULATED SUGAR
2 TEASPOONS (10 G) INVERT SUGAR (PAGE 185)
½ CUP (120 G) HEAVY CREAM
¼ CUP (60 G) AGED BALSAMIC VINEGAR

thai basil ice cream

MAKES ABOUT 1 QUART

Thai basil is spicier than sweet basil and more pungent. And that flavor pops when this ice cream is paired with cherries.

1½ CUPS (360 G) WHOLE MILK

1½ CUPS (360 G) HEAVY CREAM

PACKED ½ CUP (25 G) FRESH THAI BASIL LEAVES, CHOPPED

½ CUP PLUS 2 TABLESPOONS (125 G) GRANULATED SUGAR

2 TABLESPOONS (37 G) LIGHT CORN SYRUP

10 LARGE EGG YOLKS

4 TEASPOONS (20 G) INVERT SUGAR (PAGE 185)

Put the milk and cream in a saucepan and bring to a simmer over medium-high heat. Add the basil, turn off the heat, and infuse for 30 minutes. Mix thoroughly with an immersion blender to puree the basil; the milk should turn pale green. Strain through a fine strainer, pushing down on the solids.

Set up an ice bath in a large bowl.

Return the infused milk to the saucepan and add the 2 tablespoons granulated sugar and the corn syrup. Bring to a simmer over medium heat.

Whisk the yolks with the ½ cup granulated sugar and the invert sugar in a medium bowl. When the milk is simmering, slowly whisk about 1 cup into the yolks for about 1 minute to temper them (keep the pan off the heat while you do this). Then scrape the yolks into the saucepan and cook, stirring pretty much constantly, until the mixture reaches 180°F. Keep an eye on the color of the foam on the surface; when it turns the same color as the mixture, you're very close to the right temperature. Strain into a medium bowl and set into the ice bath. Chill completely, stirring often. Then cover with plastic wrap and refrigerate overnight for the flavors to mature.

Mix again with an immersion blender, then freeze in an ice cream maker. Pack into a plastic container and freeze for at least 2 hours before serving.

Lemongrass Ice Cream

This is a Thomas Haas signature, and it's more of a combination of ice cream and granité than just simple ice cream. I fell in love with it the first time I made it for its delicate balance of fat and acid. It pairs well with berries and would be great in a smoothie.

Crush the lemongrass with the back of a heavy chef's knife, then chop it. Put the lemongrass in a saucepan with the lime juice and sugar. Bring to a boil over medium-high heat. Stir in the corn syrup and remove from the heat. Let cool to about 115°F.

Stir in the milk and cream. Transfer to a bowl or pitcher, cover with plastic wrap, and refrigerate overnight for the flavors to mature.

Strain the mixture, then freeze in an ice cream maker. Pack into a plastic container and freeze for at least 2 hours before serving.

MAKES ABOUT 5 CUPS

5 OUNCES (150 G) FRESH
   LEMONGRASS, TRIMMED
1 CUP (240 G) FRESH LIME JUICE
1¼ CUPS (250 G) SUGAR
2 TABLESPOONS PLUS 1 TEASPOON
   (51 G) LIGHT CORN SYRUP
2 CUPS (480 G) WHOLE MILK
1 CUP (240 G) HEAVY CREAM

strawberry ice cream

My issue with fruit ice creams is not being able to taste the fruit, so to keep that flavor foremost, I cook the ice cream base on its own and then add fresh fruit. Less fat—no eggs in the ice cream base—allows the berry flavor to stand out.

1⅓ CUPS (325 G) WHOLE MILK

1 CUP PLUS 3 TABLESPOONS (285 G) HEAVY CREAM

¾ CUP (60 G) NONFAT MILK POWDER

1 TABLESPOON (30 G) INVERT SUGAR (PAGE 185)

3 TABLESPOONS (51 G) LIGHT CORN SYRUP

½ CUP PLUS 2 TABLESPOONS (125 G) GRANULATED SUGAR

14 OUNCES (375 G) FRESH STRAWBERRIES

Combine the milk, heavy cream, milk powder, invert sugar, corn syrup, and granulated sugar in a heavy saucepan. Bring to a boil over medium heat. Turn off the heat, mix thoroughly with an immersion blender, and strain into a bowl or a big measuring cup.

Hull the strawberries and put them in a food processor. Process to a smooth puree. Stir into the milk mixture, cover with plastic wrap, and refrigerate overnight for the flavors to develop.

Mix again with the immersion blender, then freeze in an ice cream maker. Pack into a plastic container and freeze for at least 2 hours before serving.

rum and coke ice cream

Who doesn't like rum and Coke? And those flavors make a great ice cream.

Set up an ice bath in a large bowl.

Put 2 tablespoons of the cola syrup in a bowl with the egg yolks.

Put the remaining ½ cup plus 2 tablespoons cola syrup and the milk in a saucepan. Whisk together and bring to a simmer. This may look curdled; don't worry, it will come together with the yolks.

Whisk the yolks and syrup until light. When the milk mixture is simmering, slowly whisk about 1 cup into the yolks for about 1 minute to temper them (keep the pan off the heat while you do this). Then scrape the yolks into the saucepan and cook, stirring pretty much constantly, until the mixture reaches 180°F. Keep an eye on the color of the foam on the surface; when it turns the same color as the mixture, you're very close to the right temperature. Strain into a medium bowl and set into the ice bath. Chill completely, stirring often.

Mix thoroughly with an immersion blender, then freeze in an ice cream maker. Add the rum just before the ice cream finishes churning. Pack into a plastic container and freeze for at least 2 hours before serving.

MAKES ABOUT 3 CUPS

¾ CUP (175 G) COLA SYRUP (SEE NOTE)
7 LARGE EGG YOLKS
2 CUPS PLUS 3 TABLESPOONS (525 G) WHOLE MILK
¼ CUP PLUS 3 TABLESPOONS (65 G) APPLETON ESTATE JAMAICA RUM OR OTHER GOLDEN RUM

NOTE: You can find cola syrup in many drugstores or online from Drugstore.com.

frozen yogurt

MAKES ABOUT 1½ QUARTS

This frozen treat combines the texture of a full-fat ice cream with the fresh flavor of a fat-free sorbet.

Use a thick, creamy yogurt for this recipe. I use the nonfat yogurt from Stonyfield Farm in the restaurant.

1 CUP LESS 1 TABLESPOON (225 G) WHOLE MILK

½ CUP PLUS 2 TABLESPOONS (150 G) HEAVY CREAM

½ CUP PLUS 2 TABLESPOONS (50 G) NONFAT MILK POWDER

½ CUP PLUS 3 TABLESPOONS (137 G) GRANULATED SUGAR

¼ CUP (72 G) LIGHT CORN SYRUP

6 TABLESPOONS (90 G) INVERT SUGAR (PAGE 185)

2¾ CUPS (640 G) PLAIN NONFAT YOGURT

JUICE OF 1 LEMON

Set up an ice bath in a large bowl.

Put the milk, cream, milk powder, granulated sugar, corn syrup, and invert sugar in a saucepan and whisk. Bring to a boil over medium-high heat. Mix thoroughly with an immersion blender and pour into a medium bowl. Set into the ice bath and chill completely, stirring often.

Add the yogurt and lemon juice and mix again with the immersion blender.

Freeze in an ice cream maker, then pack into a plastic container and freeze for at least 2 hours before serving.

Bitter chocolate sorbet

This sorbet is very smooth and not too sweet. Keep some in the freezer for a quick chocolate fix.

Set up an ice bath in a large bowl.

Whisk the water and milk powder together in a saucepan. Place over medium heat and warm to 104°F. Whisk in the invert sugar and granulated sugar and warm to 122°F. Add the cocoa powder and chocolate and cook, whisking, until the chocolate is melted and smooth and the mixture reaches 180°F. Mix thoroughly with an immersion blender and pour into a medium bowl. Set into the ice bath and chill completely, stirring often.

Freeze in an ice cream maker. This can take a long time in a home ice cream maker. Pack into a plastic container and freeze for at least 2 hours before serving.

3 CUPS LESS 2 TABLESPOONS (690 G) WATER

¼ CUP (20 G) NONFAT MILK POWDER

1½ TABLESPOONS (45 G) INVERT SUGAR (PAGE 185)

¾ CUP (150 G) GRANULATED SUGAR

¼ CUP (25 G) UNSWEETENED COCOA POWDER (PREFERABLY VALRHONA)

3¾ OUNCES (110 G) UNSWEETENED CHOCOLATE (PREFERABLY VALRHONA COCOA PASTE), FINELY CHOPPED

Green Apple Sorbet

MAKES ABOUT 1½ QUARTS

This may be the epitome of freshness, a perfect balance of sweet and tart, with the crispness of the apple apparent, even in sorbet form.

Be prepared: This can take a very long time to freeze in a home ice cream maker.

⅔ CUP (130 G) WATER

3 TABLESPOONS (51 G) LIGHT CORN SYRUP

5 TEASPOONS (25 G) INVERT SUGAR (PAGE 185)

1 CUP PLUS 2 TABLESPOONS (230 G) GRANULATED SUGAR

1 TABLESPOON (14 G) FRESH LEMON JUICE

7 OR 8 GRANNY SMITH APPLES

Set up an ice bath in a large bowl.

Put the water, corn syrup, and invert sugar in a saucepan and bring to a boil over medium-high heat. Add the granulated sugar, stirring until the sugar dissolves. Pour into a medium bowl, set into the ice bath, and chill quickly, stirring often.

Put the lemon juice in the container that will be catching the apple juice.

Core the apples and put them through a juicer. Skim the foam and pour the juice through a fine strainer into the container with the lemon juice. Measure out 3⅓ cups and add to the syrup.

Freeze immediately in an ice cream maker. Pack into a plastic container and freeze for at least 2 hours before serving.

Lemon-Basil Sorbet

Serve a scoop of this bright and refreshing sorbet over a bowl of sliced summer peaches. Or add it to your favorite gazpacho.

MAKES ABOUT 5 CUPS

Put the water and basil in a saucepan and bring to a boil over medium-high heat. Remove from the heat and infuse for 30 minutes.

Pour into a blender and whirl until the basil is completely pulverized. Strain into a measuring cup and add water if necessary to make 2⅓ cups.

Return the basil water to the saucepan and add the granulated sugar, corn syrup, invert sugar, and milk powder. Bring to a boil over medium-high heat.

Pour the mixture into a medium bowl. Cover with plastic wrap and refrigerate overnight for the flavors to mature.

Add the lemon juice and mix with an immersion blender.

Freeze in an ice cream maker. Pack into a plastic container and freeze for at least 2 hours before serving.

2⅓ CUPS (560 G) WATER
PACKED ¾ CUP (37 G) FRESH BASIL
    LEAVES
1¼ CUPS PLUS 2 TABLESPOONS
    (275 G) GRANULATED SUGAR
¼ CUP (68 G) LIGHT CORN SYRUP
SCANT 1 TABLESPOON (12 G)
    INVERT SUGAR (PAGE 185)
GENEROUS 2 TABLESPOONS (12 G)
    NONFAT MILK POWDER
1⅓ CUPS (320 G) FRESH LEMON
    JUICE

meyer lemon sorbet

MAKES ABOUT 1½ QUARTS

The intriguing lemony/orangey flavor of Meyer lemons is so refreshing; this sorbet captures the fruit's essence and perfume. The Salt Butter Shortbread (page 202) is great with it, but, really, this sorbet needs no accompaniment.

2 CUPS (480 G) WATER
½ CUP (40 G) NONFAT MILK POWDER
3 TABLESPOONS (45 G) INVERT SUGAR (PAGE 185)
2 CUPS PLUS 3 TABLESPOONS (437 G) GRANULATED
    SUGAR
2 TABLESPOONS (34 G) LIGHT CORN SYRUP
GRATED ZEST OF 6 MEYER LEMONS
2 CUPS (480 G) FRESH MEYER LEMON JUICE

Set up an ice bath in a large bowl.

Put the water, milk powder, invert sugar, granulated sugar, and corn syrup in a saucepan and bring to a boil, whisking to dissolve the milk powder and sugar, over medium heat. Strain into a medium bowl and set into the ice bath to chill quickly, stirring often.

Add the zest and lemon juice and mix with an immersion blender.

Freeze in an ice cream maker. Pack into a plastic container and freeze for at least 2 hours before serving.

passion sorbet

MAKES ABOUT 3 CUPS

The jolting flavor of passion fruit really explodes on the palate. Serve this with passion fruit seeds on a hot day. Or combine it with some meringues and strawberries.

1 CUP (240 G) WATER
4 TEASPOONS (8 G) NONFAT MILK POWDER
1 TABLESPOON (15 G) INVERT SUGAR (PAGE 185)
4 TEASPOONS (24 G) LIGHT CORN SYRUP
⅓ CUP PLUS 2 TABLESPOONS (75 G) GRANULATED
    SUGAR
1¼ CUPS (275 G) PASSION FRUIT PUREE (SEE PAGE 276)

Set up an ice bath in a large bowl.

Put the water, milk powder, invert sugar, corn syrup, and granulated sugar in a saucepan and whisk. Bring to a boil over medium heat.

Strain into a medium bowl and set into the ice bath. Chill quickly, stirring often. Add the passion fruit puree and mix with an immersion blender.

Freeze in an ice cream maker. Pack into a plastic container and freeze for at least 2 hours before serving.

rhubarb sorbet

Rhubarb is paired with strawberry so often, but I like showcasing the pungent, tangy flavor all on its own. Combining this sorbet with White Chocolate Ice Cream (page 221) softens the edge. If your rhubarb isn't very ripe and red, you may want to adjust the color with a few drops of pomegranate juice.

Set up an ice bath in a large bowl.

    Cut the rhubarb into small pieces and juice it in a juicer. The fibers can clog the juicer, so you may need to clean it about halfway through this process. Strain the juice and measure out 3 cups.

    Pour the water into a saucepan and add the granulated sugar, corn syrup, invert sugar, and milk powder and whisk. Bring to a boil over medium-high heat.

    Transfer to a medium bowl, set into the ice bath, and mix thoroughly with an immersion blender. Once this is cool, add the rhubarb juice and mix again with the immersion blender.

    Freeze in an ice cream maker. Pack into a plastic container and freeze for at least 2 hours before serving.

MAKES ABOUT 1½ QUARTS

2 POUNDS (900 G) VERY RIPE RHUBARB

1 CUP PLUS 2 TABLESPOONS (270 G) WATER

1¼ CUPS PLUS 2 TABLESPOONS (280 G) GRANULATED SUGAR

2 TABLESPOONS PLUS 1 TEASPOON (51 G) LIGHT CORN SYRUP

5 TEASPOONS (25 G) INVERT SUGAR (PAGE 185)

¼ CUP PLUS 1 TEASPOON (25 G) NONFAT MILK POWDER

strawberry sorbet

MAKES ABOUT 3 CUPS

The goal when making any sorbet is to capture the purity of ripe fruit while making the smoothest texture possible. This sorbet does that beautifully for ripe summer strawberries.

½ CUP (120 G) WATER
½ CUP PLUS 2 TABLESPOONS
(125 G) SUGAR
18 OUNCES (500 G) FRESH
STRAWBERRIES, HULLED

Pour the water into a saucepan. Add the sugar and bring to a full boil. Remove from the heat and let the simple syrup cool to room temperature.

Working in batches, puree the strawberries with the simple syrup in a blender until perfectly smooth. Refrigerate until cold.

Mix again with an immersion blender, then freeze in an ice cream maker. Pack into a plastic container and freeze for at least 2 hours before serving.

This strawberry sorbet has been combined with Balsamic Ice Cream.

tomato sorbet

Tomatoes are technically a fruit, and that's how I treat them. This sorbet, which should be made at the height of tomato season with the ripest fruits, showcases that characteristic sweet-acid tomato flavor in its coldest form.

A scoop of this sorbet can be the start of a not-so-traditional Bloody Mary, and it could also find its way into a bowl of gazpacho. Try pairing it with the Raspberry-Rose Water Soup (page 62), too.

Core the tomatoes and cut them into chunks. Put them in a food processor and process to a smooth puree. Strain into a bowl.

Pour the water into a saucepan with the granulated sugar, corn syrup, invert sugar, and milk powder and whisk. Bring to a boil over medium-high heat. Pour into the tomato puree and mix with an immersion blender. Let cool. Cover with plastic wrap and refrigerate overnight.

Mix again with the immersion blender, then freeze in an ice cream maker. Pack into a plastic container and freeze for at least 2 hours before serving.

GENEROUS 1½ POUNDS (0.75 KG) RIPE SUMMER TOMATOES

1½ CUPS (360 G) WATER

¾ CUP (150 G) GRANULATED SUGAR

6 TABLESPOONS (102 G) LIGHT CORN SYRUP

2 TEASPOONS (10 G) INVERT SUGAR (PAGE 185)

2 TABLESPOONS PLUS 1 TEASPOON (12 G) NONFAT MILK POWDER

Here, Tomato Sorbet is mixed with Lemon-Basil Sorbet.

champagne sorbet

MAKES ABOUT 3 CUPS

I love champagne and it's a natural in desserts. This sorbet captures the airiness and effervescence of the wine, and adding a hint of lemon makes it super-refreshing.

Champagnes differ in their sugar contents, which will affect whether or not the sorbet will freeze, so be sure to use Veuve Clicquot yellow label for this recipe.

1 (375 ML) BOTTLE VEUVE
   CLICQUOT CHAMPAGNE,
   CHILLED
1 CUP (240 G) COLD WATER
⅔ CUP (165 G) SIMPLE SYRUP
   (PAGE 184), CHILLED
GRATED ZEST AND JUICE OF HALF
   A LEMON

Stir the champagne, water, simple syrup, and lemon zest and juice together.

Freeze in an ice cream maker. Pack into a plastic container and freeze for at least 2 hours before serving.

strawberry-moscato granité

SERVES 6 ON ITS OWN OR
8 TO 9 AS PART OF A FOURPLAY

Dessert wines are usually too sweet for me, so I introduce the natural acids of fresh fruit or berries for balance, as in this granité.

Serve this over berries or add it to a margarita.

1 POUND (454 G) FRESH STRAWBERRIES
1/2 CUP (120 G) MOSCATO, SUCH AS FORTETO DELLA LUJA, CHILLED
1/3 CUP (75 G) SIMPLE SYRUP (PAGE 184), CHILLED
GRATED ZEST AND JUICE OF HALF A LEMON

Hull the strawberries and process them in a food processor to a very fine puree. Work through a fine strainer and measure out 2 cups puree (discard the solids).

Add the moscato, simple syrup, and lemon zest and juice to the strawberry puree and mix thoroughly. Pour into a baking dish and freeze for at least 8 hours.

To serve, scrape across the top of the granité with a fork to make small crystals.

tangerine-campari granité

SERVES 8 ON ITS OWN OR
12 AS PART OF A FOURPLAY

The combination of bitter Campari and sweet tangerine couldn't be more refreshing.

2 CUPS (470 G) FRESH TANGERINE JUICE
1/4 CUP (50 G) SUGAR
1/3 CUP (75 G) CAMPARI

Put 1/2 cup of the tangerine juice in a small saucepan with the sugar and heat, stirring, until the sugar is dissolved. Combine with the remaining 1 1/2 cups juice and the Campari.

Pour into a baking dish and freeze for at least 8 hours.

To serve, scrape across the top of the granité with a fork to make small crystals.

raspberry-fig sangria granité

SERVES 8 ON ITS OWN OR
12 AS PART OF A FOURPLAY

I love sangria in the summertime and always thought about turning it into a slushy. Here, I've taken it one step further and made granité. The acid from the raspberries both brightens and enhances the flavors of the wines.

¾ CUP (187 ML) RED WINE
¾ CUP (187 ML) RUBY PORT
2 CUPS PLUS 2 TABLESPOONS (500 G) WATER
9 OUNCES (255 G) FRESH RASPBERRIES, PUREED IN A
    FOOD PROCESSOR
9 OUNCES (255 G) FRESH MISSION FIGS, QUARTERED
1 LEMON, CUT INTO EIGHTHS
½ CUP PLUS 2 TABLESPOONS (125 G) SUGAR
1½ CUPS (375 G) FRESH ORANGE JUICE

Put the wine and port in a large nonreactive saucepan and bring just to a simmer. Ignite, carefully, with a match, cover the pot halfway, and allow the alcohol to burn off. Once the flames have died, add the water, raspberry puree, figs, lemon, and sugar. Simmer, stirring once in a while, until the fruit has broken down, about 20 minutes. Take off the heat and add the orange juice. Let cool to room temperature.

Strain the sangria through a fine strainer and pour into a baking dish. Freeze overnight.

To serve, scrape across the top of the granité with a fork to make small crystals.

pedro ximenez granité

SERVES 8 ON ITS OWN OR
14 TO 15 AS PART OF A FOURPLAY

The caramel notes of this sherry lend themselves well to the fruits available in autumn.

3¼ CUPS (780 G) WATER
⅔ CUP (130 G) SUGAR
1¼ CUPS (300 G) PEDRO XIMENEZ SHERRY

Combine the water and sugar in a small saucepan. Bring to a boil over medium heat, stirring until the sugar is completely dissolved. Let cool completely.

Stir in the sherry, pour into a baking dish, and freeze for at least 8 hours.

To serve, scrape across the top of the granité with a fork to make small crystals.

pear-cumin granité

The warm richness of pear and the earthiness of cumin combine to create a new flavor that to me is the epitome of fall. This granité isn't too sweet, so you could also serve it as a middle course of a big dinner, before the meat.

You could substitute sparkling apple cider mixed with an equal amount of pear puree for the pear cider.

Set up an ice bath in a large bowl.

Pour about 3 tablespoons of the pear cider into a small bowl. Sprinkle the gelatin over the surface and let sit for at least 1 minute. Microwave for 45 seconds or heat gently in a saucepan until melted.

Put the water and sugar in a saucepan. Bring to a boil over medium-high heat. Whisk in the gelatin and strain into a medium bowl. Gradually stir in the remaining cider and the cumin and set into the ice bath, stirring to chill quickly.

Pour into a baking dish and freeze for at least 8 hours.

To serve, scrape across the top of the granité with a fork to make small crystals.

SERVES 6 TO 8 ON ITS OWN OR 10 AS PART OF A FOURPLAY

1 (750 ML) BOTTLE SPARKLING PEAR CIDER, SUCH AS ERIC BORDELET POIRÉ AUTHENTIQUE OR GRANIT

1 TEASPOON POWDERED GELATIN (OR 4.5 G SHEET GELATIN; SEE PAGE 276)

2 TABLESPOONS (30 G) WATER

1¼ CUPS (250 G) SUGAR

2 TEASPOONS (4 G) FRESHLY GROUND CUMIN (DON'T GRIND IT TOO FINE)

fruits and

CHOCOLATE

slow-roasted apricots

Sometimes you don't need to manipulate an ingredient to get the most out of it. The simple roasting here gets to the best flavors in the apricots.

1 POUND (454 G) RIPE APRICOTS
1 BUNCH LEMON THYME
UNSALTED BUTTER
2 TO 3 TABLESPOONS (40-60 G)
    HONEY, PREFERABLY
    LAVENDER

Heat the oven to 325°F or 300°F on convection.

Halve the apricots and remove the pits.

Scatter half the thyme in the bottom of a baking dish. Set the apricots on top, cut side up, and put a tiny pinch of butter in each cavity. Scatter on the rest of the thyme, and drizzle with the honey, to taste.

Cover the pan with aluminum foil and bake until the apricots are just beginning to get tender. Ripe apricots will take 5 to 10 minutes; less ripe ones may take as long as 20. Keep touching them, checking for tenderness and springiness. Serve these warm or at room temperature.

slow-roasted strawberries

This simple technique yields amazing results, intensifying the flavor of the strawberries so that each one explodes on your palate.

The strawberries I use are small, local, day-neutral or "ever-bearing" varieties like Tristar, which come from local farmers. You can roast larger berries, but they will take longer and they won't be as sweet.

Hull the strawberries, slicing off a little of their tops so that the strawberries can stand up.

Toss the berries with enough of the verjus just barely to cover. Macerate for 30 minutes to 1 hour.

Heat the oven to 225°F or 200°F on convection.

Drain the strawberries over a bowl and stand them up in a baking dish just big enough to hold them comfortably. If you want, reserve the maceration liquid to serve with the berries.

Roast the berries until they have darkened, turning almost a maroon color (they should be very tender but still hold their shape), about 1 hour and 20 minutes.

Remove the berries from the dish and let cool to room temperature before serving.

SERVES 6 ON ITS OWN OR
12 AS PART OF A DESSERT

1½ PINTS (515 G) DAY-NEUTRAL
   STRAWBERRIES
ABOUT 1 CUP (240 G) RED VERJUS
   (PREFERABLY 8 BRIX; SEE
   NOTE)

NOTE: 8 Brix is sold in some gourmet markets and is available online from Amazon. If you're not using 8 Brix, you may want to add a few drops of balsamic vinegar to balance the acidity of the berries.

brandied cherries

Fresh sour cherries are best, but you can also make this recipe with frozen morello cherries. These cherries will keep in the refrigerator for several months and are fantastic spooned over ice cream or a simple cake or even dropped into a glass of champagne with a little of their syrup.

2½ CUPS (500 G) SUGAR
3 CUPS (720 G) WATER
1½ CUPS (375 G) BRANDY OR
   COGNAC, OR MORE TO TASTE
1½ POUNDS (680 G) SOUR
   CHERRIES, PITTED

Put the sugar and water in a large saucepan and bring to a boil, stirring to dissolve the sugar. Reduce the heat and add the brandy and cherries. Bring to a simmer and cook for 15 minutes. Remove the cherries carefully with a slotted spoon. Continue to simmer the liquid for 30 minutes, reducing the liquid to give it some body.

Take the pan off the heat and return the cherries to the liquid. Let cool to room temperature. Taste and add more brandy if you want. Store in the refrigerator.

poached pears

While I serve these pears with Semolina Pancakes (page 97), you could spoon them over any pancake and replace the traditional maple syrup accompaniment with this poaching liquid instead. Poached pears are also great in a simple trifle, with layers of ice cream and crisp cookies.

Poaching is a long, gentle cooking process, so firm fruit is what you want. Choose pears of equal ripeness for poaching, and they will all be equally tender.

Crack the star anise, cloves, and peppercorns in a mortar and pestle or on the counter with the bottom of a small, heavy skillet.

Put the honey in a medium saucepan. Bring to a boil over medium-high heat and cook until the honey caramelizes slightly. Stir in the cracked spices. Pour in the water—carefully, because this will sputter—and stir until the mixture is smooth and the honey is completely dissolved. Add the salt, lemon and orange zests, and ginger and bring to a simmer.

Peel the pears and lower them into the poaching liquid. Cut a round of parchment the size of the pan and lay it over the pears. Top with a lid or plate that is smaller than the pan so the pears remain submerged and completely covered by the poaching liquid. Simmer very gently, keeping the temperature between 181° and 185°F, until the pears are tender, about 2 hours.

Let cool and store in the refrigerator in the poaching liquid. Serve cold.

7 STAR ANISE

10 WHOLE CLOVES

8 BLACK PEPPERCORNS

1¼ CUPS (375 G) HONEY

6½ CUPS (1,560 G) WATER

2¼ TEASPOONS (9 G) COARSE SALT

GRATED ZEST OF 1 LEMON

GRATED ZEST OF 1 ORANGE

2 OUNCES (57 G) FRESH GINGER, PEELED AND SLICED

4 SLIGHTLY UNDER-RIPE PEARS (BOSC OR BARTLETT)

poached quinces

MAKES 4; SERVES 4 TO 8

The trick to cooking quinces is to maintain their fragrance and delicate flavor while you coax them into tenderness. Gentle poaching is an ideal way to achieve this goal. Use poached quinces interchangeably with poached pears. They're great with chocolate, with cheese, or with walnuts and arugula as a salad.

If you've saved vanilla pods from other recipes, use them here in place of fresh beans.

6 CUPS (1,440 G) WATER
2¹/₂ CUPS (500 G) SUGAR
9 STAR ANISE, CRACKED
2 VANILLA BEANS, SPLIT AND SCRAPED
4 QUINCES

Put the water, sugar, star anise, and vanilla pods and seeds in a saucepan and bring to a boil over medium-high heat, stirring until the sugar is dissolved.

Peel the quinces and lower them into the poaching liquid. Cut a round of parchment the size of the pan and lay it over the quinces. Top with a lid or plate that is smaller than the pan so the quinces remain submerged and completely covered by the poaching liquid. Simmer very gently, keeping the temperature between 181° and 185°F, until the quinces are tender, about 1¹/₂ hours.

Let cool and store in the refrigerator in the poaching liquid. Serve cold.

port-poached rhubarb

MAKES ABOUT 3 CUPS

This simple preparation replaces the bitterness of raw rhubarb with the musty richness of port while maintaining a special crispness in flavor.

You could put this out with cheese. Or pair it with Pink Peppercorn Meringues (page 38), fresh berries, ice cream, and whipped cream for a deconstructed vacherin.

1 POUND (454 G) RIPE RHUBARB
1¹/₂ CUPS (375 ML) RUBY PORT, SUCH AS SIX GRAPES
1¹/₂ CUPS (375 ML) DRY RED WINE
1¹/₄ CUPS (250 G) SUGAR

Peel the rhubarb and cut it into neat batons about 1¹/₂ inches long and ¹/₃ inch wide. Place in a flat-bottomed casserole.

Bring the port and wine to a boil in a nonreactive saucepan. Ignite the wine—carefully—and let it burn for 1 minute. Put the lid on the pan to extinguish the flames. Whisk in the sugar, stirring until it dissolves. Pour over the rhubarb, cover with plastic wrap, and let cool to room temperature.

Transfer with the poaching liquid to a plastic container and chill for at least 2 hours before serving.

Rhubarb pickles

There were always barrels of pickles at the flea markets my parents took me to when I was growing up. My dad loved half-sours; my mom loved sweet pickles; I loved both. Mom would cut both kinds in half and stick them together, so I'd get two flavors in every bite. This is my homage to those days, made with one of my favorite ingredients.

Peel the rhubarb and cut it into neat batons about 1½ inches long and ⅓ inch wide. Place in a flat-bottomed casserole.

Put the vinegars, honey, grenadine, salt, and star anise in a saucepan and bring to a rolling boil over high heat. Turn off the heat and let cool for about 5 minutes. Pour over the rhubarb and cover with plastic wrap. Let cool to room temperature. Taste the pickles for texture. If they're too crisp for your taste, drain the liquid into a clean saucepan, bring it back to a simmer, let it cool for a few minutes, then pour it over the rhubarb again—with the star anise.

Store in the refrigerator in the liquid. Serve cold.

MAKES ABOUT 3 CUPS

1 POUND (453 G) RIPE RHUBARB
GENEROUS ½ CUP (125 G) SHERRY VINEGAR (SEE NOTE)
GENEROUS ½ CUP (125 G) RICE VINEGAR (SEE NOTE)
1 CUP PLUS 1 TABLESPOON (315 G) HONEY
3 TABLESPOONS (45 G) GRENADINE
1 TABLESPOON (12 G) COARSE SALT
2 STAR ANISE

Note: If you can find persimmon vinegar in a Korean market, use it in this recipe, as I do. Add ½ cup, and reduce the amount of the sherry and rice vinegars to ¼ cup each.

strawberry-rhubarb compote

MAKES ABOUT 1¼ CUPS

This compote is a perfect balance of opposite flavors: sweet, soft strawberries and bitter, astringent rhubarb. It fills the mochi on page 23, but it would also be very nice with Fromage Blanc Panna Cotta (page 37), mixed into thick plain yogurt, or as a bed for Vanilla Bean Ice Cream (page 220) and fresh berries.

5.6 OUNCES (156 G) FRESH STRAWBERRIES

5.6 OUNCES (156 G) RIPE RHUBARB

⅓ CUP (75 G) POMEGRANATE JUICE

⅓ CUP (65 G) SUGAR

⅓ TEASPOON POWDERED GELATIN (OR 1.4 G SHEET GELATIN; SEE PAGE 276)

⅓ TEASPOON (0.6 G) AGAR

⅔ TABLESPOON (8.75 G) FRESH LEMON JUICE

Hull the strawberries and cut in half (or in quarters if you're using large strawberries). Peel the rhubarb and cut into 2-inch pieces.

Put the strawberries and rhubarb in a saucepan with the pomegranate juice and ¼ cup of the sugar. Bring to a simmer and cook gently until the berries and rhubarb just start to break down, about 10 minutes. Let cool for about 20 minutes. Strain through a fine strainer into a clean saucepan. Spoon out 2 tablespoons of the juice into a small bowl and sprinkle the gelatin over the surface. Reserve the berries and rhubarb in a medium bowl.

Add the remaining ¼ cup sugar and the agar to the juice in the saucepan and bring to a boil over medium-high heat. Reduce the heat and simmer for 1 minute. Microwave the gelatin for 30 seconds or heat it gently in a separate saucepan until it melts. Whisk the gelatin into the juice in the saucepan, then whisk in the lemon juice.

Pour the juices over the strawberries and rhubarb, whisking to break up any clumps and to make sure the juices are well incorporated. Cover with plastic wrap and chill for at least 1 hour before serving.

papaya-lime compote

MAKES ABOUT ¾ CUP

I love the burst of flavor when I combine this compote with Cream Cheese Ice Cream (page 223), but you could also put it out for brunch, with bagels and cream cheese and smoked salmon, to bring that acidic tang you'd usually get from a ripe summer tomato.

HALF A PAPAYA, SEEDED AND CUT INTO TINY DICE
2 TABLESPOONS (35 G) SIMPLE SYRUP (PAGE 184)
GRATED ZEST AND JUICE OF 1 LIME

Mix the papaya, simple syrup, and lime zest and juice together in a small bowl. Cover with plastic wrap and chill for at least 1 hour before serving.

cherry jam

MAKES ABOUT 3½ CUPS

I developed this jam for Cherry-Chocolate Linzer Tarts (page 76), but it's great on fresh Brioche (page 194) that's been slathered with butter.

1¾ POUNDS (794 G) SOUR CHERRIES
½ CUP (120 G) WATER
⅓ CUP PLUS 2 TABLESPOONS (90 G) SUGAR
4 TEASPOONS (9.5 G) POWDERED APPLE PECTIN
2 TABLESPOONS PLUS 2 TEASPOONS (25 G) RASPBERRY
    VINEGAR

Pit the cherries and put them in a saucepan with the water and bring to a simmer over medium heat. Reduce the heat and continue to simmer until the cherries start to soften, about 4 minutes.

Mix the sugar and pectin together and add to the cherries along with the vinegar. Stir until the sugar dissolves. Turn up the heat and bring to a boil. Boil until the jam reaches 220°F.

Pour into a clean jar and let cool. This will keep in the refrigerator for 2 to 3 weeks.

mango soup

This is one of the first desserts I learned from François Payard. It's complex in flavor yet simple in ingredients and technique. Put it in the freezer for a while until it's so cold that it's slushy, and serve it with assorted tropical fruits.

4 RIPE MANGOES

1¼ CUPS (225 G) UNSWEETENED CANNED COCONUT MILK

¾ CUP (225 G) SIMPLE SYRUP (PAGE 184)

6 TABLESPOONS (75 G) FRESH LIME JUICE

¼ CUP (50 G) MALIBU COCONUT RUM

Peel, seed, and chop the mangoes. Put in a food processor and process to a fine puree. Strain and measure out 2 cups.

Return the 2 cups puree to the food processor with the coconut milk, simple syrup, lime juice, and rum. Pulse until well combined. Chill in a covered container for at least 2 hours and up to 6 hours before serving.

strawberry gelée

This brightly flavored jelly would make a delicious layer in a birthday cake. Pour it into the cake pan you're using for the cake and let it set.

Run a 9 x 12-inch rimmed baking sheet under cold water and shake off the excess. Line the damp pan neatly with plastic wrap. (The water will help the plastic stick to the pan.)

Cut enough of the strawberries into tiny dice to measure ¼ cup.

Put the remaining strawberries in a food processor and process to a very smooth puree. Strain and measure out 2 cups.

Pour about ½ cup of the puree into a small bowl and sprinkle the gelatin over the surface. Let sit for at least 1 minute.

Pour the water into a saucepan and whisk in the agar. Add ½ cup of the strawberry puree and bring to a boil over medium-high heat. Add the puree with the gelatin and whisk for at least 1 minute to dissolve the gelatin. Remove the pan from the heat and add the remaining 1 cup puree, the sugar, the Triple Sec, and the diced strawberries. Taste for sugar and stir in more if needed.

Skim any froth. Pour into the baking sheet and refrigerate for at least 2 hours to set. To serve, turn out onto a cutting board and cut into small squares. Or use a whisk to break the gelée up into irregular shapes.

1½ POUNDS (680 G) STRAWBERRIES, HULLED
4½ TEASPOONS POWDERED GELATIN (OR 20.25 G SHEET GELATIN; SEE PAGE 276)
½ CUP (120 G) WATER
2½ TEASPOONS (15 G) AGAR
⅓ CUP PLUS 2 TABLESPOONS (90 G) SUGAR, OR MORE TO TASTE
2 TABLESPOONS (25 G) TRIPLE SEC (OR OTHER ORANGE-FLAVORED LIQUEUR)

pear gelée

MAKES ONE 9 X 12-INCH PAN

¼ CUP (50 G) WATER

3 TEASPOONS POWDERED GELATIN
   (OR 13.5 G SHEET GELATIN; SEE
   PAGE 276)

1 CUP (300 G) SIMPLE SYRUP
   (PAGE 184)

⅔ CUP (150 G) PEAR EAU-DE-VIE,
   SUCH AS POIRE WILLIAM

GRATED ZEST OF 1 ORANGE

I use this as a garnish for Chocolate-Pear Cake (page 98), but it would be delicious in the bottom of a glass of champagne.

Run a 9 x 12-inch rimmed baking sheet under cold water and shake off the excess. Line the damp pan neatly with plastic wrap. (The water will help the plastic stick to the pan.)

Put the water in a small bowl and sprinkle with the gelatin. Let sit for at least 1 minute. Microwave for 30 seconds or heat gently in a saucepan until melted.

Combine the simple syrup and eau-de-vie in a large measuring cup. Add the gelatin and whisk for about 45 seconds. Whisk in the zest.

Pour into the baking sheet and refrigerate for at least 2 hours to set. To serve, turn out onto a cutting board and cut into small squares. Or use a whisk to break the gelée up into irregular shapes.

pear mousse

I use this as a component in Chocolate-Pear Cake (page 98), but it's delicious served by itself or garnished with diced Poached Pears (page 247).

Set up an ice bath in a large bowl.

Measure the eau-de-vie into a small bowl and sprinkle the gelatin over it.

Put the pear puree and the vanilla seeds and pod in a saucepan. Bring to a simmer over medium heat. Stir in the milk powder and bring to a boil, whisking to make sure the milk doesn't clump.

Whisk the yolks with the 1 tablespoon sugar in a medium bowl. When the pear puree is boiling, slowly pour about half into the yolks and whisk for about 1 minute to temper them (keep the pan off the heat while you do this). Then scrape the yolks into the saucepan and cook over medium heat, stirring pretty much constantly, until the sauce reaches 180°F. Keep an eye on the color of the foam on the surface; when it turns the same color as the mixture, you're very close to the right temperature. Strain the sauce into a medium bowl and set into the ice bath.

Microwave the eau-de-vie and gelatin for 30 seconds or heat gently in a saucepan until melted. Stir into the pear sauce and let cool to room temperature.

Whip the cream to medium peaks.

Put the egg whites in the bowl of a standing mixer fitted with the whisk. Turn it on to low, and beat the whites gently for 2 minutes, to start establishing a structure. The whites will look frothy but still a bit wet. Turn the speed up to medium and add 2 teaspoons of the sugar. Beat until the whites have body and are just shy of having soft peaks. Add the remaining 2 teaspoons sugar and continue beating until the whites have formed firm peaks.

Fold the cream into the pear sauce, then fold in the egg whites.

If you are making the chocolate-pear cake, use the mousse while it is at room temperature. Spoon leftovers into small bowls, cover with plastic wrap, and refrigerate for up to 3 days.

If you are serving the mousse on its own, spoon it into 6 to 8 small bowls or ramekins, cover with plastic wrap, and chill for at least 2 hours before serving.

SERVES 6 TO 8

2 TABLESPOONS PLUS 1 TEASPOON (25 G) PEAR EAU-DE-VIE, SUCH AS POIRE WILLIAM

1¼ TEASPOONS POWDERED GELATIN (OR 5.6 G SHEET GELATIN; SEE PAGE 276)

⅔ CUP (166 G) PEAR PUREE (SEE PAGE 276)

½ VANILLA BEAN, SPLIT AND SCRAPED

3 TABLESPOONS (15 G) NONFAT MILK POWDER

3 LARGE EGG YOLKS

1 TABLESPOON PLUS 4 TEASPOONS (29 G) SUGAR

¾ CUP PLUS 2 TABLESPOONS (210 G) HEAVY CREAM

SCANT ¼ CUP (40 G) EGG WHITES

coconut cream

MAKES ABOUT ¾ CUP

This coconut cream is light and fluffy, but it has a truly rich body, which comes from the coconut curd base.

You can use this cream—or even the curd on its own—as a filling for tarts and top with fresh berries, mango, or papaya. Serve the leftover curd on toast or toasted brioche.

For the Coconut Curd

9 TABLESPOONS (126 G) UNSALTED BUTTER

½ CUP (100 G) SUGAR

½ CUP (112 G) CANNED COCONUT MILK

8 LARGE EGG YOLKS

¾ TEASPOON POWDERED GELATIN (OR 3.3 G SHEET GELATIN; SEE PAGE 276)

Set up an ice bath in a large bowl.

Combine the butter, sugar, and coconut milk in a saucepan over medium heat. Bring to a boil.

Meanwhile, whisk the egg yolks in a bowl.

Slowly pour half the hot coconut mixture over the yolks, whisking as you pour, to temper the yolks. Return the entire mixture to the saucepan and bring to a quick boil, whisking constantly. Sprinkle the gelatin over the surface, then whisk for at least 1 minute to dissolve the gelatin. Strain the curd into a medium bowl and mix with an immersion blender.

Press a piece of plastic wrap on the surface of the curd and chill completely in the ice bath.

For the Coconut Cream

¼ TEASPOON POWDERED GELATIN (OR 1.12 G SHEET GELATIN; SEE PAGE 276)

2 TABLESPOONS (30 G) MALIBU COCONUT RUM

SCANT ⅓ CUP (75 G) HEAVY CREAM

½ CUP PLUS 1 TABLESPOON (150 G) COCONUT CURD

Sprinkle the gelatin over the rum in a small glass bowl or a cup. Let sit for at least 1 minute. Microwave for 30 seconds or heat gently in a small saucepan until melted.

Whip the cream to stiff peaks in a medium bowl. Whisk the gelatin into the whipped cream. Add the coconut curd and fold together gently but thoroughly. Cover with plastic wrap and chill for at least 2 hours before serving.

citrus curd

MAKES ABOUT 1 CUP

These days, I like to carbonate my curds (see page 134, for example), but you could serve this one, with its mix of lemon, lime, and orange, as is, spooned over berries or over sorbet, or both.

¼ CUP (50 G) SUGAR
5 LARGE EGG YOLKS
⅓ CUP (80 G) FRESH LEMON JUICE
⅓ CUP (80 G) FRESH LIME JUICE
¼ CUP (60 G) FRESH ORANGE JUICE
5 TEASPOONS (25 G) WATER

Set up an ice bath in a large bowl.

Whisk the sugar and egg yolks in a heatproof bowl until the sugar dissolves. Stir in the juices and water and set the bowl over a pot of simmering water. Cook, stirring often with a heatproof rubber scraper, until the curd reaches 180°F.

Mix the curd with an immersion blender and strain into a bowl. Set into the ice bath to chill completely. Cover with plastic wrap and refrigerate until you're ready to serve it.

lemon confit

There are so many uses for this preserve, which captures the zing of the citrus. Chop it up and use it as a garnish for sweet sorbets or as a marmalade on buttered Brioche (page 194). Or wrap a strawberry or a piece of melon with a slice of this lemon, stick a toothpick through it, and you've got a fruit canapé.

I'm not giving a yield or amounts here, because you can make as much of this classic preserve as you wish. If they're in season, Meyer lemons are what you want.

ORGANIC LEMONS (PREFERABLY MEYER LEMONS)
SUGAR

Heat the oven to 150°F.

Scrub the lemons and cut off the ends to expose the flesh. Cut into ⅛-inch-thick slices and remove the seeds.

Weigh the lemons, then weigh out an equal amount of sugar.

Sprinkle a layer of sugar in the bottom of a baking dish. Arrange a layer of lemon slices on top, overlapping slightly. Sprinkle with sugar. Arrange another layer of lemons and sprinkle again with sugar. If you want, you can make one more layer of lemons and sugar, but there should be no more than three layers. Barely cover with water.

Cut a piece of parchment to fit the dish and cover the lemons. Bake until the lemons are slightly transparent, about 2 hours.

Let cool and store in the refrigerator. The confit will keep for a couple of weeks.

candied lemon zest

MAKES ABOUT 1 CUP

I candy Etrog citrons in the restaurant, but I've adapted the recipe for good old lemons. You could chop this up and fold it into whipped cream. Or serve over ice cream.

2 LARGE LEMONS
1 CUP (280 G) SIMPLE SYRUP (PAGE 184)
1 TABLESPOON (17 G) LIGHT CORN SYRUP

Cut off the tops and bottoms of the lemons with a thin, sharp knife, to the point where you expose the flesh. Remove the zest with a vegetable peeler, leaving only the smallest amount of white pith on the zest. Cut the zest into neat ⅛-inch-wide batons. (Reserve the lemons for another use.)

Bring a small pot of cold water to a boil. Add the zest, bring back to a boil, and drain. Repeat this blanching process two more times.

Put the simple syrup and corn syrup in a small saucepan and bring to a simmer over medium heat. Add the zest and bring back to a simmer. Reduce the heat and poach the zest gently until it's slightly translucent, about 20 minutes.

Let cool in the syrup. Store covered in syrup in a small glass jar in the refrigerator for up to 6 weeks.

candied kumquats

MAKES ABOUT 2 CUPS

I think aromatic kumquats walk a line between oranges and lemons, and they aren't bitter at all when you cook them properly.

You could chop these up and bake them in a sponge cake, or fold them into a mousse that could use a shot of acidity. Fill them with soft cheese or mousse and put them out after dinner as petits fours. Or just serve with ice cream.

1 PINT KUMQUATS
2 CUPS SIMPLE SYRUP (PAGE 184)
2 TABLESPOONS (34 G) LIGHT CORN SYRUP

Cut the kumquats in half lengthwise. Scoop out the seeds with a melon baller or small spoon and discard.

Bring a pot of water to a boil. Add the kumquats, bring back to a boil, and drain. Repeat this blanching process two more times.

Put the simple syrup and corn syrup in a saucepan and bring to a simmer over medium heat. Add the kumquats and bring back to a simmer. Reduce the heat and poach the kumquats gently until they're slightly translucent, about 25 minutes.

Let cool in the syrup. Store covered in syrup in a glass jar in the refrigerator for up to 6 weeks.

mandarin carpaccio

Gregory Gourreau, my cooking partner when I was sous-chef at Daniel, worked on a dish where he froze citrus into something that resembled a mosaic. I loved the idea and played with it for a while, until I came up with this refreshing block of oranges.

I like to use a 4-inch square plastic tube to form the citrus mixture, but you could just as easily use two 15-ounce cans. Remove the tops and bottoms and wash them well.

Set up an ice bath in a large bowl.

Remove the zest from 3 of the mandarin oranges with a very sharp vegetable peeler. Cut the zest into the thinnest strips possible and put them in a metal bowl. Cover with boiling water and let sit for 1 minute. Drain the zest.

Set a strainer over another bowl. Segment all of the oranges (see page 115), letting the segments drop into the strainer. Squeeze the citrus membranes over the bowl after you've removed the segments from each. Measure out 1 cup of the juice for the carpaccio and drink the rest.

Pour ¾ cup of the juice into a small saucepan. Add the honey, banana, star anise, and vanilla seeds (rinse, dry, and save the vanilla pod for another use). Bring to a simmer, then adjust the heat so the juice will simmer actively for 7 minutes. Strain into a medium bowl.

Sprinkle the gelatin over the remaining ¼ cup juice and let sit for at least 1 minute. Microwave for 30 seconds or heat gently in a saucepan until melted. Stir the gelatin and zest into the flavored juice. Set into the ice bath until very cold and just about to set.

Seal one end of each plastic tube with a couple of layers of plastic wrap, and if you want to be safe, secure it with a rubber band. Fill the tube, alternating layers of citrus segments and juice. Seal the top with more plastic wrap and freeze for at least 3 hours, but overnight is best.

To serve, push the carpaccio out of the tube and cut into slices.

SERVES 8 ON ITS OWN OR
12 AS PART OF A DESSERT

4 MANDARIN ORANGES OR
    CLEMENTINES
4 CARA CARA OR NAVEL ORANGES
GENEROUS 2 TABLESPOONS (45 G)
    HONEY
¼ RIPE BANANA, MASHED WITH
    A FORK
1 STAR ANISE
¼ VANILLA BEAN, SPLIT AND
    SCRAPED
¾ TEASPOON POWDERED GELATIN
    (OR 2.75 G SHEET GELATIN; SEE
    PAGE 276)

crispy tangerine sticks

MAKES ABOUT 40 STICKS

Using the newer technologies that are available in the kitchen, we're now able to create textures without diluting the flavor of the prime ingredient. The Methocel in this recipe turns tangerine juice—or any juice—into an airy foam that I pipe into sticks and then dehydrate to make the sticks crisp.

These are great as a garnish for ice cream, as well as being an integral part of the Lemongrass Ice Cream dessert on page 115.

5 TABLESPOONS (62 G) SUGAR
3 G METHOCEL F50
0.5 G XANTHAN GUM
0.5 G CITRIC ACID
1 CUP (240 G) FRESH TANGERINE
   JUICE

Heat the oven to 150°F. Line a baking sheet with a Silpat or parchment.

Combine the sugar, Methocel, xanthan gum, and citric acid in a small bowl and blend well.

Pour the tangerine juice into the bowl of a standing mixer fitted with the whisk. Turn on to medium high and add the dry ingredients a few grains at a time, so they won't clump. Continue to beat until the foam has increased to about eight times the original volume.

Fit a pastry bag with a plain tip (#802 or #803 is ideal). Fill the bag with the tangerine foam and pipe 3-inch-long sticks onto the baking sheet. Dry in the oven until crisp, 9 to 10 hours.

Store in an airtight container.

NOTE: If you have a dehydrator, use it for this recipe. Line the trays with acetate, set the dehydrator to 135°F, and dry the sticks for 12 hours.

Apple Tempura

I love all things fried, so I had to add a sweet tempura to my dessert menu. The batter comes out of the fryer crisp and full of flavor—a great foil for the sweet and tangy dipping sauce.

Break the tamarind into small pieces and put it in a bowl. Cover with simmering water. When the water has cooled, drain. Discard the water. Pass the tamarind through a food mill fitted with the fine disk.

Mix the tamarind with the salt, maple syrup, and honey. Taste and adjust to your preference.

Put the water, vinegar, and sesame and grapeseed oils in a mixing bowl and whisk well.

In a separate bowl, whisk the rice flour, salt, baking powder, and baking soda together. Add gradually to the wet ingredients, whisking slowly, and continue to whisk until the batter is smooth.

Heat 3 inches of canola oil in a saucepan to 350° to 365°F. Set a baking sheet with a rack on top next to the stove.

Meanwhile, peel and core the apples; cut each into 8 wedges. Stick a skewer lengthwise into each wedge of apple.

Working in batches, dip each apple wedge into the batter and let the excess dribble off. Lower into the oil partway and hold for about 10 seconds.

Then lower the wedge in the rest of the way and lean the skewer against the side of the pan. This two-stage process ensures that the tempura won't stick to the bottom of the pan. Fry until the batter is pale gold and crisp, about 3 minutes. Drain on the rack and serve hot, with the dipping sauce.

SERVES 4 ON ITS OWN OR
10 AS PART OF A DESSERT

For the Dipping Sauce
MAKES ABOUT 1 CUP

8 OUNCES (227 G) BRICK TAMARIND

1 TEASPOON (4 G) COARSE SALT, OR MORE TO TASTE

$\frac{1}{2}$ CUP (130 G) MAPLE SYRUP, OR MORE TO TASTE

$\frac{1}{4}$ CUP (74 G) HONEY, OR MORE TO TASTE

For the Tempura

$\frac{1}{2}$ CUP PLUS 2 TABLESPOONS (150 G) COLD WATER

2 TEASPOONS (11 G) SHERRY VINEGAR

2 TEASPOONS (10 G) SESAME OIL

1 TEASPOON (6 G) GRAPESEED OIL

$1\frac{1}{3}$ CUPS (140 G) RICE FLOUR

$\frac{1}{2}$ TEASPOON (4 G) COARSE SALT

$\frac{1}{4}$ TEASPOON (1 G) BAKING POWDER

$\frac{1}{8}$ TEASPOON (1 G) BAKING SODA

CANOLA OIL FOR FRYING

2 ROYAL GALA APPLES

chocolate mousse

SERVES 6 TO 8

This light, rich mousse literally melts in your mouth. It is a component of the Chocolate-Pear Cake (page 98), but you can serve it on its own.

2 TEASPOONS DARK RUM

$^1/_2$ TEASPOON POWDERED GELATIN (OR 2.25 G SHEET GELATIN; SEE PAGE 276)

3 LARGE EGG YOLKS

GENEROUS 1 TABLESPOON (14 G) SUGAR

7.8 OUNCES (225 G) BITTERSWEET CHOCOLATE (PREFERABLY VALRHONA MANJARI 64% CACAO), CHOPPED

2 CUPS (480 G) HEAVY CREAM

Measure the rum into a small glass bowl and sprinkle the gelatin on top.

Put the egg yolks and sugar in the bowl of a standing mixer and set over a saucepan of simmering water; the bottom of the bowl should not touch the water. Whisk until the sugar has dissolved and the yolks have tripled in volume. Move the bowl to the standing mixer.

Microwave the rum and gelatin for 30 seconds or heat gently in a saucepan until melted. Scrape into the egg yolks and beat with the whisk attachment until the mixture is slightly warmer than room temperature.

Put the chocolate in a large heatproof bowl and melt in the microwave in 30-second bursts or over the pan of simmering water. Let the chocolate cool to 115°F.

In a separate bowl, beat the cream to medium peaks.

Fold half the cream into the chocolate. It will start to seize. Microwave for 10 seconds or so or put over the pan of simmering water to restore the temperature. Fold in the egg mixture, then fold in the rest of the cream.

If you are making the chocolate-pear cake, use the mousse while it is at room temperature. Spoon leftovers into small bowls or ramekins, cover with plastic wrap, and store in the refrigerator for up to 3 days.

If you are serving the mousse on its own, spoon it into 6 to 8 small bowls or ramekins, cover with plastic, and chill for at least 2 hours before serving.

chocolate crème chiboust

A chocolate pastry cream lightened with meringue, this crème chiboust is an elegant topping for a bowl of warm roasted berries. When I make this to finish Meyer Lemon Tarts (page 121), I freeze it and cut it into disks.

If making the Meyer lemon tarts, line a 9 x 12-inch rimmed baking sheet with a Silpat.

Put the milk in a saucepan and bring almost to a simmer. Whisk the cocoa powder and gelatin together and add to the milk. Whisk until smooth.

Whisk the egg yolks in a medium bowl until creamy. Mix the cornstarch with the 2 tablespoons sugar and add to the yolks. Whisk until light. Slowly add about ½ cup of the simmering milk to the yolks and whisk for about 1 minute to temper them (keep the pan off the heat while you do this). Then scrape the yolks into the saucepan and whisk well. Return the pan to the heat and cook, whisking just about constantly so the chocolate cream doesn't scorch. The mixture will become very thick. Watch for the cream to bubble up, almost like lava. Once you see the first bubble erupt, cook for another minute, still whisking. Remove from the heat and mix with an immersion blender, scraping the pan often, until very creamy.

Put the egg whites in the bowl of a standing mixer fitted with the whisk. Add the egg white powder, a pinch of cream of tartar, and 2 tablespoons of the sugar. Beat the whites at the lowest speed while you make the sugar syrup.

Combine the remaining ½ cup plus 2 tablespoons sugar and the water in a small saucepan. Mix with your fingers until the sugar is like wet sand. Cook over medium-high heat until the syrup reaches 250°F. Once the sugar comes to a boil, increase the mixer speed on the egg whites to medium. You want the whites not quite at soft peaks when the syrup is ready.

MAKES ABOUT 3 CUPS

1 CUP (240 G) WHOLE MILK
½ CUP (50 G) UNSWEETENED
   COCOA POWDER
1½ TEASPOONS POWDERED
   GELATIN (OR 6.75 G SHEET
   GELATIN; SEE PAGE 276)
5 LARGE EGGS, SEPARATED
¼ CUP (30 G) CORNSTARCH
¾ CUP PLUS 2 TABLESPOONS
   (175 G) SUGAR
1 TABLESPOON (6 G) EGG WHITE
   POWDER
CREAM OF TARTAR
2 TABLESPOOONS (30 G) WATER

CONTINUES . . .

With the mixer still at medium speed, pour the syrup in a steady stream into the whites, avoiding the whisk and the sides of the bowl. Turn the speed to high and beat the whites until the sides of the bowl feel cool.

Mix the chocolate cream again with the immersion blender. Mix about one-quarter of the whites into the cream to lighten it, then scrape into a large bowl. Fold in the remaining whites.

Spread the chiboust into the baking sheet and even it out. Cover with plastic wrap and freeze for about 2 hours.

If you are making the chiboust to serve on its own, just put it into a bowl, cover with plastic wrap, and refrigerate for up to 2 days.

TEMPERING CHOCOLATE

While it isn't essential for you to temper chocolate for the recipes in this book, the bright, shiny surface of tempered chocolate will give your dessert a beautiful, professional look. Use the best-quality chocolate, preferably Valrhona.

Chop 5 ounces (142 g) bittersweet chocolate into small, even pieces. Reserve 1 ounce (28 g).

Put the 4 ounces of chocolate into a heatproof bowl and set over a saucepan of barely simmering—not boiling—water. Melt the chocolate, stirring often with a heatproof rubber scraper to keep the temperature even.

When the chocolate is melted and has reached about 110°F, stir in the reserved chocolate. When the new chocolate has melted—this will happen very quickly—move the bowl to the counter and let the chocolate cool to 88°F to 90°F and keep the chocolate at this temperature.

To test it, dip a small offset spatula into the chocolate. The chocolate should set within 4 minutes.

If the chocolate has cooled down below 88°F, you can zap it for a second or two in a microwave, but be careful not to bring the temperature above 90°F.

chocolate décor

Here you'll find instructions for two versions of chocolate decorations for your dessert plate. In the restaurant, we call the swirls "Scooby-doos." The name dates back to when I first worked with François Payard. He could never remember the word swirl, *and so would make a swirling gesture with his index finger and say, "You know, like Scooby-doo." I use the squares as the top layer for the Strawberry Gelée dessert on page 49.*

I always use tempered chocolate for décor. You can certainly use plain melted chocolate, but you will need to refrigerate it for the chocolate to set. And it just won't shine.

Wipe a 12 x 18-inch plastic cutting board with a wet cloth and place a 12 x 18-inch piece of acetate on top (the damp surface will keep the acetate from moving around). Smooth the acetate out completely.

Pour the chocolate into the center of the acetate and use a large offset spatula to spread the chocolate into an even layer that covers the acetate completely. Make long, even sweeps with the spatula, from the center out to the sides and corners. When the chocolate starts to set but is not yet hard, follow these instructions to make squares, rectangles, or swirls.

To make squares or rectangles: Score the chocolate into 2½-inch squares or 1½ x 3-inch rectangles with the back of a knife (you don't want to cut through the acetate). Cover the chocolate with a piece of parchment, transfer it to a baking sheet, and weight it with another baking sheet. Leave it overnight for the best shine.

To make swirls: Run a cake trowel over the chocolate to create strips. Cut the acetate into 2-inch strips that are about 8 inches long. Before the chocolate sets, lift the strips with the tip of a knife and curl them so they look like opened toilet paper tubes. Set the curls in baguette molds and leave overnight for the best shine. Unwrap the acetate just before using.

5 OUNCES (142 G) BITTERSWEET CHOCOLATE (PREFERABLY VALRHONA GUANAJA 70% CACAO), TEMPERED (SEE OPPOSITE)

sauces

chocolate sauce

MAKES ABOUT 1⅓ CUPS

This building block in the pastry kitchen can't really stand on its own, yet so many desserts depend on it. Use this intense sauce as a layer in a parfait, as a chocolate fondue, as plate decoration, and—of course—on ice cream.

1 CUP (240 G) WATER
¾ CUP PLUS 1 TABLESPOON (168 G) SUGAR
SCANT ¾ CUP (70 G) UNSWEETENED COCOA POWDER (PREFERABLY VALRHONA)
½ CUP PLUS 2 TABLESPOONS (150 G) HEAVY CREAM

Set up an ice bath in a large bowl.

Put the water and sugar in a small saucepan and bring to a boil to dissolve the sugar.

Put the cocoa powder in a small heatproof bowl and whisk in the syrup a little at a time, until smooth. Return to the saucepan and bring to a boil. Add the cream, lower the heat to a simmer, and cook, stirring often with a heatproof rubber scraper, until thick, about 30 minutes. Watch for scorching.

Pour the sauce through a fine strainer into a medium bowl and cool it in the ice bath. Store in a jar in the refrigerator for up to 1 week.

black peppermint crème anglaise

The clean, refreshing note of black peppermint always says summer to me.

Churn this sauce in an ice cream maker and you'll have a great peppermint ice cream.

Put the cream, vanilla pod and seeds, and mint in a saucepan. Bring to a boil over medium-high heat. Remove from the heat and infuse for 20 minutes. Remove the vanilla pod. Mix the cream with an immersion blender.

Set up an ice bath in a large bowl.

Add the 1 tablespoon sugar to the peppermint cream. Bring to a simmer over medium heat.

Whisk the yolks with the ¼ cup sugar in a medium bowl. When the cream is simmering, slowly whisk about ½ cup into the yolks for about 1 minute to temper them (keep the pan off the heat while you do this). Then scrape the yolks into the saucepan and cook, stirring pretty much constantly, until the sauce reaches 180°F. Keep an eye on the color of the foam on the surface; when it turns the same color as the sauce, you're very close to the right temperature.

Strain the sauce into a medium bowl and set into the ice bath. Chill completely, stirring often. Cover with plastic wrap, and store in the refrigerator for up to 1 week.

MAKES ABOUT 1½ CUPS

1⅓ CUPS (320 G) HEAVY CREAM
½ VANILLA BEAN, SPLIT AND
   SCRAPED
PACKED ⅔ CUP (25 G) BLACK
   PEPPERMINT LEAVES
¼ CUP PLUS 1 TABLESPOON (62 G)
   SUGAR
4 LARGE EGG YOLKS

Hazelnut caramel sauce

MAKES ABOUT 2 CUPS

You could double this recipe and have extra caramel on hand to spoon over cheesecake or ice cream.

I like to chop nuts before roasting them, since chopping exposes more surface area. The more area that gets toasted, the more flavor. So coarsely chop the hazelnuts or pound them with the end of a rolling pin in a deep container to break them up.

9 OUNCES (225 G) HAZELNUTS, COARSELY CHOPPED

2½ OUNCES (70 G) MILK CHOCOLATE (PREFERABLY VALRHONA JIVARA 40% CACAO), CHOPPED

4 TEASPOONS (28 G) HONEY

½ CUP (100 G) SUGAR

1½ TABLESPOONS (26 G) LIGHT CORN SYRUP

GENEROUS ¼ TEASPOON (1.5 G) COARSE SALT, OR MORE TO TASTE

⅓ CUP (80 G) HEAVY CREAM, HEATED

Heat the oven to 350°F.

Spread the nuts out on a baking sheet and bake for 10 to 15 minutes, until toasted and fragrant. Lift the nuts off the baking sheet, leaving any nut powder behind; it will be a little bitter and won't feel right in your mouth.

Put the chocolate in a heatproof bowl and drizzle in the honey. Pour the sugar into a deep skillet and sprinkle it with a tablespoon or two of cool water. Drizzle on the corn syrup, add the salt, and cook over high heat. Leave the pan alone until the sugar starts to color, then pick up the pan and swirl the sugar in it so it colors evenly. Cook until the sugar is dark amber. Remove the skillet from the heat and pour in the hot cream; this will boil up and spatter, so be careful. Return the pan to the heat and cook, rolling the caramel in the pan, until the caramel comes back to a boil and is completely smooth again.

Pour the caramel over the chocolate and honey and leave it for about 1 minute. Then stir and fold with a heatproof rubber scraper until the chocolate has melted completely. Fold in the nuts. Taste for salt; it should be on the salty side.

You can make the nut caramel days in advance and refrigerate it, covered with plastic wrap, for up to 2 days. Heat it up in the microwave or a double boiler before you use it.

apricot sauce

MAKES ABOUT ½ CUP

You could invent your own melba with this sauce; all you'd need is some crunchy meringues, ice cream, and fresh apricots. It is also great with pancakes and waffles.

1 CUP (250 G) APRICOT PUREE
2 TABLESPOONS (30 G) WATER

Put the apricot puree and water in a small saucepan and bring to a simmer over medium heat. Reduce the heat to low and simmer gently, stirring often with a heatproof rubber scraper, until reduced by half. Don't let this scorch.

Cover with plastic wrap and chill for at least 2 hours before serving.

pineapple-spice sauce

MAKES ABOUT 1 CUP

I'd serve this sauce with any sweet cake, like toffee pudding, or use it as a topping for a summer sundae.

1 OUNCE (28 G) FRESH GINGER
PACKED ⅓ CUP (80 G) LIGHT BROWN SUGAR
2 CUPS (480 G) PINEAPPLE JUICE
15 WHOLE CLOVES
2 CINNAMON STICKS

Peel and chop the ginger. Put it in a saucepan with the sugar, pineapple juice, cloves, and cinnamon and bring to a boil. Reduce the heat and simmer until the sauce is syrupy and reduced by half, about 1 hour. Strain, cover with plastic wrap, and store in the refrigerator for up to 3 days.

Serve warm.

strawberry sauce

MAKES ABOUT 1 CUP

Sure you can spoon this sauce over ice cream, but you can also make it to serve with waffles or pancakes. Or even as a dip for toasted Brioche (page 194).

10 OUNCES (285 G) FRESH
   STRAWBERRIES, HULLED
2 TABLESPOONS (25 G) SUGAR
¾ TEASPOON (2.5 G) POWDERED
   APPLE PECTIN
1 TEASPOON (5 G) FRESH LEMON
   JUICE

Put the strawberries in a food processor and process to a very smooth puree. Strain and measure out 1 cup. Transfer to a small saucepan and heat to 115°F over medium heat.

Mix the sugar and pectin together and stir into the strawberry puree. Bring to a boil. Strain the sauce and stir in the lemon juice. Cover with plastic wrap, and chill for at least 2 hours before serving, or for up to 2 days.

Raspberry-Beet Sauce

When you tame the slight acidity of raspberries with the natural sweetness of beets, you come up with a flavor profile like none other.

In addition to serving this sauce with Chocolate-Beet Cake (page 29), you could use it as the start of a trifle. Try one with crumbled Chocolate Meringues (page 209) and fresh berries and unsweetened whipped cream, maybe with a layer of Strawberry Sorbet (page 236). You could also serve this sauce with yogurt and granola.

Put the raspberries in a food processor and process to a very smooth puree. Strain and measure out 1 cup (discard the solids).

Put the raspberry puree, beet puree, and vanilla pod and seeds in a small saucepan and bring to a boil over medium heat.

Mix the sugar and pectin together and stir into the puree. Bring back to a boil. Strain, cover with plastic, and chill for at least 2 hours before serving, or for up to 2 days.

MAKES ABOUT 1 CUP

18 OUNCES (510 G) FRESH RASPBERRIES

¼ CUP (55 G) BEET PUREE (SEE PAGE 30)

½ VANILLA BEAN, SPLIT AND SCRAPED

1 TABLESPOON (12.5 G) SUGAR

¾ TEASPOON (2.5 G) POWDERED APPLE PECTIN

ABOUT MEASUREMENTS AND MEASURING

I've always worked in a professional kitchen, so weighing ingredients comes naturally to me. And if you want to be exact in your baking, you should weigh your ingredients, too.

That said, I've given measurements in cups and tablespoons and teaspoons for most of the recipes in this book. The exceptions are my few forays in the book into what Harold McGee calls the "scientific study of deliciousness." My guess is that if you are going to try those recipes, you already have the all-important scale. And exact measurements are particularly important for those recipes.

If using cups and tablespoons and teaspoons, here are some guidelines that will help make sure your measurements match mine.

⊚ Use metal measuring cups for dry ingredients, and metal measuring spoons. Plastic reacts to changes in temperature by expanding and contracting, and you can't be sure of exact measurements.

⊚ Use heatproof glass measuring cups for liquids.

⊚ Sift dry ingredients before measuring. The exceptions here are granulated sugar, unless it has clumped, and nut flours. But flour, cocoa powder, and confectioners' sugar should all be sifted onto a piece of waxed paper before you measure.

⊚ Spoon and swipe. Once you have your dry ingredient sifted, spoon it into the measuring cup lightly, filling the cup to overflowing. Then use the back of a knife to swipe off the excess. Don't rap the measuring cup on the table or shake it; that will compact the ingredient in the cup.

⊚ Spices and baking powder and baking soda don't really need to be sifted—unless they've clumped. But aerate them first by stirring. Then fill the measuring spoon to overflowing and swipe off the excess. Again, don't compact the ingredient in the spoon.

⊚ Measure liquids on a level surface, and don't lift the cup to check the measurement—the cup won't be level. Bend over so you're eye level with the cup. There are newer-style cups with gradations inside, so you can look down to check your measurements, but they're plastic and inexact.

Do me a favor, though. Get a scale for your kitchen.

the Basics

FLOURS. The basic flour in my kitchen is unbleached all-purpose flour. You will find some specialty flours in some of my recipes, though.

- Semolina flour is available at many good grocery stores and gourmet markets. You can also purchase it online from Bob's Red Mill.

- Potato starch shouldn't be confused with potato flour. You can find it at good grocery stores and online from Bob's Red Mill and Amazon.

- Nut flours (almond, hazelnut, and peanut, for example) are simply natural nuts ground to a fine powder. You'll find them at good grocery stores, natural food shops, and online from Bob's Red Mill, Amazon, and Byrd Mill.

SUGARS. The basics are granulated and confectioners' sugars. I also use turbinado sugar (Sugar in the Raw) and demerara sugar to finish cookies and biscuits (usually combined with sea salt). I like their crunch and texture.

- Honey plays an important role in many of my recipes. I like using single varietal honeys, such as cranberry honey—which are available at gourmet markets and online from Bee Raw—when I can pair the flavor of the honey with that of the rest of the dessert. For other recipes, I recommend pure clover honey.

- Fondant is a confection usually used to ice petits fours and éclairs. I like playing with it, turning it into the base for tuiles. It's available as a mix from baking supply stores and from Ateco.

In addition, I use the following sugars in my ice cream recipes:

- Invert sugar (such as Trimoline) is a sucrose syrup treated with an enzyme or an acid, which splits the sucrose molecule into fructose and glucose. It helps make ice cream less likely to crystallize. You can buy invert sugar online, but I've also included an easy recipe for it.

SALT. I love the taste of salt in sweets, but salt is also very important since it opens the taste buds. I always use coarse kosher salt in my recipes. For finishing a dish, my choice is fleur de sel, but I also like pink salt, for its color, and flaky Maldon salt, for its texture.

MILK. I use whole milk in all my recipes.

NONFAT MILK POWDER. I add this to many of my ice creams and sorbets. It absorbs water in the mixture and is another way to eliminate crystallization.

HEAVY CREAM. I've developed these recipes with pasteurized heavy cream that has 36 percent butterfat. Avoid ultrapasteurized cream if you can, as it just doesn't have the flavor.

YOGURT. I've developed these recipes using a creamy nonfat yogurt. I use Stonyfield Farm yogurt in the restaurant.

BUTTER. I use unsalted butter. Softened butter should still be cool to the touch. When you press it, your finger should leave a mark. But if the butter slumps or feels greasy instead, it's too soft.

VANILLA BEANS. All my vanilla comes from my friend Mr. Recipe, who sources the best beans from Madagascar and picks through them one by one to make sure he sells the best. There is no substitute for a good vanilla bean. Buy the best you can find (Amadeus Vanilla Beans is a good online source) and store them airtight in a cool spot.

CHOCOLATE. I use several brands of chocolate in the restaurant, but these recipes were all tested with Valrhona chocolate, and that's what you should use at home for the best results.

@ Cacao nibs are cleaned, roasted, and lightly crushed cacao beans. They add a nice crunch and intense flavor to recipes. You can buy them online from Chocosphere.

@ Chocolate pearls ("Les Perles") are dark chocolate drops from Valrhona, perfectly round and smaller than chocolate chips. I prefer the crunchy ones ("Les Perles Croquantes"). These are also available from Chocosphere.

GELATIN. I use Gelita sheet gelatin (available online from Pastry Chef Central) in the restaurant, but for the home cook, the recipes have been tested with unflavored powdered gelatin.

WORKING WITH SHEET GELATIN

Sheets of Gelita gelatin are thinner than most commercially available sheet gelatin, so I give weights instead of numbers of sheets in the recipes in case you are using a different brand.

Sheet gelatin must be softened before being added to recipes. Fill a bowl with ice water and add the gelatin, sheet by sheet so it doesn't stick together. When it's soft and flexible, after 8 minutes, lift it out, squeeze out all the water, and leave it in a strainer until you need to add it to the recipe.

Sheet gelatin must be added to a hot liquid and should be stirred or whisked until it melts.

The professional pantry

FRUIT PUREES. The benefit of using fruit purees—and I use apricot, calamansi, mango, passion fruit, and pear purees in the book—is consistency of flavor and texture. These products usually have 10 percent added sugar, which is something to keep in mind if you choose to puree your own fruit at home. Boiron purees are available at many gourmet stores and online from 1-800-Gourmet.

FEUILLETINE. These extremely thin dried and crushed crêpes give crunch to several of my desserts. You can find this product online from L'Epicerie.

PRALINE PASTE. In the restaurant, I use Ancienne Praline, which is made with a mix of almonds and hazelnuts, and pistachio praline paste. They're available only to professional kitchens, but you can substitute any 60 percent nut praline paste (40 percent sugar), such as the hazelnut praline paste from L'Epicerie.

EGG WHITE POWDER. Pure egg white powder helps stabilize meringues. You can find it in some grocery stores (like Whole Foods) and online from Terra Spice Company.

AGAR. This thickener (derived from red seaweed) sets more firmly than gelatin, and its setting powers are heat stable to a point (85°C or 185°F). It also has a more brittle texture than gelatin. I use Telephone brand (which is available at Asian markets) for fluid gels, but you can use any agar powder available at gourmet markets for the recipes in this book.

APPLE PECTIN. Used for setting jellies, powdered apple pectin is available at some grocery stores and online from L'Epicerie.

XANTHAN GUM. I use this natural ingredient (a product of glucose fermentation) as a thickener and stabilizer. It's available at many good grocery stores and online from Bob's Red Mill.

TAPIOCA MALTODEXTRIN (N-ZORBIT M). This powder is derived from tapioca and used to turn high-oil or fatty foods into a free-flowing powder. You can find it online from Terra Spice Company.

GELLAN GUMS. High-acyl gellan creates gels that are springy and elastic; low-acyl gellan is used for gels that are firm and brittle. Buy it online from Terra Spice Company or Le Sanctuaire.

LECITHIN (SOY). This is traditionally used as an emulsifier for commercial chocolates; I use it to create airy bubbles in liquids. You can buy it at stores such as GNC or at Le Sanctuaire.

HYDROLYZED SOY PROTEIN (VERSA-WHIP 600K). This whipping agent can create a very light and stable foam in pureed ingredients. It's available online from Terra Spice Company.

SODIUM ALGINATE. Processed from brown seaweed, sodium alginate creates a strong gel that is completely heat-stable when put into a solution that contains calcium, meaning it will retain its form and not melt. It's available online from Terra Spice Company and Le Sanctuaire.

METHOCEL (F50 AND A16-SG). These cellulose derivatives, often made from cotton (Methocel is a brand of Dow Chemical), are used primarily for gelling and whipping. F50 is particularly effective for creating foams. You'll find them online from Terra Spice Company and Le Sanctuaire.

CALCIUM SALTS (CALCIUM CHLORIDE AND CALCIUM LACTATE). Used in combination with alginates, calcium salts assist in forming gels (with molecular structures like egg cartons) that are very stable. You'll find them online from Terra Spice Company and Le Sanctuaire.

I expect you'll have some of these items in your kitchen already. Some of them can be found at good kitchenware shops, and everything can be ordered (see "Online Sources" on page 281).

Electrics

STANDING MIXER. A handheld mixer won't be sturdy enough for most of my recipes.

FOOD PROCESSOR. You'll need this for making some doughs, for making purees, and for making powders.

BLENDER. In the restaurant kitchen, I use a Vita-Mix, which can liquefy practically anything in seconds. At home, you can use a standard blender, but take the time to make sure you have a very smooth puree.

IMMERSION BLENDER. I use this piece of equipment for everything from making emulsions to creating foams.

JUICER. I use a Champion juicer for juicing apples, beets, rhubarb, and other fruits and vegetables. I prefer the Sunkist juicer for citrus.

SPICE GRINDER. You'll need this not only for grinding spices but also for making some of the tuiles. I recommend a clean coffee grinder reserved solely for spices.

DEHYDRATOR. This is ideal for making fruit leather and Crispy Tangerine Sticks (page 260).

Bakeware

RIMMED SHEET PANS. You'll need half and quarter sheet pans, which are 12 x 18 x 1 inch and 9 x 12 x 1 inch, respectively. These are sometimes called jelly roll pans.

SILPATS. These nonstick mats, made of fiberglass and silicone, are invaluable for lining pans. You can substitute parchment in many cases, but they're well worth the investment.

Molds, Rings, and Forms

PASTRY CUTTER SET. A twelve-piece set from Ateco has cutters that range in size from $7/8$ inch to $4\,7/16$ inches.

$2^{1}/_{4}$-INCH TART RINGS. Have twelve on hand for tarts and some cakes.

2 X 2-INCH RING MOLDS. Have twelve on hand for some cakes and frozen desserts.

$1^{1}/_{2}$-INCH SQUARE MOLDS. I use these as cutters and as molds.

TIMBALE MOLDS. You'll need eight to nine 1-ounce aluminum molds for the Citrus-Almond Sponge Cake (page 118).

CANNOLI FORMS. These are needed for the Corn Panna Cotta (page 83).

FLEXIPAN SAVARIN MOLD. If making Frozen Cranberry Nougat (page 105), you'll need two of the 2¾-inch molds (6 cavities).

FLEXIPAN MINI SAVARIN MOLDS. For Warm Crispy-Creamy Chocolate "Doughnuts" (page 170) you'll need one half-size mold (30 cavities).

cookware

HEAVY SMALL SAUCEPANS. I recommend a 1½-quart pan and a smaller one. A ½-quart butter warmer is invaluable for making small amounts of sugar syrup.

HEAVY SKILLET OR SAUTÉ PAN. I use this when making caramel.

HOTEL PANS AND PERFORATED HOTEL PANS. These are also known as steam-table pans. A half-size (10⅛ x 12¹¹⁄₁₆ x 2½) is all you need for home use. These are useful for making granités, Port-Poached Rhubarb (page 248), and Rhubarb Pickles (page 249). The perforated pan (combined with the solid one) is useful for Strawberry Soda (page 44) and essential for Two Chocolate Consommés (page 168).

gadgets

SODA SIPHON AND SODA CHARGERS (CO_2). You'll need these for making Strawberry Soda (page 44) and some of the foams. You can buy them at good housewares and kitchenware stores.

WHIPPED CREAM MAKER AND CREAM WHIPPER CHARGERS (N_2O). To make aerated foams, you'll need these, which are available at good housewares and kitchenware stores.

CULINARY TORCH. I use a regular torch, but the small ones you can now buy in kitchenware stores will work fine at home for caramelizing sugar. (Alternatively, you can use your broiler in some cases.)

SPAETZLE MAKER. You'll need this for Chocolate Spaetzle (page 172).

ICE CREAM SCOOP. I use a small one (1-tablespoon capacity) to ensure uniformity when I make Almond Tuiles (page 205), though it is not strictly necessary. You could use a tablespoon measure instead.

supplies

PARCHMENT. For lining pans and rolling dough and tuiles, this paper is essential in the pastry kitchen.

CHEESECLOTH. This is great for clarifying and straining soups and purees.

PASTRY BAGS. Have a supply of 18-inch disposable bags on hand. I don't always use tips when I'm filling molds, but you will need a plain round tip (#802 or #803) for piping meringues and Crispy Tangerine Sticks (page 260).

ACETATE. This clear plastic cake wrap is the best way to line molds for frozen desserts to prevent them from sticking to the molds. You can find it in art supply and craft stores.

NONTOXIC SILICA PACKETS. These are designed to control moisture and great to use when you're storing fruit leather and crystallized herbs and even tuiles for more than a day or so in humid climates. You can buy them at J.B. Prince.

miscellaneous

KITCHEN SCALE. I think a digital scale (one that converts from metric to imperial) is one of the most important pieces of equipment in a pastry kitchen. For the new, cuisine-tech recipes, you'll also need a scale that is accurate to 0.1 g.

INSTANT-READ THERMOMETER. I rely on temperature when I'm cooking sugars or making an anglaise (not a cue like "coats the back of a spoon"), because it's the most accurate way of cooking.

OFFSET SPATULAS. Large and small ones are both useful to spread everything from batters to icings evenly.

HEATPROOF RUBBER SCRAPERS. Have these in a variety of sizes so you can use them for everything from making a crème anglaise to folding flavorings into egg whites.

MICROPLANE. This long sharp rasp is essential for finely grating citrus zest.

CHINOIS OR FINE STRAINER. You need one of these—double mesh—in your kitchen to make the smoothest sauces, ice creams, and purees.

ROLLING PIN. Get one that's heavy and has a barrel that's at least 12 inches long. With bearings (handles) or without—it's up to you.

online sources

AMADEUS VANILLA BEANS
www.amadeusvanillabeans.com
310-670-9731
   Bulk vanilla beans from Madagascar, Uganda, Tahiti, and Indonesia.

AMAZON.COM
www.amazon.com
   A good source for kitchen equipment as well as many specialty ingredients.
   Champion juicers, kitchen scales, instant-read thermometers, soda siphons, whipped cream makers, standing mixers, culinary torches, sheet pans (half- and quarter-sized), and pastry cutter sets, as well as potato starch, beet and yogurt powders, 8 Brix verjus, fruit purees, and more.

ATECO
www.atecousa.net
August Thomsen Corp.
36 Sea Cliff Avenue
Glen Cove, NY 11542
800-645-7170
   Cake decorating supplies and pastry tools. Ateco also sells fondant mix.

BEE RAW HONEY
www.beeraw.com
888-660-0090
   American varietal honeys.

BIGTRAY
www.bigtray.com
800-244-8729
   Restaurant equipment and supplies; hotel pans and perforated hotel pans.

BOB'S RED MILL
www.bobsredmill.com
800-349-2173
   Whole grain products as well as almond flour, hazelnut flour, semolina flour, and potato starch.

BRIDGE KITCHENWARE
www.bridgekitchenware.com
   Imported cookware for the professional. Request a catalog.
   Ring molds, tart rings, timbale molds, ice cream scoops, and more.

BRITISH DELIGHTS
www.britishdelights.com
978-392-0077
   Bird's custard, Belvoir elderflower cordial.

BROADWAY PANHANDLER
www.broadwaypanhandler.com
65 East 8th Street
New York, NY 10003
866-266-5927
   Bakeware, cookware (including butter warmers), culinary torches, kitchen electrics (including spice grinders, standing mixers, food processors, and blenders).

BYRD MILL
www.byrdmill.com
888-897-3336
   Peanut flour.

CHOCOSPHERE
www.chocosphere.com
877-992-4626
   A fine chocolate purveyor in Portland, Oregon.
   Valrhona products, including Les Perles (chocolate pearls) and cacao nibs (Valrhona and Scharffen Berger). Many of the Valrhona chocolates you will need for the recipes in this book are sold as "chefs' products."

1-800-GOURMET
www.1800gourmet.com
800-GOURMET
   Boiron fruit purees.

IMPORTFOOD.COM

www.importfood.com

888-618-THAI

Thai ingredients, including white sticky rice and black sticky rice.

J.B. PRINCE COMPANY

www.jbprince.com

36 East 31st Street

New York, NY 10016

800-473-0577

J.B. Prince bills itself as the source for the "World's Finest Chefs' Tools & Equipment," and they really do have a full line of supplies. Ask for a catalog. They specialize in selling to the industry, though, so there is a $50 minimum.

Acetate, silica desiccant packs, Flexipan molds, sheet pans (half- and quarter-sized), tart rings, and more.

KALUSTYAN'S

123 Lexington Avenue

New York, NY 10016

www.kalustyans.com

800-352-3451

A wide selection of spices and vinegars. Also sweet rice flour.

L'EPICERIE

www.lepicerie.com

866-350-7575

Sugars, specialty ingredients, and a small molecular gastronomy section; dextrose, glucose, glucose powder (atomized glucose), invert sugar, feuilletine, freeze-dried strawberry powder, gianduja, praline paste, and more.

LE SANCTUAIRE

www.le-sanctuaire.com

315 Sutter Street

San Francisco, CA 94108

415-986-4216

Herbs and spices, freeze-dried fruit powders, and specialty ingredients (sold under the heading "molecular gastronomy").

NEW YORK CAKE SUPPLIES

www.nycake.com

56 West 22nd Street

New York, NY 10010

800-942-2539

212-675-7099 (fax)

This store offers bakeware, essential baking supplies like pastry bags, and specialty ingredients like fondant and edible decorations. They accept orders only by phone or fax.

PASTRY CHEF CENTRAL

www.pastrychef.com

561-999-9483

They call themselves a superstore "for the baker in all of us," and they have a very wide selection of baking equipment—including many hard-to-find molds and rings.

They're also a good source for ingredients like instant pastry cream, fondant, feuilletine, praline, invert sugar, glucose, and powdered glucose. The drawback is that they sell commercial quantities, but they do sell Gelita sheet gelatin, which is the brand I use in the restaurant.

QUICKSPICE.COM

www.quickspice.com

323-728-4762

Asian ingredients, including mochiko flour.

SUR LA TABLE

www.surlatable.com

A fine source for bakeware, baking tools, and electrics, with many brick-and-mortar locations.

TERRA SPICE COMPANY

www.terraspice.com

574-586-2600

This full-line spice and dry goods company has a particularly strong line of specialty ingredients.

Agar powder, calcium chloride, calcium lactate, calcium lactate gluconate, dextrose, lecithin, malt powder, Methocel F50, tapioca maltodextrin, and xanthan gum, as well as birch beer extract, cacao nibs, rose water, tamarind paste, and vanilla beans.

WILLIAMS-SONOMA

www.williams-sonoma.com

877-812-6235

A fine source for bakeware, baking tools, and electrics, with many brick-and-mortar locations.

acknowledgments

From Johnny . . .

Where do I start? I have been very lucky in my career to have worked with so many talented, generous, and patient people. From the very beginning, by chance, I was afforded rare and special opportunities.

First, I need to thank my parents, who really believed in me and encouraged me to follow my dream no matter what the path, as long as it made me happy. I am so grateful to have had them as parents, because of their virtues, their respect, and their integrity. My father is a workhorse; his energy and determination truly amaze me. My mother was dedicated and loyal and always found a way to make things work. Thanks Joseph, Josh, and Fran—the rest of my family—for your love and support.

I look back over the years and it seems like only yesterday I was graduating from high school and taking on a full-time job in a professional kitchen. Many people have had a hand in melding me into who I am today. I truly need to thank the chefs I have worked for and worked with over the years for sharing their knowledge and their own experiences with me and for creating a thirst and hunger deep inside of me for more. Their influence is apparent in my technique, style, recipes, and my approach and respect for ingredients.

I have to thank Chef Brad Goulden for seeing something in a long-haired high school troublemaker and for keeping me busy. I have lost track of him, but I hope someday he will see this and it will make him proud. Thank you, Chef Joe McKenna and Peter Greweling; your special tutelage throughout my days at the C.I.A. has not been forgotten. I worked only a short time with Chef Lincoln Carson, although we have remained close friends; you made me realize that if I want to ever be one of the best, there are no shortcuts. Also for taking me to buy my

first street motorcycle. It was your goodwill and a simple phone call that changed the direction of my career and, ultimately, my life. That call was to Chef François Payard, my mentor. François is a very complex man, a ball of emotion, an encyclopedia of knowledge, and an amazing pastry chef. He has probably forgotten more than I will ever know. I am forever indebted to him. While working with François, I was also working with Chef Daniel Boulud. In the more than seven years I worked for him, he treated me like a son. He believed in me, and he is the most charming, benevolent man I've ever met. Chef Alex Lee taught me simplicity of ingredients and importance of pure flavor. Chef Thomas Haas, the ultimate technician, is so thrifty, so energetic! My days with him were always exciting and are forever treasured; he really taught me how to create. Thank you, Pierre Hermé, for inviting me into your kitchen at Ladurée all those years ago and sharing so many techniques and recipes with me. I am forever grateful. Chef Jean-Georges Vongerichten is the most diversified chef I have ever met. So keen, so sharp, such an expansive palate; you taught me the importance of "everything must pop!" Thank you for allowing me to run with this project and for giving me the ultimate platform to create at restaurant Jean Georges.

Many of my generation of chef friends have inspired me and pushed me to be a better chef: Dave Arnold, Sean Brock, Dave Chang, Will Goldfarb, Gregory Gourreau, Adam Perry Lang, Paul Liebrandt, Sam Mason, George Mendes, Aaron Sanchez, Brad Thompson, Zohar Zohar. A special thanks to my good friend Wylie Dufresne for inspiring me to think in new directions as well as for his time in working with me on new techniques and recipes. I need to thank my teams from over the years for their dedication to the team and the house and for their enthusiasm. A special note of gratitude to Jason Casey "Tang," Elizabeth Katz, Daniel Skurnick, "Captain S." Chris Szczeniowski, Emily Wallend-jack, and AJ Bellarosa—my sous-chefs past and pres-ent—who really helped me realize my goals and maintain the highest level of quality. Thanks to my colleagues at restaurant Jean Georges—Chef Danny Del Vecchio, Chef Gregory Brainin, Chef Mark Lapico, and Philippe Vongerichten for their standard of excellence and camaraderie. Thanks as well to all the savory sous-chefs who have come and gone through my life.

Thanks to my homeboy David Arnold for your ability to build crazy equipment and help bring my ideas to life.

I'd like to thank Harold McGee—aka McGizz—for his friendship and for allowing me to access his mental database at all times.

Thank you to three special women who have seen this project come to fruition: Taylor, for encouraging me to start this project and convincing me someone will buy it; Olyia, for helping and pushing me along the way and keeping me focused; and Lucinda, for her creativity and for promising me that in the end I will be glad I did it.

Thanks to Roy Finamore, my coauthor and amigo, for harnessing my energy and for being able to translate it to these pages. He is a very wise man and I have learned a great deal from him. I know it hasn't been easy, but I'm glad it was you!

Dorie Greenspan for her advice, knowledge, and experience, and for treating me like her second son.

Thanks to all our farmers and purveyors who grow and find us the freshest, highest quality ingre-dients and products to work with, especially Franca Tantillo, Rick and Nicole Bishop, "Tomato" Tim Eck-erton, Nancy McNamarra, Alex Paffenroth, Cherry Lane Farm, Ronnybrook Farm Dairy, Locust Grove Farm, Stokes Farm, Joel Somerstein, Ben Friedman, Aaron Isaacson—aka Mr. Recipe—and Arnold Schneider.

From Johnny and Roy . . .

We've been very lucky to have had a terrific group of supporters for *Dessert FourPlay*.

Thanks first to David Black, who brought us together and found us a home. Joy Tutela has been our rock throughout the process, and David Larabell was ever ready to keep things running smoothly.

Gregor Halenda made the photographs we dreamed of for this book. So sharp, so clean! What an eye for detail. Thank you, Gregor. Thanks as well to Jeff Elkins for keeping it all running smoothly on set and to Anais Brielle for keeping the visual record of the making of the photographs.

A very talented group of young chefs contributed their time and efforts. Thanks to Justin "Mr. Binni-gans" Binnie, Anna "Banana" Bolz, Lindsay "Bear" Busanich, Geoff "Gooey Kooey" Koo, Lina "Babooshka" Kulchinsky, Alina Martell, Michal "Mickey" Shelkowitz, Lucinda Sterling, and Emily "WallenMcQuackers" Wallendjack. Also, Katherine Wardle (the original angel) and Carolyn Coopersmith for their time, eyes, and input in the manuscript.

William DeJesus and Hollywood are the drivers and go-to men who have made many things possible. Thanks, guys. You rock!

Thank you, Rica Allannic, for welcoming us to Clarkson Potter and for believing in the book. Marysarah Quinn has outdone herself with her witty and elegant design. The legendary Joan Den-man worked her magic with the printers. Thank you, both. We're grateful to Patricia Bozza, Ashley Phil-lips, and Selina Cicogna. And thanks to Lauren Shakely for your support.

From Roy . . .

Thanks to Carole Walter and Dorie Greenspan for your ready advice and encouragement.

My parents are always a source of encourage-ment, as is my sister Marie.

Thanks to Molly Stevens for more than I can say.

I am ever grateful to Marian Young for her good sense and support.

And thanks, Johnny, for letting me share this book with you. It's been quite a ride.

index